THE
FAILURE OF
PRESIDENTIAL
DEMOCRACY

Volume 1

Comparative
Perspectives

THE
FAILURE OF
PRESIDENTIAL
DEMOCRACY

*Comparative
Perspectives*

Edited by
Juan J. Linz and Arturo Valenzuela

The Johns Hopkins University Press

Baltimore and London

©1994 The Johns Hopkins University Press
All rights reserved
Printed in the United States of America
on acid-free paper
2 4 6 8 9 7 5 3

The Failure of Presidential Democracy is published in a hardcover edition
and in two paperback volumes:
The Failure of Presidential Democracy, vol. 1,
Comparative Perspectives and *The Failure of Presidential Democracy,* vol. 2,
The Case of Latin America.

The Johns Hopkins University Press
2715 North Charles Street
Baltimore, Maryland 21218-4363
www.press.jhu.edu

ISBN 0-8018-4640-4

Library of Congress Cataloging-in-Publication Data
will be found at the end of this book.

A catalog record for this book is available
from the British Library.

To the memory of

Charles Guy Gillespie

and Carlos Nino

Contents

Preface

IN THE LAST DECADE of the twentieth century, the eyes of the world have focused on the former Soviet Union and Eastern Europe, where a succession of events have had profound implications for the course of human history. In a largely peaceful process, centrally planned, socialist regimes have succumbed to economic and political stagnation, and the way has been opened for elections and democratic reform.

With less drama, democracy has also begun to make headway in other areas of the world, such as Africa, where, after independence, the promise of self-government led to despotic rule. In 1989, when Brazil and Chile elected presidents openly and competitively for the first time since their independence, all of the Ibero-American nations except Cuba had elected heads of state.

There may be grounds for cautious optimism about the future of democracy, particularly in countries where the challenges of economic and political reform are less daunting and experience with democratic institutions longer standing. The growing consensus favoring free-market economic policies has helped reduce polarization and conflict about the fundamental organization of economic life. Except where it is being overwhelmed by nationalist, religious, or ethnic challenges, democracy is no longer challenged as a form of government by alternative ways of organizing the political community.

And yet the long-term viability of democratic governments in several countries remains questionable. Much of the recent scholarship dealing with democratic "governability" has focused on these challenges and on state efforts to implement critical policies designed to correct economic imbalances, address deep social problems, and promote growth. Less attention has been given to the design and performance of democratic institutions per se. There is an implicit assumption among reformers that all democratic rules and procedures are similar in design, that the institutional dimensions of representative government are constants. It is also assumed that democratic institutions affect different societies in similar ways, depending only on the particular social and economic conditions.

These assumptions are not fully tenable. There is substantial variation in the formal and informal political architecture of democratic regimes and the contexts in which they operate. Democratic governments can be organized along unitary or federal lines, with wide variations in the degree of administrative decentralization and local autonomy. Leaders can be elected through winner-take-all or proportional representation systems. Political competition can be organized in two-party or multiparty configurations, which can in turn be either moderately differentiated or polarized.

The most important difference among democratic regimes concerns the generation and accountability of executive authority. In presidential regimes based on the U.S. doctrine of separation of powers, executive authority is generated by direct or indirect elections and is not accountable politically to the legislature. In parliamentary regimes, which evolved gradually in Western Europe, the executive is generated by the legislature and is accountable to legislative majorities for its political survival.

Nor is it the case that all democratic rules and procedures have similar impact. Federal schemes may be more relevant in societies with strong regional or local traditions, while electoral systems based on proportional representation may be more responsive to the realities of highly divided societies.

It is significant that with the notable exception of Latin American countries, few democracies have opted for the U.S. model of presidentialism. In the immediate aftermath of World War II, Karl Loewenstein observed that "the economic and technological prestige of the United States is not equaled by the popularity of its form of government. In this period of hectic political reconstruction remarkably few among the nations seem inclined to follow the constitutional pattern commonly spoken of as presidentialism under the separation of powers. . . . This is not surprising in view of the fact that in the past the transplantation of the American model was likewise the exception and that, in its primary area of adoption, Latin America, it rarely if ever produced lasting political stability."[1]

It is curious that some countries in Eastern Europe, notably Russia and Poland, are toying with the option of establishing presidential regimes when many Latin Americans are having serious doubts about the impact of presidentialism on their continent. The vast majority of the contemporary world's stable democracies have had parliamentary forms of government. Only in Latin America, the continent of presidentialism, have a few presidential regimes had long periods of democratic continuity.

In this day of democratic crafting, the academic literature provides little insight and guidance for reformers concerned with the impact of differing forms of constitutional structure and governmental arrangements for alternative national realities. That is, political scientists are uncertain about the degree to which different formal rules, practices, and governmental structures of democracy encourage or hinder regime efficacy and stability in particular societies. In particular, little is known about the implications for governmental efficacy and stability of the two principal forms of democratic government, presidential and parliamentary, and their contemporary variations.[2] Does it make a difference whether societies seek to strengthen democratic institutions according to the U.S. constitutional principal of separation of powers or to some form of European parliamentarism?

Such questions were of central importance to classical political theorists and constitutional scholars, but they have been neglected by contemporary social scientists. This neglect resulted in part from the postwar revolution that shifted scholarly attention away from public law and formal organizations to such themes as political behavior, political culture and socialization, parties and interest groups, public policy formulation, and the relationship between politics and markets. This behavioral approach took hold in countries in which institutional and constitutional dimensions were taken for granted.

The Eurocentric focus of much of the literature in comparative politics reinforced the neglect of institutional dimensions. Work contrasting democratic institutions and policy outcomes in various national contexts was valuable, but it did not systematically address the relative merits of presidential and parliamentary governments simply because it considered only one example of presidentialism—the United States—which thus became a peculiar "deviant case" with no common referents elsewhere.[3]

Despite the vast body of literature on the U.S. presidency, there is very little serious work on comparative presidentialism, and no studies systematically compare presidential regimes with parliamentary ones. A review of 94,000 articles abstracted in the *International Political Science Abstracts* from 1975 to 1991 reveals that only 141 dealt with the presidency or presidential systems outside of the United States, and of these only 22 dealt with presidentialism in Latin America, the continent of presidentialism.[4]

The lack of consideration of Latin American presidential democracies, some of which have had longer periods of democratic rule than many European countries, has impoverished our understanding of the relationship between regime type and democratic stability in varying political contexts. For example, Latin America has several presidential regimes that have functioned with multiparty systems, leading to a pattern of coalition politics very dissimilar to that of the United States and more comparable to that of European countries. This variation in presidential regimes casts a different light not only on coalition behavior but on the broader literature dealing with political parties.

While institutional factors were taken for granted in the European literature, in Latin America they were dismissed as irrelevant. Influenced by neo-Marxist and structuralist perspectives, scholars focused on social classes and movements and on political actors such as the church and the military. Politics was analyzed from the point of view of broad social forces, and democracy or its promise was viewed as nonexistent. Studies of Latin American authoritarianism were principally concerned with explaining the underlying causes of military regimes and the political economy of authoritarian regimes. Governmental institutions, constitutions, and the rules of the game were viewed as irrelevant or epiphenomenal. The question of the fit of certain institutional forms with the social and political realities of a given country was not posed.

The concern for institutional dimensions of democratic stability expressed in this book had its origins in the research project on the breakdown of democracy begun in the early 1970s by Juan Linz. In developing his theoretical writings on the subject, Linz drew primarily from the European experience. The Latin American cases, however, could not be ignored when the breakdown of democratic regimes was addressed. The insights derived from the Chilean and Brazilian case studies by Arturo Valenzuela and Alfred Stepan, respectively, and the work of Guillermo O'Donnell on the Argentine conundrum entered into his thinking. The 1978 volume on democratic breakdowns edited by Juan Linz and Alfred Stepan departed from the general orthodoxy of the time by highlighting the importance of political variables, leadership, and choice and stressing the importance of the institutional context and the formal rules of the game in explaining democratic failures.[5]

Although the relationship between regime type and democratic breakdown was not made fully explicit in the "breakdown" project, Linz concluded that the nature of presidential regimes had to be considered an important variable in accounting for regime crisis. In his own contribution to the volume, he added an excursus noting that the rigidities of presidentialism played a significant role in defining the "impossible" political game in Argentina, one that precluded the consolidation of a viable democracy.[6]

That work stressed the importance of the need to account for the broader institutional and political context that framed the process leading to the collapse of democracy.[7] From this perspective politics and institutions are viewed as independent variables in their own right, not simply as epiphenomena reflecting underlying economic and social forces. Complex organizations are more than aggregates of individual behavior; they are social structures with their own autonomy and logic, affecting and constraining individual behavior and human choice. Political options and decisions are mediated by the rules and structures of the game, rules with closely related formal and informal dimensions.

This perspective should not be viewed as a kind of primitive institutionalism that reifies formal rules and procedures as the fundamental determinants of politics. We would be the first to argue that institutional forms are not magic formulas capable of solving all problems. Indeed this work is primarily behavioral, in that it focuses on the interplay between institutions and political roles, on how the latter are affected by the former and vice versa. Nor is much attention placed on constitutional texts as such. Indeed, they are cited infrequently. We are as concerned with public opinion, political roles, rhetoric, the image and self-assessment of leaders, among other phenomena, as with formal rules. Our premise, however, is that formal rules cannot be ignored in examining political behavior. There is a complex dialectic between rules and behavior.

Invited to present a paper at a 1984 symposium on "Political Parties and Democratic Transition" organized by the Woodrow Wilson International Center for Scholars, Linz turned his attention to a more systematic examination of the implications for democratic stability of presidential versus parliamentary democracy. Arturo Valenzuela, at the same workshop, drew on his own earlier work on the Chilean breakdown to suggest that the crisis of Chilean politics was exacerbated by a lack of congruence between a polarized multiparty system and a presidential regime.

Subsequent to the Wilson Center meeting, Linz and Valenzuela organized a broader research effort, including the commissioning of a range of country case studies and analytical pieces, to examine the questions posed in Linz's 1984 paper. That effort resulted in a research symposium entitled "Presidential or Parliamentary Democracy: Does It Make a Difference?" held at Georgetown University in May 1989 as part of the university's bicentennial celebration. The symposium provided an opportunity to discuss the first drafts of individual papers and to debate the relative merits of presidential and parliamentary forms of government.

In addition to the scholars represented in this volume, we wish to acknowledge the valuable contributions to the symposium made by Ergun Ozbudun and Oyeleye Oyeridan, who shared their perspectives on the cases of Turkey and Nigeria, respectively, and by Fred Riggs, who made an outstanding contribution bringing the U.S case into the comparison. We regret that space limitations made it impossible to include their papers in the final volume. The symposium was enriched by the attendance of Seymour Martin Lipset, Matthew Shugart, Scott Mainwaring, Douglas Chalmers, John Bailey, Carol Lancaster, Colin Campbell, Michael Hudson, and Oscar Godoy as discussants and panel chairs.

The Georgetown symposium aroused considerable attention in Chile, where, in the aftermath of General Augusto Pinochet's defeat in a plebiscite, the issue of constitutional reform had moved to the forefront of public debate. The Institute of Political Science of the Catholic University of Chile, directed by Oscar Godoy, and the Center for Latin American Studies at Georgetown organized a conference in Santiago, Chile, in September 1990 with the participation of Linz, Valenzuela, Arend Lijphart, Giovanni Sartori, and a group of distinguished Chilean political scientists and leaders. Draft versions of the papers by Linz, Lijphart, and Valenzuela were published by the Institute of Political Science at the Catholic University.[8]

In Argentina, a change from a presidential to a semipresidential system was proposed by President Raúl Alfonsín, drawing on the impressive work done by the Comisión para la Consolidación de la Democracia. Although both major parties were close to an agreement on constitutional reforms, fear that Alfonsín was making use of the issue for personal political advantage, combined with Argentina's mounting economic crisis, led to failure of the reform effort.

The country for which the question of the relative merits of presidential and parliamentary government became most salient was Brazil, as Bolivar Lamounier describes in chapter 8 of this volume. In a national referendum held in April 1993, Brazilians chose to retain a presidential regime, rejecting parliamentary and monarchical options. The first drafts of the papers by Linz, Lijphart, Lamounier, and Valenzuela were published in Portuguese in a volume edited by Lamounier; they contributed to the debate on regime change in Brazil.[9] Linz and Valenzuela participated in two international symposia on the issue organized by Lamounier in Brasília.

Together with Bolivar Lamounier and Carlos Nino of the Centro de Estudios Constitucionales of Buenos Aires, Argentina, Linz and Valenzuela participated in a two-year-long project advising the Fundación Milenio in La Paz, Bolivia, on constitutional reform issues. Working with a distinguished panel of Bolivian constitutional scholars, they helped draft a constitutional proposal for Bolivia that responds to some of the issues raised in this volume.[10] We wish to thank Gonzalo Sánchez de Lozada and Jorge Balcazar for their extraordinary hospitality during our time in Bolivia.

The debate on regime type has also been prominent in Italy, where many critics of the Italian political system have urged a move away from parliamentary government to some form of semipresidential system. Giovanni Sartori has played an important role in this debate. Earlier versions of his essay, and those of Linz and Valenzuela, were published in Rome in a special issue of *Arel,* the journal of the Agenzia di Ricerche e Legislazione.[11]

In October 1992 the Council of Europe, European Commission for Democracy through Law, organized in cooperation with the government of Turkey and the Turkish Democracy Foundation a conference on "Constitution Making as an Instrument of Democratic Transition" with the participation of representatives from most of the Commonwealth of Independent States and political scientists from Europe and Turkey in which Linz presented the chapter included in this volume.

In the United States, the *Journal of Democracy* published a short summary of Juan Linz's chapter with critiques by Donald Horowitz and Seymour Martin Lipset and a reply by Juan Linz. The article has been translated into several languages. The *Journal of Democracy* also published a summary by Arturo Valenzuela of the findings of this research project with respect to the "crisis" of Latin American democracy.[12]

We have referred to the long history of this project and our activities since 1985 in order to highlight the interest generated in academic and political circles even before the publication of the present complete and revised text.

We want to thank Louis Goodman, then Secretary of the Latin American Program at the Woodrow Wilson International Center for Scholars, for convening the original conference that began this project and Richard Bloomfield of the World Peace Foundation for his support of a very important effort to bring academics and prominent political leaders from Latin America together in the difficult days before the "democratic transitions" took place. We also want to acknowledge our gratitude to Shepard Forman and the Ford Foundation for the foundation's generous support of the research effort and to the Georgetown symposium that made this project possible. We are particularly honored that the symposium was included as part of Georgetown University's official bicentennial celebrations and are grateful to Charles L. Currie, S.J., and Kathleen Lesko for the magnificent support of the Bicentennial Office.

The National Endowment for Democracy supported research efforts and conferences in Chile, Brazil, and Bolivia directly related to the central debate of this volume. Jeanne O'Neil, Administrative Director of the Center for Latin American Studies at Georgetown, deserves special thanks for her magnificent contributions to the project from start to finish, including the management of several grants. We are also grateful to Henry Tom of the Johns Hopkins University Press who, once again, has patiently waited for a manuscript that seemed to go through endless revisions. Terry Schutz worked patiently and with skill in copy editing a difficult and unwieldy manuscript.

Finally, Juan Linz acknowledges support from the Wissenschaftskolleg zu Berlin for a fellowship in 1990–91 that enabled him to complete the final draft of his contribution. Arturo Valenzuela acknowledges support from the Heinz Foundation and the Fulbright Fellowship Program, which permitted him to update his contribution to this volume.

Notes

1. Karl Loewenstein, "The Presidency Outside the United States: A Study in Comparative Political Institutions," *Journal of Politics* 11, no. 3 (1949): 462.

2. Richard Gunther and Anthony Mughan, "Political Institutions and Cleavage Management," in R. Kent Weaver and Bert A. Rockman, eds., *Do Institutions Matter? Government Capabilities in the United States and Abroad.* (Washington, D.C.: Brookings Institution, 1993), pp. 272–301.

3. The splendid comparative work on democracy by Arend Lijphart and G. Bingham Powell, Jr., is not fully exempt from this criticism. See Arend Lijphart, *Democracies: Patterns of Majoritarian and Consensus Government in Twenty-one Countries* (New Haven: Yale UP, 1984) and G. Bingham Powell, Jr., *Contemporary Democracies: Participation, Stability and Violence* (Cambridge, Mass.: Harvard UP, 1982).

4. *Presidential Studies Quarterly* focuses exclusively on the United States; since 1977 only three articles have had comparative themes. *Legislative Studies Quarterly* has had no articles dealing with the presidency outside of the United States since its founding in 1976.

5. See Juan J. Linz and Alfred Stepan, eds., *The Breakdown of Democratic Regimes* (Baltimore: Johns Hopkins UP, 1978). This work was published in one hardback volume and four paperback versions: Juan J. Linz, *The Breakdown of Democratic Regimes: Crisis, Breakdown and Reequilibration;* Juan J. Linz and Alfred Stepan, eds., *The Breakdown of Democratic Regimes: Europe;* Juan J. Linz and Alfred Stepan, eds., *The Breakdown of Democratic Regimes: Latin America;* and Arturo Valenzuela, *The Breakdown of Democratic Regimes: Chile.*

6. See Linz, *Breakdown of Democratic Regimes: Crisis,* pp. 72–74.

7. For a criticism of the "breakdown of democracy" project for its emphasis on democratic procedures and institutions in their own right and its normative ("extremist") bias in favor of procedural democracy as opposed to "substantive democracy" see Phillippe C. Schmitter's review of *The Breakdown of Democratic Regimes* in *American Political Science Review* 74, no. 3 (Sept. 1980): 849–52.

8. See Juan Linz, Arend Lijphart, and Arturo Valenzuela, *Hacia una democracia estable: La opción parlamentaria* (Santiago: Editorial Universidad Católica de Chile, 1991), prologue by Oscar Godoy. Drafts of essays presented at the Georgetown conference by Juan Linz, Arend Lijphart, and Fred Riggs were published in Consejo para la Consolidación de la Democracia, eds., *Presidencialismo vs. parlamentarismo: Materiales para el estudio de la Reforma Constitucional* (Buenos Aires: Eudeba, 1988).

9. Bolivar Lamounier, *A opçào parlamentarista* (Sao Paolo: IDESP-Editora Sumaré, 1991).

10. Fundación Milenio, *Una constitución para Bolivia* (La Paz: Fundación Milenio, 1993).

11. See *Arel* Quaderni Istituzionali 6 (Rome, May 1991). Sartori has expanded his views of the subject with respect to the Italian experience in his *Seconda Repubblica? Sì, Ma Bene* (Milan: Rizzoli, 1992.)

12. Juan Linz, "The Perils of Presidentialism," *Journal of Democracy* 1 (1990): 51–69. Arturo Valenzuela, "Latin America: Presidentialism in Crisis," *Journal of Democracy* 4 (1993): 3–16.

Part I
Introduction

JUAN J. LINZ

Presidential or Parliamentary Democracy: Does It Make a Difference?

In RECENT DECADES renewed efforts have been made to study and understand the variety of political democracies, but most of those analyses have focused on the patterns of political conflict and more specifically on party systems and coalition formation, in contrast to the attention of many classical writers to institutional arrangements.[1] With the exception of the large literature on the impact of electoral systems on the shaping of party systems generated by the early writings of Ferdinand Hermens and the classic work by Maurice Duverger, followed by the writings of Douglas Rae and Giovanni Sartori, Rein Taagepera, and Matthew Shugart among others,[2] political scientists have paid little attention to the role of political institutions, except in the study of particular countries. Debates about monarchy and republic, parliamentary and presidential regimes, the unitary state and federalism have receded into oblivion and not entered the current debates about the functioning of democratic institutions and practices, including their effect on party systems. When a number of countries initiate the process of writing or rewriting constitutions, some of those issues should regain saliency and become part of what Sartori has called political engineering, in an effort to set the basis of democratic consolidation and stability.

Undoubtedly, the constitutional innovations of the postwar period, the German constructive nonconfidence vote, and the constitution of the French Fifth Republic, whose semipresidential regime reinforces the executive to counter the weaknesses of assembly parliamentarism, have attracted imitators and scholarly attention. But we lack a more systematic and behavioral study of the implications for the political process of different institutions on which to base some of the ongoing debates about institutional and constitutional reform. With the notable exception of the book by Kaltefleiter, in which the cases of a bipolar executive like the Weimar

Republic and the French Fifth Republic are analyzed; the paper by Stefano Bartolini,[3] on cases of direct election of the head of state in Europe; the writings of
Maurice Duverger and the new book by Matthew Soberg Shugart and John M.
Carey,[4] the differences between parliamentary, presidential, and semipresidential
regimes have not attracted much attention from political scientists. These differences receive only limited attention in the two most recent works comparing contemporary democracies, those of Bingham Powell and Arend Lijphart,[5] who has,
however, written an excellent chapter on the implications of presidential regimes
for this volume.

The neglect is largely due to the fact that with the outstanding exception of the
United States, most of the stable democracies of Europe and the Commonwealth
have been parliamentary regimes and a few semipresidential and semiparliamentary, while most of the countries with presidential constitutions have been unstable
democracies or authoritarian regimes and therefore have not been included in
comparative studies of democracy.[6] Since many social, economic, cultural, and
political factors appeared central in the analysis of the crisis and breakdown of
democracy in those countries, we find practically no mention of the role of institutional factors in those crises. Only in the case of Chile has there been some reference to the conflict between President Allende and the congress in the analysis of
the breakdown of democracy.[7] It might or might not be an accident that so many
countries with presidential regimes have encountered great difficulties in establishing stable democracies, but certainly the relationship between the two main types
of democratic political institutions and the political process seems to deserve more
attention than it has received. It would have been interesting to turn back to earlier
debates of constitutionalists and intellectuals, particularly in Latin America, about
presidentialism and parliamentarism.[8] But we suspect they would not be particularly helpful for our present concerns because they would reflect, on the one side,
admiration for the great American democratic republic and its presidential government, ignoring to some extent what Woodrow Wilson described as congressional government, and on the other, probably bitter criticism of French parliamentarism from the Latin American legal literature.

In my own work on the breakdown of democratic regimes, at the stage of cor-
recting proofs I was struck in rereading O'Donnell's analysis of the impossible
game in post-Peronist Argentina by the extraordinary difficulty of integrating or
isolating the Peronists in contrast to the Italian communists, which in spite of all
the strains in Italian democracy never led to comparable consequences. As a result
I wrote a brief excursus on the political implications of presidentialism and parliamentarism that I expanded and that constitutes the basic theme of this essay.[9] The
ideas I intend to develop require further research using empirical evidence from
different countries, particularly in Latin America but also the Philippines, South
Korea, Nigeria, and perhaps Lebanon. The essays in this volume represent an important contribution in this direction. Further work on the problem would require

research on the perceptions of both political elites and the public of presidents and legislatures in those regimes.

It is striking that most of the discussion of presidential government in classic works on democratic politics is limited to the United States and comparison between that country and the United Kingdom. There is practically no reference to long experience with presidential regimes in Latin America.[10] This gap in the literature inevitably weakens my analysis in this essay. It should be taken as a stimulus for further and more systematic thinking and research.

Presidentialism: Principles and Realities

It has been argued that the terms *presidentialism* and *parliamentarism* each cover a wide range of political institutional formulas, and that the variety among those formulas is such that it is misleading to generalize about either term. Even two "pure" presidential systems like that of the United States and Argentina, despite the influence of the U.S. Constitution on the constitution Argentina adopted in 1853, are legally quite different—and even more so in practice—so that Carlos Nino contrasts the hyperpresidentialism of his country with a more balanced division of powers in the United States.[11] The same is probably even truer of parliamentary systems when we compare the *gouvernement d'assemblée* of the Third and Fourth Republics in France with the *Kanzlerdemokratie* of the Bundesrepublik.[12] There is the temptation in a debate about the two systems to turn to the extreme—and therefore most questionable—cases for or against the merits of each. As I will show, there are in modern democracies (even leaving aside the so-called semipresidential or semiparliamentary hybrids) some convergencies between the practices of presidentialism in conflictual multiparty systems (like Bolivia's) and parliamentary systems with a personalization of power or leadership similar to presidentialism when one party has an absolute majority or as in Germany with the "rationalized parliamentarism" of the Basic Law (the Bonn Constitution).

However, this should not obscure the fundamental differences between the two systems. All presidential and all parliamentary systems have a common core that allows their differentiation and some systematic comparisons. In addition, most presidential democracies are probably more similar to each other than the larger number of parliamentary democracies are alike, partly because all presidential democracies were inspired by the U.S. model and partly because the societies with such systems (with the outstanding exception of the United States) have some common characteristics. In parliamentary systems the only democratically legitimated institution is the parliament and the government deriving its authority from the confidence of the parliament, either from parliamentary majorities or parliamentary tolerance of minority governments, and only for the time that the legislature is willing to support it between elections and, exceptionally, as long as the parliament is not able to produce an alternative government.

Presidential systems are based on the opposite principle. An executive with considerable powers in the constitution and generally with full control of the composition of his cabinet and the administration is elected by the people (directly or by an electoral college elected for that purpose) for a fixed period of time and is not dependent on a formal vote of confidence by the democratically elected representatives in a parliament; the president is not only the holder of executive power but the symbolic head of state and cannot be dismissed, except in rare cases of impeachment, between elections.

Two features stand out in presidential systems:

1. Both the president, who controls the executive and is elected by the people (or an electoral college elected by the people for that sole purpose), and an elected legislature (unicameral or bicameral) enjoy democratic legitimacy. It is a system of "dual democratic legitimacy."

2. Both the president and the congress are elected for a fixed term, the president's tenure in office is independent of the legislature, and the survival of the legislature is independent of the president. This leads to what we characterize as the "rigidity" of the presidential system.

Most of the characteristics and problems of presidential systems flow from these two essential features. Some other nondefining features of presidentialism are often associated with it and are discussed below, such as term limits or no reelection, automatic succession by a vice president, freedom in appointing and (even more) in dismissing a cabinet, sameness of head of state and head of government. One characteristic so normal that it is often included in the definition is that the presidency is a unipersonal office. There have been only two cases of directly elected pluripersonal "presidencies": the two-person Cypriot administration (1960–63) and the Uruguayan Colegiado (which governed twice—1918–33 and 1952–67).[13]

Dual Democratic Legitimacy

The basic characteristic of presidentialism is the full claim of the president, to democratic legitimacy. Very often the claim has strong plebiscitary components although sometimes it is based on fewer popular votes than are received by many prime ministers in parliamentary systems heading minority cabinets that are perceived by contrast as weakly legitimated by the electorate. To mention just one example: Allende with a 36.2 percent plurality obtained by a heterogeneous coalition (1973) was certainly in a very different position from Adolfo Suárez with 35.1 percent of the vote (1979), as were the opponents Alessandri with 34.9 percent and Felipe González with 30.5 percent, and the less successful contenders Tomic with 27.8 percent and Fraga and Carrillo with respectively 6.1 and 10.8 percent. A presidential system gives the incumbent, who combines the qualities of head of state representing the nation and the powers of the executive, a very different aura and self-image and creates very different popular expectations than those redounding to a prime minister with whatever popularity he might enjoy after receiving the same number of votes.[14]

The most striking fact is that in a presidential system, the legislators, particularly when they represent well-organized, disciplined parties that constitute real ideological and political choices for the voters, also enjoy a democratic legitimacy, and it is possible that the majority of such a legislature might represent a different political choice from that of the voters supporting a president. Under such circumstances, who, on the basis of democratic principles, is better legitimated to speak in the name of the people: the president, or the congressional majority that opposes his policies? Since both derive their power from the vote of the people in a free competition among well-defined alternatives, a conflict is always latent and sometimes likely to erupt dramatically; there is no democratic principle to resolve it, and the mechanisms that might exist in the constitution are generally complex, highly technical, legalistic, and, therefore, of doubtful democratic legitimacy for the electorate. It is therefore no accident that in some of those situations the military intervenes as *"poder moderador."*

It could be argued that such conflicts are normal in the United States and have not led to serious crisis.[15] It would exceed the limits of this essay to explain the uniqueness of American political institutions and practices that have limited the impact of such conflicts, including the unique characteristics of the American political parties that lead many American political scientists to ask for a more responsible, disciplined ideological party system.[16] In my view, the development of modern political parties, in contrast to the American type of parties, particularly in socially or ideologically polarized societies, is likely to make those conflicts especially complex and threatening.

Without going into the complexities of the relationship between the executive and the legislature in different presidential regimes,[17] the relative dangers of predominance of one or the other, and the capacity to veto or stalemate decisions on legislation, there can be no doubt that presidential regimes are based on a dual democratic legitimacy and that no democratic principle can decide who represents the will of the people in principle. In practice, and particularly in developing countries with great regional inequalities in modernization, it is likely that the political and social composition and outlook of the legislature differs from that of the supporters of the president. The territorial principle of representation, sometimes reinforced by inequalities in the districting or the existence of a senate in federal republics, tends to give stronger weight in the legislature to representatives of rural areas and small towns of the provinces than to the metropolises. And it is easy to claim that the democratic credentials of representatives of backward areas are dubious and that these representatives are local oligarchs elected thanks to their clientelistic influences, their social and economic power. Independently of the truth of this claim and of the degree to which a democracy would disqualify voters who, rather than being influenced by trade unions, neighborhood associations, and party machines, are loyal to local notables, tribal leaders, priests, and even bosses, urban progressive elites are tempted to question the representativeness of those elected by them. In such a context, it becomes easy for a president encountering resistance to his program in the legislature to mobilize the people against the oligarchs, to claim true democratic legitimacy, deny it to his opponents, and confront his opponents with his capacity to mobilize his supporters in mass demonstrations.[18]

It is also conceivable that in some societies the president might represent the more traditional or provincial electorates and might use that support to question the right of the more urban and modern segments in a minority to oppose his policies. In the absence of any logical principle to define who really has democratic legitimacy, it is tempting to use ideological formulations to legitimize the presidential component of the system and delegitimize those opposing him, transforming what is an institutional conflict into serious social and political conflicts.

The different "legitimacies" of a popularly elected president and a congress are already well described in this text of 1852:

> While the votes of France are split up among the seven hundred and fifty members of the National Assembly, they are here, on the contrary, concentrated on a single individual. While each separate representative of the people represents only this or that party, this or that town, this or that bridgehead, or even only the mere necessity of electing some one of the seven hundred and fifty, in which neither the cause nor the man is closely examined, he is the elect of the nation and the act of his election is the trump that the sovereign people plays once every four years. The elected National Assembly stands in a metaphysical relation, but the elected President in a personal relation, to the nation. The National Assembly, indeed, exhibits in its individual representatives the manifold aspects of the national spirit, but in the President this national spirit finds its incarnation. As against the Assembly, he possesses a sort of divine right; he is President by the grace of the people.

Incidentially this is not the analysis of an institutionalist (or political psychologist) but of the "sociologist" Karl Marx in his "Eighteenth Brumaire of Louis Bonaparte."[19]

Election for a Fixed Term: The "Rigidity" of Presidentialism

The second main institutional characteristic of presidential systems is the fact that presidents are elected for a period of time that, under normal circumstances cannot be modified: not shortened and sometimes, due to provisions preventing reelection, not prolonged. The political process therefore becomes broken into discontinuous, rigidly determined periods without the possibility of continuous readjustments as political, social, and economic events might require. The duration of the mandate of a president becomes an essential political factor to which all actors in the political process have to adjust, and this has many important consequences. If I had to summarize the basic differences between presidential and parliamentary systems, I might point to the rigidity that presidentialism introduces into the political process and the much greater flexibility of that process in parliamentary systems. This rigidity might appear to the proponents of presidentialism as an advantage because it reduces some of the incertitudes and unpredictability inherent to parliamentarism, in which a larger number of actors, parties, their leaders, even the rank-and-file legislators, including those changing loyalties, can at any time between elections make basic changes, see to realignments, and above all, change the head of the executive, the prime minister. The search for strong power and predictability would seem to favor presidentialism, but paradoxically, unexpected events from the death of the incumbent to serious errors in judgment, particularly when faced with changing situations, make presidential rule less predictable and often weaker than that of a prime minister, who can always reinforce his authority and democratic legitimacy by asking for a vote of confidence.

The uncertainties of a period of regime transition and consolidation no doubt make the rigidities of a presidential constitution more problematic than a parliamentary system, which permits flexible responses to a changing situation.

One of the presumed advantages of a presidential regime is that it assures the stability of the executive. This has been contrasted with the instability of many parliamentary governments, which undergo frequent crises and changes in the prime ministership, particularly in multiparty European democracies. It would seem that the image of governmental instability in the French Third and Fourth Republics, in Italy today, and more recently in Portugal has contributed to the negative image of parliamentarism held by many scholars, particularly in Latin America, and their preference for presidentialism. In such a comparison it is often forgotten that parliamentary democracies have been able to produce stable governments. Under their apparent instability, the continuity of parties in power, the reshuffling of cabinet members, the continuation of a coalition under the same premier, and the frequent continuity of ministers in key ministries in spite of cabinet crises tend to be forgotten.[20] It is also overlooked that the parliamentary system allows for removal of the prime minister who has lost control of his party or is involved in a scandal, whose continuation in office might create a serious political crisis. He might be replaced by his party, by the formation of a new coalition, or by the withdrawal of support of parties tolerating the minority government, without a major constitutional crisis. Unless parliamentary alignments make the formation of a democratically based government impossible, parliament with more or less difficulty and with more or less delay should be able to produce a new prime minister. In some cases of more serious crisis, there is always the alternative of calling for new elections, although they often do not resolve the problem but, as in Germany in the early 1930s, compound it.

In contrast, presidents are elected for a fixed term in office. The kind of changes that produce government crises and the substitution of one executive by another are excluded for that time. But this entails a rigidity in the political process that makes adjustment to changing situations extremely difficult; a leader who has lost the confidence of his own party or the parties that acquiesced to his election cannot be re-placed. He cannot be substituted with someone abler to compromise with the oppo-sition when polarization has reached an intensity that threatens violence and an ille-gal overthrow. The extreme measure of impeachment, which is in the constitutional texts, is difficult to use compared to a vote of no confidence. An embattled president is tempted to, and can, use his powers in such a way that his opponents might not be willing to wait until the end of his term to oust him. But there are no mechanisms to remove him without violating the constitution, unless he is willing to resign.[21]

Voluntary resignation under the pressure of party leaders and public opinion would be one way of avoiding the implications of the rigidity of the presidential mandate without the rumbling of tanks or violence in the streets. However, it is an unlikely outcome given the psychology of politicians. Moreover, in a presidential system, particularly one without the possibility of reelection, the incumbent can-not vindicate himself before the electorate. It is difficult for his former supporters to encourage him to such a step, particularly when some consider a vice president, who would automatically succeed him, even less desirable than the incumbent (as in the Fernando Collor crisis in Brazil in mid-1992). After two years and ten months and the complete failure of his administration, President Siles Suazo resigned, pre-venting another breakdown of civilian rule. Pressure from the opposition parties, the MNR (Movimiento Nacional Revolucionario) and the ADN (Alianza Demo-crática Nacional), which had the majority in the congress, the hostility of the major business organizations, and rumors of a possible coup had reduced his mandate in a little more than a year. It was exceptional in Bolivian politics because instead of a coup, the crisis led to an election in July 1985 in which ADN gained 28.57 percent of the votes and MNR 26.42 percent (an election in which the trade union movement and the radical left advocated abstention or void voting). Paz Estenssoro of MNR was elected president, and a period of democratic stability was initiated. Suazo's resignation is today widely recognized as a patriotic act.

Even "voluntary" resignation under pressure is likely to generate a serious polit-ical crisis because the segment of the electorate that brought the president to power might feel cheated of its choice and rally publicly to the incumbent's support. It is difficult to imagine political leaders resolving the issue without bringing the peo-ple into the debate and without using the threat of nondemocratic institutions, like the courts, and, more frequently, of political intervention by the armed forces. The intense conflict underlying such crises cannot be contained within the corridors and smoke-filled rooms of the legislature, as the nonconfidence vote (or more often the threat of it) against a prime minister or a party leader can be.

Identifiability and Accountability

One of the positive characteristics attributed to presidentialism is accountabil-ity and identifiability. The voter in casting his ballot knows whom he or she is vot-ing for and who will govern should this candidate win. The person voting for representatives of a party in a parliamentary system presumably does not know who the party will support to be prime minister, and if it is a multiparty system in which the party cannot expect to gain an absolute majority, the voter does not know what parties will form a governing coalition.

In reality neither of these statements is true or all the truth the voter would need to know in order to make a "reasonable" choice.

In presidential elections the voter may know much less about who will govern than the voters of a party in most parliamentary systems. The presidential candidates do not need and often do not have any prior record as political leaders. They may not be identified with a party with an ideology or program and record, and there may be little information about the persons likely to serve in a cabinet. The choice is often based on an opinion about *one* individual, a personality, promises, and—let's be honest—an image a candidate projects, which may be an image chosen by advisers (who are not necessarily politicians). This is even more the case in our age of "videopolitics."[22]

It may be argued that the voters of PASOK (Panhellenic Socialist Movement) voted for Papandreou, the British Conservatives voted for Mrs. Thatcher, the PSOE (Partido Socialista Obrero Español) voted for Felipe González, and so forth, although some might have voted for those parties in spite of their leaders or the other way around. Personalization of leadership is not exclusive to presidential politics. There is, however, a difference: leaders in parliamentary systems are not likely to have proposed themselves to the voters without having gained, and sometimes retained over many years, the leadership of their parties, either in power or in the opposition (something far from easy in the competitive world of politics). These leaders represent their parties. In addition, the voter knows that those who will form a cabinet will come from the party and, more often than not, are well-known leaders of the party with an accumulated experience in politics. A prime minister today is quite free in selecting his cabinet but certainly not as free as most presidents.

The argument that in a parliamentary system the voter does not know who will govern is not true in most cases because parties are identified with highly visible leaders. Those leaders appeal directly to the voters, and the campaigns increasingly are focused on the leader who aspires to be prime minister or chancellor. No Conservative voter could ignore that he was voting for Mrs. Thatcher, no PSOE voter that he was casting his ballot for Felipe González, no CDU (Christlich Demokratische Union) voter that Helmut Kohl would form the government. It could be argued that the party's parliamentary group or the notables of the party could remove the chosen leaders, that those who voted for Mrs. Thatcher, for example, had for the remainder of the legislature to accept Major as prime minister. But why would a party change leaders after the investment made in building them up, unless there is a feeling that they have proved inadequate? After all, the parliamentarians and party leaders have much to lose if the voters disapprove; they can be held accountable.

As to the indeterminacy of who will govern when coalitions are necessary in multiparty systems, with some exceptions, this again is not true. Parties commit themselves to an alliance, such as the CDU-CSU-FDP (CSU, Christlich Soziale Union; FDP, Frei Demokratische Partei) before the elections, and the voter for any of those parties knows that a particular person will be chancellor and also that unless one party wins an absolute majority (and even then) the government will include representatives of all the parties in the coalition. This is particularly interesting to those wanting a minor coalition party, such as the FDP, to have an influence. Voters do not know the exact composition of the coalition cabinet—which cabinet posts will go to which parties and leaders—but they know much more than voters for a president in the United States or Brazil know. Parties in parliamentary systems often have a well-known shadow cabinet, while a president-elect starts naming a cabinet only after the election. The identifiability in presidentialism is of *one* person; in parliamentary government most of the time it is of a pool of people and often a number of well-known subleaders.

Let us assume a multiparty system, no absolute majority, no previous coalition agreement. The voter still knows that the prime ministership will go to the leader (or one of the top leaders) of the largest party and knows which are the likely coalition partners of that party. The voter may not like one or the other of the parties, their leaders, or their positions but is likely to know more about the possible cabinets than voters for most presidents know. The voter for a major party hopes that it might govern alone. The voter for a minor party (eligible to enter coalitions) knows it and its leader will not govern alone but hopes that the vote will give it a greater share of power. After all only a limited number of coalitions are possible, and noncontiguous coalitions are exceptional. A Catalan nationalist voter for CiU (Convergéncia i Unió) in a Spanish parliamentary election knows that this party will not form a government but also that if no party has an absolute majority CiU representatives can influence the formation of a government and might even enter it. The voter certainly knows more about who and what to vote for than if he only had the choice between two presidential candidates. Should his CiU representative enter a coalition he disapproves the party is more accountable than the party of a president who would disappoint Catalanist sentiments to which he might have appealed.

Accountability to the voters for performance is presumably enhanced by the fact that a president is directly and personally responsible for policies—not the cabinet, not a coalition, and not the leaders of the party that might have occupied the prime minister's office in a succession. Only *one* person is clearly identified as governing for the entire period of a mandate. There are no confused or shared responsibilities. So the argument goes.

Let us analyze this argument. First of all there is no way to hold accountable a president who cannot be presented for reelection. Such a president can neither be punished by the voters by defeat nor rewarded for success by reelection with the same or a larger vote than in the previous election. A president who cannot be reelected is "unaccountable."

This is the case in thirteen presidential systems (counting those that provide for one or two interim terms) compared to six systems that have no limit on reelection or a two-term limit. We could add to these the semipresidential (or premier-presidential systems) of France and Finland, which do not limit reelection, and Portugal, which has a two-term limit.[23]

It could be argued that in the case of no reelection the party that supported the election of the president would be held accountable, but in fact that party's new presidential candidate is the person accountable. He would try to identify with his successful predecessor or to disidentify from him in case of failure. In a personalized election this might be easier than when the voter has to support a party that has not changed its leadership or has done so belatedly. Besides, it is partly unfair to punish a party for the actions of a president who, after the election, could govern independently of its confidence.

When reelection is possible, the incumbent president who is perceived negatively paradoxically can try, more or less successfully, to escape blame by shifting it to the congress, particularly if it was dominated by the opposition but even if his own party was in the majority. Just before the election he can propose legislation that the congress rejects and can claim that if his policies had been approved he would have been successful. A prime minister with a majority cannot play such a game. The division of powers can therefore provide an alibi for failure. The congress, even the president's party in the congress, can play a similar game by blaming the executive for not implementing policies it has approved or not submitting the measures necessary to deal with problems.

In conclusion, accountability with separation of powers is not easy to enforce. In a parliamentary system the party with a majority, or even a stable coalition of parties, can easily be made accountable to the voters, as long as the voters do not exclude in principle a vote for parties in the opposition.

The objection that in a parliament, parties, their leaders, and the prime ministers they support cannot be made accountable is valid only under certain conditions: when there are many unstable governments or shifting (and even contradictory) coalitions, and when no party has played a central role in the coalition-making process.

This might have been the case in the Third French Republic and in the "third force" governments of the Fourth Republic. Even in such a fractionalized parliamentary system as the Italian, I surmise that the voters had not much doubt until recently that the Democrazia Cristiana was responsible for governing and could have been made accountable if a sufficient number of voters had considered potential alternative coalitions (which probably were impossible without the participation of the Communists). In addition, in the case of coalitions the minor parties can be and have been held accountable for entering or not entering them, and the major parties for including or not including the minor ones.

However, in many parliamentary systems parties can be made fully accountable.

This is true in Westminster-type majoritarian democracies, particularly when a two-party system has emerged, and also in multiparty systems with coalition or minority governments. Voters in such situations often have voted for parties committed to form a particular coalition. The parties campaign with such a commitment although the voters may give more or less weight in the process of policy formation to one or another member of the coalition (checking perhaps the threat of hegemonic rule by one party). This has been the case in the Federal Republic of Germany. Moreover, the coalition parties can be and have been made accountable in the next election. Obviously one party might break out of the coalition, even change sides for the next election, but voters can reward or punish it for its behavior.

Another problem in presidential systems is not to be ignored: even in the case of possible reelection, the voters have to wait for the end of the presidential term to demand accountability. A prime minister can be made accountable to the parliament and his own party by a vote of no confidence at any time; the party becomes accountable to the voters at the end of the period or even earlier should the leadership crisis in parliament or the governing party lead to anticipated elections.

Winner Take All

In a presidential election whatever the plurality gained the victorious candidate takes over the whole executive branch, while a leader aspiring to be prime minister whose party gains less than 51 percent of the seats might be forced to share power with another party or to constitute a minority government. With some 30 percent of the seats he could not form a noncoalition government, while a president with the same vote could (although he might have a hard time getting the congress to support his policies). The control of the executive in presidential systems is in principle "winner take all."

In addition it is "loser loses all" for defeated presidential candidates, who might end without any public office after the election and, unless they have strong positions as leaders of their party, might have gambled away all their political resources. Where is Michael Dukakis or Vargas Llosa today? The loser often loses all.

Adam Przeworski commenting on this point has written:

> Linz (1984) has developed a number of arguments in favor of parliamentary, as opposed to presidential, systems. I am particularly persuaded by his observation that presidential systems generate a zero-sum game, whereas parliamentary systems increase total payoffs. The reasons are the following. In presidential systems, the winner takes all: He or she can form a government without including any losers in the coalition. In fact, the defeated candidate has no political status, as in parliamentary systems, where he or she becomes the leader of the opposition. Hence, in terms of the model developed above, under *ceteris paribus* conditions (under which $W + L = T$ is the same in both systems), the value of victory, W, is greater

and the value of defeat, L, is smaller under presidential than under parliamentary systems. Now, assume that political actors discount the future at the rate of r per annum. Under the presidential system, the term is fixed for some period ($t =$ PRES), and the expected value of the next round is $r^{PRES} (pW + (1 - p)L)$. Under the parliamentary system, the winner governs only as long as he or she can maintain sufficient support in the parliament, say for the period $t =$ PARL, so that the expected value of the next round is $r^{PARL} (pW + (1 - p)L)$.

Elementary algebra will then show that unless the tenure expected under parliamentarism is notably longer than under presidentialism, the loser has a greater incentive to stay in the democratic game under parliamentarism.[24]

My critics, however, are right that with the division of powers a successful presidential candidate might not "take all" because his party might be in the minority in the congress. They are also totally right that when in a parliamentary system a disciplined party gains a majority or more of the seats, it is truly a "winner-take-all" situation. This is likely in a Westminster-type parliamentary system where single-member districts might assure a party a disproportionate number of seats in a culturally homogeneous country. As Mainwaring and Shugart put it, the purest examples of what Lijphart calls majoritarian democracy, in which the winner takes all, are parliamentary rather than presidential democracies.[25] However, this is true only when a party is able to gain an absolute majority of seats, something that does not happen often.

Even when a party in a parliamentary democracy gains an absolute majority of seats—a "winner-take-all" situation, which is likely to happen in a Westminster-type democracy—the party leader or premier may not be in the same position as a president. To stay in office the prime minister has to pay attention to his supporters in the parliamentary party; rebellion of backbenchers or of the barons of the party can terminate his tenure. The fate of a powerful, once popular leader, such as Mrs. Thatcher, is paradigmatic: Mrs. Thatcher's party under the new leadership of John Major could win a subsequent election. Nothing similar could have happened when the failure of Alán García of Peru became apparent, and APRA (Alianza Popular Revolucionaria Americana) had to pay the price in the elections.

One of the possible outcomes of a presidential election is that the defeated candidate loses all. This is likely, and probably desirable, for the "amateur" challenger without party support. But it also is likely in a two-party contest. The defeated candidate, regardless of the number of votes obtained, is not likely to be considered a desirable candidate for the next presidential election and therefore probably will have lost his leadership position in the party. In fact, sometimes the defeated party is left leaderless until a candidate is nominated for the next election. Only in highly ideological and structured parties, or in some multiparty situations, do defeated presidential candidates retain a leadership position. Leaders of parties in parliamentary systems, however, are practically always assigned seats in the legislature and sometimes have the status of "leader of the loyal opposition" (although growing personalization in the campaigns might also lead to their resignation from leadership of the party).

No Reelection and Its Implications

The principle of no reelection or of no immediate reelection is not a defining characteristic of presidentialism, but it is clearly the predominant pattern. Shugart and Carey list eight countries (several of dubious democratic credentials) that allow no reelection, four with no immediate reelection, and one—Venezuela—with two interim terms. Among those allowing immediate reelection, five limit the presidency to two terms and six have no limit (including two semipresidential or, in their terminology, premier-presidential systems).[26]

The importance assigned to the no-reelection principle is reflected in the fact that the General Treaty of Peace and Amity signed by all Central American governments at Washington on February 7, 1927, provided that: "The Contracting Parties obligate themselves to maintain in their respective Constitutions the principle of non-reelection to the office of President and Vice President of the Republic, and those of the Contracting Parties whose Constitutions present such reelection, obligate themselves to introduce a constitutional reform to this effect in their next legislative session after the notification of the present Treaty."[27]

The principle of no reelection in many countries has acquired a strong symbolic importance. The memory of lifelong rule by nondemocratic rulers, caudillos and dictators, led to demands of no reelection, like that of Madero against the Porfiriato in Mexico. Attempts to change constitutional provisions barring reelection, efforts to assure what the Latin Americans call *continuismo*, have mobilized public opinion and led to riots and coups not only in Latin America but South Korea.[28] The prospect of reelection of an incumbent in the winner-take-all game often has united presidential hopefuls of quite opposite ideological positions, as some powerful Brazilian governors were united against Goulart.

The continuous support of the electorate for a particular party election after election, which we find in quite a few parliamentary democracies (Scandinavia, the United Kingdom, Italy, India, and Japan) sometimes has assured permanence in the office of prime minister. But it has not led to a demand to limit the term in office and never to violent protest and regime crises comparable to those provoked by efforts of *continuismo*. This tells us something about the different political culture generated by presidentialism and parliamentarism. The stakes in theory are different although in practice parliamentarism might lead to greater continuity in office of highly respected party leaders.

Democracy is by definition a government pro tempore, a government in which the electorate at regular intervals can make those governing accountable and impose a change.[29] The maximum time limit for any government between elections is probably the greatest guarantee against omnipotence and abuse of power, the last hope for those in the minority position. The requirement of periodic elections, however, in principle does not exclude the possibility that those in power might again obtain the confidence of the electorate. A turnover in power can also have dysfunctional consequences, because no government can be assured the time to implement promises, to carry through between the two elections major programs of social change, to achieve irreversible changes in the society. This is even more true when there is term limitation, as in many presidential systems. And all governments, democratic and nondemocratic, would like to assure themselves continuity over a long period of time.

The concentration of power in a president has led in most presidential regimes to attempts to limit the presidency to one or at most two terms. Those provisions have been frustrating for ambitious leaders, who have been tempted to assure *continuismo* legally. Even in the absence of such ambitions, the consciousness that time to carry out a program associated with one's name is limited must have an impact on political style in presidential regimes. The fear of discontinuity in policies and distrust of a potential successor encourage a sense of urgency, of what Albert Hirschman has called "the wish of *vouloir conclure,*"[30] that might lead to ill-designed policies, rapid implementation, impatience with the opposition, and expenditures that otherwise would be distributed over a longer period of time or policies that might contribute to political tension and sometimes inefficacy. A president wants to be sure that he can inaugurate his Brasilia before leaving office, implement his program of nationalizations, and so forth. A prime minister who can expect his party or the coalition supporting him to win the next election is not likely to be under the same pressure; we have seen prime ministers staying in office over the course of several legislatures without any fear of dictatorship arising because removal could take place anytime without recourse to unconstitutional means. Term limits and the principle of no reelection, whose value cannot be questioned, mean that the political system has to produce a capable and popular leader periodically and that the political capital accumulated by a successful leader cannot be used beyond the leader's term of office.

All political leadership is threatened by the ambitions of second-rank leaders, by their positioning themselves for succession, and sometimes by their intrigues. But inevitably the prospect of a succession at the end of a president's term is likely to foster those tendencies and suspicions of them on the part of the incumbent. The desire for continuity, on the other hand, leads a president to look for a successor who will not challenge him while he is in office. Such a person is not necessarily the most capable and attractive leader. The inevitable succession also creates a distinctive tension between the ex-president and his successor, who will be tempted to assert his independence and his differences with his predecessor, even when both belong to the same party—a process that might become quite threatening to the unity of the party. The person who has been president, with all the power, prestige, and adulation accompanying that office, will always find it difficult to relinquish power and to be excluded from the prospect of regaining it in the case of failure of the successor. That frustration might have important political consequences, such as an attempt to exercise power behind the scenes, to influence the next presidential succession by supporting a candidate different from the one supported by the incumbent, and so forth.

When a president is barred from immediate reelection but can run again after an interim period, as in Venezuela, conflict is likely to develop between the incumbent and his predecessor of the same party. The case of Carlos Andrés Pérez and President Lusinchi, discussed by Michael Coppedge (chapter 12) comes readily to mind.

Certainly similar problems emerge in parliamentary systems when a prominent leader leaves the premiership but finds himself capable of and willing to return to power. But probably the need to maintain party unity, the deference with which such a leader is likely to be treated by other leaders of his party and by the successor, and the successor's awareness of needing the cooperation of a powerful leader outside of government might facilitate an alternative positioning of the two leaders of the same party. The departing leader knows that he might be called back into office at any time, and his successor also knows that such a possibility exists. The awareness of both leaders that a confrontation between them might be costly to both creates a situation that very often leads to a sharing of power.

Political Style in Presidential and Parliamentary Democracies

The preceeding discussion has focused on the institutional dimensions of our problem. Some of the legal provisions in presidential constitutions and some of the unwritten rules that differentiate the types of democracies have been referred to. Other aspects that need to be addressed are the way in which political competition is structured in a system in which the people directly elect the president, the style in which authority and power are exercised, the relations among a president, the political class, and the society, and the way in which power is likely to be exercised and conflicts to be resolved. Our assumption is that the institutional characteristics to which we have referred directly or indirectly shape the whole political process and the way of ruling.

Perhaps the most important implication of presidentialism is that it introduces a strong element of zero-sum game into democratic politics with rules that tend toward a "winner-take-all" outcome. A parliamentary election might produce an absolute majority for a particular party, but more normally it gives representation to a number of parties. One perhaps wins a larger plurality than others, and some negotiations and sharing of power become necessary for obtaining majority support for a prime minister or tolerance of a minority government. This means that the prime minister will be much more aware of the demands of different groups and much more concerned about retaining their support. Correspondingly different parties do not lose the expectation of exercising a share of power, an ability to control, and the opportunity to gain benefits for their supporters.

The feeling of having independent power, a mandate from the people, of independence for the period in office from others who might withdraw support, including the members of the coalition that elected him, is likely to give a president a sense of power and mission that might be out of proportion to the limited plurality that elected him. This in turn might make resistances he encounters in the political system and the society more frustrating, demoralizing, or irritating than resistances usually are for a prime minister, who knows from the beginning how dependent he is on the support of his party, other parties, other leaders, and the parliament. Unless the prime minister has an absolute majority, the system inevitably includes some of the elements that become institutionalized in what has been called consensus and sometimes consociational democracy.

Certainly there have been and are multiparty coalition governments in presidential systems, based on the need for "national unity," but they are exceptional and often unsatisfactory for the participants. The costs to a party of joining others to save a president in trouble are high. If the endeavor succeeds, the president gets the credit; if it fails, the party is blamed; and the president always has power to dismiss the ministers without being formally accountable for his decision. Those considerations entered into the decision of Fernando Henrique Cardoso not to serve in the cabinet of President Collor in 1992.

In this context it is important to notice that when democracy was reestablished in two Latin American countries with presidential constitutions in difficult circumstances, the political leaders of the major parties turned to consociational types of agreements to obviate some of the implications of giving one party the entire authority associated with the presidency and the zero-sum implications for those not gaining that office. However the difficulty in forming true coalition governments in presidential regimes has led to more formalized and rigid arrangements. The Colombian *Concordancia*, a form of consociationalism, although democratically legitimized after being agreed to by the politicians, established a system that preempted the rights of the voters to choose which party should govern. To prevent the zero-sum implications of presidentialism, which were feared by the politicians, a system of dubious democratic legitimacy was chosen. The Venezuelan *pacto de punto fijo* had the same purpose but not the rigid constitutionalization of the Colombian solution.[31]

The zero-sum character of the political game in presidential regimes is reinforced by the fact that winners and losers are defined for the period of the presidential mandate, a number of years in which there is no hope for shifts in alliances, broadening of the base of support by national unity or emergency grand coalitions, crisis situations that might lead to dissolution and new elections, and so forth.[32] The losers have to wait four or five years without access to executive power and thereby to a share in the formation of cabinets and without access to patronage. The zero-sum game raises the stakes in a presidential election for winners and losers, and inevitably increases the tension and the polarization.

Presidential elections have the advantage of allowing the people to choose directly who will govern them for a period of time. Many multiparty systems with parliamentary institutions leave that decision to the politicians. Presumably, the president has a direct mandate from the people. If a minimal plurality is not required and a number of candidates compete in a single round, the person elected might have only a small plurality; the difference between the successful candidate and the runner-up might be too small to justify the sense of plebiscitary popular support that the victor and his supporters might sincerely feel. To eliminate this element of chance the electoral laws sometimes require a minimal plurality for the victor and some procedure for choosing when no one reaches that minimum.[33] Those requirements might frustrate the supporters of the most successful candidate. More frequent is the pattern in which the election turns into a confrontation between two leading candidates, either in a first or a second round. Such a bipolar choice under certain conditions is likely to produce considerable polarization. One of the consequences in multiparty systems of the confrontation of two viable candidates is that before the elections, broad coalitions are likely to be formed in which extremist parties with some strength cannot be ignored because success might depend on even the small number of votes they might be able to provide. A party system in which significant numbers of voters identify strongly with such parties gives these voters disproportionate presence among the supporters of the candidates. It is easy for the opponent to point to the dangerous influence of the extremists, and the extremists have a possible blackmail power over a moderate candidate. Unless a strong candidate of the center rallies wide support against those who engage in an alliance with extreme segments of the political spectrum and finds widespread support in the center that cuts into the more clearly defined alternatives, a presidential election can encourage centrifugal and polarizing tendencies in such an electorate.

Where there is great fear of polarization, the politicians may agree on a compromise candidate whom they respect and who does not generate antagonism. Such a candidate may be chosen more for his personal qualities than for the policies he advocates, and he is more likely to be a leader of a small than a large party. Such an option can serve the purpose of making a smooth transition to democracy, with its competition among parties and policies, or of reequilibrating a system in crisis. However, it is very doubtful that such an ad hoc coalition of politicians would want to or could give the president it helped to elect full support to govern, to make difficult decisions that alienate many erstwhile supporters and run counter to their ideological commitments. This problem would be particularly serious in the late years of the mandate. Such a compromise president might therefore provide weak leadership and be left without support in the congress. Many of his former supporters may dissociate themselves from him (without paying the price of a government crisis, as in a parliamentary system) to prepare themselves for legislative elections and the next presidential election.

It can be argued that in a society where the bulk of the electorate places itself at the center of the political spectrum, shares basically moderate positions, agrees on the exclusion of the extremists, and differs only moderately between left of center and right of center, the potentially negative consequences of presidential competition are excluded. With an electorate of overwhelmingly moderate centrist leanings, anyone making an alliance or taking a position that seems to lean toward an extreme is unlikely to win an election, as Goldwater and McGovern discovered on election night. However, most societies facing serious social and economic problems probably do not fit the model of U.S. presidential elections. They are likely instead to be divided in their opinions about an authoritarian regime that had significant support at some point and to have parties that are perceived as extremist with strong organizations and considerable appeal.

In a single-round election, none of the leading candidates in a somewhat polarized society with a volatile electorate can ignore those forces with whom he would otherwise not be ready to collaborate without the very great risk of finding himself short of a plurality. Let us retain for our analysis the potential for polarization and the difficulty of isolating politically extremist alternatives disliked intensely by significant elites or segments of the electorate.

A two-round election with a runoff between leading candidates reduces the uncertainty and thereby might help to produce a more rationally calculated outcome, on the part of both the candidate and the voters. The candidates can point to their own strengths and calculate how much their alliances can contribute to a winning coalition, and those tending more toward the extremes are aware of the limits of their strength. This in some ways would come closer to the process of coalition formation in a parliament in search of a prime minister.

The runoff election would seem, in principle, to be the solution in the case of multiparty presidential systems in which candidates might gain only small pluralities and in which, contrary to "rational" expectations, no broader coalitions are formed to obtain a majority. In a runoff in which only the two leading candidates are allowed to compete, one of them inevitably receives an absolute majority.

However, a number of dysfunctional consequences derive from this method of election:

1. In a highly fragmented system the two leading candidates might enjoy only small pluralities with respect to other candidates and might represent positions on the same segment of the political spectrum.

2. One of the candidates might be an outsider to the party system with no congressional party base.

3. The "majority" generated might not represent a politically more or less homogeneous electorate or a real coalition of parties.

4. The winner, although initially the choice of a small proportion of the electorate, is likely to feel that he represents a "true and plebiscitary" majority.

5. The expectation of a runoff increases the incentive to compete in the first run, either in the hope of placing among the two most favored or of gaining bargaining power for support in the runoff of one of the two leading contenders. Therefore, rather than favoring a coalescence of parties behind a candidate, the system reinforces the existing fragmentation.

Excursus: What Difference Would Presidentialism Have Made in the Spanish Transition to Democracy?

To illustrate this argument, let us assume that, in 1977 in Spain, the first free election after Franco had been presidential rather than parliamentary. In fact, of course, a referendum on political reform had called for a parliamentary monarchy, and the election was for a constituent parliament.[34] But what would the implications of a presidential election at that juncture have been?

First, in the absence of a record of the distribution of preferences of the electorate, despite all the information provided by public opinion surveys, which politicians would have tended to disregard, the prevailing incertitude would have made it difficult to form coalitions. And certainly the potential front-runners would have been forced to form more than winning coalitions. Assuming that the democratic opposition to Franco would have united behind a single candidate, Felipe González, something that would not have been assured at the time, González would not have been able to run independently in the way he did in the parliamentary election, given the expectations that prevailed about the Communist strength and the more or less 10 percent of the electorate that Communists actually represented. A Popular Front image would have dominated the campaign and probably obliterated the identities of the different political forces from the extreme left to the Christian Democratic center and the moderate regional parties. As it was, these forces could maintain their identities in most districts, except for some senatorial elections.

The problem would have been even more acute for the Center Right, those who had supported the *reforma* and particularly the *reforma pactada* exit from the authoritarian regime. It is not sure that, in spite of the great popularity gained by the prime minister of the transition, Adolfo Suárez, he could have united and would have wished to unite all those to the right of the Socialists. At that point, many Christian Democrats, including those who in 1979 ran on the Unión de Centro Democrático ticket, would have been unwilling to abandon their political friends from the years of opposition to Franco. On the other hand, it would have been difficult for Suárez to present himself with the support of Alianza Popular, which appeared to be a continuist alternative to Franco led by former Franco cabinet members; nor does it seem logical that the AP would have supported a leader ready to legalize the Communist party.

Excluding the possibility that the candidate of the Right would have been

Manuel Fraga, later the accepted leader of the opposition, it would have been very difficult for Suárez to sustain in a presidential campaign his distinctive position as an alternative to any thought of continuity with the Franco regime. In fact, the campaign in 1977 of the UCD was directed as much against the AP as against the Socialists and given the incertitudes about the strength of the AP and the fears and hostility it generated on the Left, much of the campaign was centered on the AP's leader, Fraga. This focus reduced the potential polarization between the longtime democrats "*de toda la vida*" and the neophytes of democracy who constituted an important part of the UCD. Inevitably, in a presidential election, the candidate of the Center Right and Right would have concentrated his attack on the dangerous supporters of the democratic left candidate, the role of the Communists and the peripheral nationalists among his supporters, and the compromises he would have made with them. The candidate of the Center Left and democratic left inevitably would have had to bring up his opponent's continuity with the Franco regime, the importance among his supporters of unreconstructed Francoists, and the absence among his coalition partners of democrats of even the moderate center, those who after the election in 1977 and in the years of constitution making and the first constitutional government after the 1979 election would play a prominent role in supporting the Suárez governments, such as the moderate Catalanists.

There can be no question that a presidential election in 1977 would have been much more polarized than the parliamentary elections that took place on June 15. Should Prime Minister Suárez have rejected an understanding with the AP, or Fraga have rejected an alliance with the Suaristas based on his bloated expectations and his vision of a natural majority of the Right and a two-party system, the outcome would have been either highly uncertain or, more likely, a plurality for the leftist candidate. A leftist president with popular backing, even with a different outcome of congressional elections, would have felt legitimated to undertake the making of a more partisan constitution and radical changes in the polity and the society. He probably would have made more changes than the Socialist prime minister Felipe González would undertake in 1982. González had been a member of parliament for five years, and his party had governed municipalities. The more utopian left wing of his party had been defeated in a party congress, and the main goal of the 1982 campaign was to win votes in the center of the spectrum, where previous elections had shown the bulk of the electorate placed itself. In my view there can be no doubt that the process of transition and consolidation of democracy in Spain would have been very different and probably more difficult with a Socialist victory in 1977. Comments by Felipe González about what a victory of his party even in 1979 would have meant confirm this.[35]

Let me caution that some of the negative consequences of polarization implicit in a presidential competition are not inherent to such a system and are not inevitable. They may be avoided when a massive consensus of the population favors moderate positions to the right and left of center and when the limited weight of the extremes is quite apparent so that no one is particularly interested in alliances with them. This situation is likely when there is a consensus to isolate the extremes, or when they themselves opt for running alone in order to make their propaganda and their presence conspicuous. But I doubt that these conditions would be found in many societies in the process of democratization and consolidation of democracy.

The Ambiguities of the Presidential Office

I have been discussing some of the implications of presidentialism for the electoral process. Some might feel that the election is one thing and what the incumbent does after being elected with all the powers granted to him by the constitution is another. Why should he or she not be ready to overcome the polarization of the campaign, heal the wounds generated, offer the defeated an opportunity to collaborate, ignore and isolate the allies on the extremes of the spectrum, and become the president of all the people? Such a policy and style of governing cannot be excluded, but whether such a policy and style are chosen depends on the personalities of the leader and the opponents. Before an election no one can be assured that this will be the choice of the new incumbent, and certainly the process of political mobilization in a plebiscitary context is not likely to facilitate such a turn of events. Moreover, such a stance might weaken rather than strengthen the new president because it risks alienating the more extremist components of his coalition, who are still in competition with the dominant, more moderate party of the alliance in the congress and other arenas for the support of the electorate. The possibility that extremists might claim betrayal makes it difficult to ignore their demands. In addition, if such a stance is not reciprocated by the defeated candidates, the incumbent's position is likely to be weakened. If a public offer has been made, a refusal may lead him to a more intransigent stand identifying even moderate opponents with the least legitimate members of the coalition that supported his opponent and thus reinforcing the rhetoric generated during the campaign.

Some of the most important consequences of a presidential system for political style result from the nature of the office itself: the powers associated with it and the limits imposed on it, particularly those derived from the need for cooperation with the congress, which might be of a different partisan composition than the winning presidential coalition, and above all the sense of time that an election for a limited number of years with no right of succession often imposes on presidents.

The presidential office is by nature two-dimensional and in a sense ambiguous because a president is the representative of a clear political option, a partisan option, and of his constituency, sometimes in addition representing his party within the coalition that brought him to power. But the president is also the head of state.

The symbolic and deferential dimension of power—those aspects of authority that Bagehot[36] saw represented in the monarchy and sometimes successfully incarnated by presidents in parliamentary regimes (as recently by Sandro Pertini in Italy, or by Theodor Heuss in the early years of the Federal Republic of Germany)—is difficult to combine with the role of the partisan politician fighting to implement his program. It is not always easy to be at the same time the president of all Chileans and the president of the workers, to be the elegant and well-mannered president in La Moneda and the demagogic orator at the mass rallies in a stadium. Many voters and key elites are likely to see the second role as a betrayal of the role of head of state, who is somewhat above party and a symbol of the continuity of the state and the nation that is associated with the presidency. A presidential system, by comparison with a parliamentary monarchy or republic with a prime minister and a head of state, does not allow a differentiation of these roles.

Perhaps the most important consequence of the direct relationship between a president and the electorate, of the absence of any dependency on politicians (to renew his power once elected by the threat of motions of no confidence and the need for confirmation of confidence), is the sense of being the elected representative of the whole people and thus the propensity to identify the people with one's constituency and to ignore those voting for one's opponents. The implicit plebiscitary component of presidential authority is likely to make the opposition and the constraints a president faces immediately in exercising his authority particularly frustrating. In this context, the president is likely to define his policies as reflecting the popular will and those of his opponents as representing narrow interests rejected by the people. This sense of identity between leader and people that encourages or reinforces a certain populism can be a source of strength and power, but it also can lead to ignoring the limited mandate that even a majority, not to say a plurality, can give to implementation of any program. It encourages certain neglect of, sometimes disrespect toward, and even hostile relations with the opposition. Unlike a president, a prime minister is normally a member of a parliament who, although sitting on the government benches, is still a member of a larger body where he is forced to interact to some extent as an equal with other politicians and leaders of other parties, particularly if he depends on their support as head of a coalition government or of a minority government. A president, given his special position as head of state, is not forced into such interactions; he is free to receive his opponents or not, and always in the context of his ceremonial status in the presidential palace.

One has only to observe the exchanges between the prime minister and the leaders of the opposition in the House of Commons, on one hand, and a president's speech before the congress, on the other. Anyone who saw the memorable session in which Mrs. Thatcher presented her resignation will recognize the difference. Even a president facing a critical or hostile congress would not face a similar situation.

In addition, in a presidential system the defeated opponent and the leaders of the opposition occupy ambiguous positions. Although publicly leaders, because they do not hold an office and are not even parliamentarians, they cannot act with respect to the president in the same way as the leader of the parliamentary opposition in Westminster.

The absence in a presidential system of a king or a president of the republic who can act symbolically as a moderating power deprives the system of a degree of flexibility and of mechanisms to restrain the exercise of power. A king or other symbolic leader can sometimes exercise a moderating influence in a crisis situation and can even, as a neutral power, facilitate a parliamentary rebellion against the prime minister and maintain contact with forces, particularly armed forces, that are ready to question the leadership of the prime minister. Even the presidents of legislative bodies who in a parliamentary confrontation between parties can exercise some restraints do not have such power over presidents; unlike a president, a prime minister sits on the government bench while the president of a legislative body presides over the chamber or the senate.

Given the inevitable institutional and structural position of a president, the people, that is, the people who support and identify with the president, are likely to feel that he has more power than he actually has or should have and to center excessive expectations on him. Moreover, they may express those sentiments if the president manipulates or mobilizes them against an opposition. The interaction between a popular president and the crowd acclaiming him can generate a political climate of tension and fear on the part of his opponents. The same can be said about the direct relationship a conservative president or a president with a military background can establish with the armed forces in his capacity as commander in chief. A president has many opportunities to interact with army leaders unencumbered by a prime minister or a minister of defense, one of whom would normally be present in a parliamentary monarchy or republic.

The Election of an "Outsider"

The personalized character of a presidential election makes possible, especially in the absence of a strong party system, the access to power of "outsiders." We mean by this candidates not identified with or supported by any political party, sometimes without any governmental or even political experience, on the basis of a populist appeal often based on hostility to parties and "politicians." The candidacy of such leaders might appear suddenly and capitalize on the frustrations of voters and their hopes for a "savior." Such candidates have no support in the congress and no permanent institutionalized continuity (due to the principle of no reelection) and therefore find it difficult to create a party organization. Only in a presidential system can candidates like Fujimori or Collor de Mello aspire to power. The same is true for military leaders like Hindenburg, Mannerheim, Eisenhower, and Eanes, although the success of these men depended upon the support of political parties. Scott Mainwaring[37] observes that in each of the four presidential elections between 1945 and 1960 in Brazil, one or both of the two top vote-getters were career officers who had no prior involvement with parties.

The "outsider," a presidential candidate running without party support, even against parties, be it Fujimori, Tyminski (who won 23.2 percent of votes against the 40.0 percent of Walesa), Aristide, Perot, or Chung Ju Yung (the founder of Hyundai) in South Korea, is not just the result of a particular crisis situation or of the ambition of particular individuals. There are structural reasons for such a candidacy.

If the purpose of a presidential election is to elect the "best" woman or man to the office and the individual voter has to make the choice, why should he or she think of parties? If voters can get sufficient information, or think they have gotten it, to make up their minds about the "personal" qualifications and positions of the candidates, they are presumably right in voting for a *candidate* irrespective of his links with a party. Voters feel that they do not need a party to tell them how to vote.

In the past this was difficult because no candidate, even one who did a lot of "whistle-stop" campaigning, could reach every voter. Today, perhaps in most countries, people can be reached through television. The "mediation" of parties, through presenting, endorsing, and supporting a candidate and organizing and financing a campaign, seem to be meddling and interfering in the relationship between the candidate and the voter. In some countries institutional changes recognize that fact: open primaries, registration of candidates rather than parties, funding of candidates by public means rather than parties, equal access to the media (either by law or by agreement of media managers) make parties less relevant in a presidential election. If in addition people are free to spend their own money to promote a candidacy—and why should citizens be deprived of this right if the money does not come from a criminal activity?—anyone may try to convince the citizenry of his or her personal qualifications for the office. After all we are supposed to vote for one person and for that person's program or positions. Why should we submit ourselves to the decisions of politicians controlling a party if we, the "sovereign" people, can vote for our candidate directly?

In a world where, for reasons we cannot discuss here, politicians and parties are the objects of relentless criticism, just and unjust, and rank very low in people's confidence, amateur outsiders are favored. In fact, it is tempting to run "against" the parties, which as continuous organizations controlling legislatures and government can easily be made responsible for the problems of a society, both solvable and unsolvable.

In addition, the crisis—not the end—of ideological certitudes and identifications, the loss of traditional party identifications mediated by class and religious identities, in a fluid, socially and culturally increasingly homogenized society, makes for volatility in party loyalties and for weaker links between interest groups—even organized groups like trade unions—and parties. The development of "outsider" candidacies should not surprise us.

It could be thought that the candidacy of an outsider with no party support, no previous experience in political office, is a Latin American phenomenon, an unlikely event in a country with well-established, traditional parties, where even an outsider would have to win the nomination of a major party, even should the primaries make it possible for a relative unknown to gain the nomination. In fact, third-party candidates in the United States generally have been supported by a splinter group from one of the parties. However, the candidacy of Ross Perot in 1992 shows that in the context of dissatisfaction with the parties, constant criticism of Congress, and the wear of primary campaigns, an outsider can appeal directly to the electorate. In the age of television, someone with wealth and popularity in a presidential system can appeal directly to the voters without having to build a party, as he or she would in a parliamentary system.

Former U.S. vice president Walter Mondale states this difference between leadership selection in parliamentary and presidential systems: "Unlike a parliamentary system whose leaders are picked by peers who know them, we have developed a self-nomination system where almost anyone with ambition can run for President. A candidate is not required to pass any test; he or she does not need any organizational base of support; it is not even necessary for him or her to have been elected to office before."[38] The problem with such patterns is that they are based on the initial fallacy that the "best" person in the office of the president—even if he or she had more power than presidents actually have—could govern without supporters in the congress, without a pool of persons with experience in office, without the support of politicians identified with his or her positions on issues. If we can accept the assumptions of the partyless presidential election, why not apply the principle (particularly in a system of single-member plurality elections) to all representative offices? In that case we could find ourselves with legislatures of *homini* and *femine nove* without prior commitments (except those made to their voters), who after election would have to aggregate their positions into something coherent to govern. We would be back at the first nineteenth-century parliaments, where those elected had to discover their affinities by meeting in coffee houses or clubs and slowly inventing the political party.

If partyless elections seem like unsound ways of assuring good government, we might ask ourselves what kind of institutional arrangements favor them or make them less likely. I would suggest that presidentialism facilitates them and that parliamentarism makes it more difficult for them to prevail.

An institutionalized party system makes it difficult for outsiders to enter into a presidential competition and even more difficult to win the competition. The decreased institutionalization of parties after authoritarian rule in Brazil, Peru, and Ecuador, in contrast to Colombia, Venezuela, Uruguay, Argentina, and Chile, supports this conclusion. However, one could also argue that the possibility and the incentives for outsiders to enter into the presidential competition has contributed to the arrest of or destroyed incipient institutionalization in Brazil and particularly in Peru.[39] In September 1988, once the discredit of Alán García had become irreparable, if APRA could have replaced him with another leader (as the Conservatives in the United Kingdom did with Mrs. Thatcher), the party's crisis might have been limited.[40] The not negligible institutionalization of parties in Bolivia and of cooperation among them since redemocratization might be threatened in the near future by the outsider, antiparty candidacy of Max Fernández.

Plebiscitary Leadership: Delegative Democracy

O'Donnell has noted that presidential elections, particularly in those cases that fit his model of "delegative democracy," are strongly individualistic but more in a Hobbesian than a Lockean variety: voters, irrespective of their identities and affiliations, are supposed to choose the individual who is most fit to take charge of the country's destiny. In his essay, "Delegative Democracy," he writes: "Delegative democracies are grounded on one basic premise: he or she who wins a majority in presidential elections (delegative democracies are not very congenial to parliamentary systems) is enabled to govern the country as he (or she) sees fit, and to the extent that existing power relations allow for the term he has been elected."

The plebiscitary character of many presidential elections, the polarization and emotionality surrounding them, the appeal beyond and sometimes above party, the sometimes uncontrolled promises made, lead often to extremely high rates of approval after the election. Approval may be as high as 70 and even 80 percent of the electorate. Such rates are not likely in parliamentary systems, in which voters identify with the parties of the opposition and the leader of the opposition continues to occupy a position of leadership. By contrast, the defeated presidential candidate often is reduced almost to the rank of a private person. The starting popularity ratings of a number of presidents and prime ministers show this pattern.

At the same time, failure and loss of support of a president is not cushioned by party loyalty. He or she is held personally responsible, and therefore we find drops in approval in the polls to very low levels, lower than most prime ministers on the way to defeat. Presidents suffer the wildest swings in popularity, as O'Donnell writes: "Today they are acclaimed as providential figures, tomorrow they are cursed as only fallen gods can be."

As examples of that dynamic in public opinion of presidents when they face difficult challenges, such as the economic crises in Latin America (inflation, the debt problem, and so forth), we might refer to opinion about Presidents Alfonsín of Argentina and Alán García of Peru. In May 1984, 82 percent of the population in greater urban centers expressed a positive opinion of Alfonsín. By August 1987 that figure had been reduced to 54 percent, and in April 1989, shortly before the May presidential election, to 36 percent. Even so, the president was always more favorably evaluated than the government, which moved from 45 percent in May 1984 to 27 percent in August 1987 and 9 percent in April 1989. Alán García, upon entering office in September 1985, enjoyed 90 percent approval; one year later in September 1986, his approval was 70 percent; in October 1987, it was 44 percent; in October 1988, 16 percent; and in January 1989 it reached a low point of 9 percent.[41]

In contrast, support for Prime Minister Adolfo Suárez never reached such high levels in spite of his role in the transition to democracy, but it also did not fall as vertiginously. At the high point in April 1977 when the transition to democracy seemed assured, it was 79 percent, and before the June 1977 first free election it was 67 percent, although the vote for his party, the UCD, was only 34.7 percent. By October 1978 it had dropped to 50 percent, and by December 1979 to 35 percent. By June 1980 it had fallen to 26 percent. The drop reflected the internal crisis of the UCD, the impact of Basque terrorism, and the economic crisis, and it ultimately led to Suárez's resignation in February 1981.[42]

Approval of Chancellor Konrad Adenauer started in the last quarter of 1949 at 33 percent. By the end of 1950, it was 24 percent. It started to move up in 1951 and 1952, rose sharply in 1953 and reached 57 percent in the last quarter, moved down in 1954, rose again in 1955 to 55 percent, and then hovered over the next years a little above 40 percent (with a low of 41 percent in 1960). The founder of the Federal Republic of Germany never could attain the massive support that Latin American presidents enjoyed, but he never experienced a great drop either, although conditions were more favorable for him to do so.[43]

General de Gaulle, despite his undoubtable charisma in the period from July 1956 to his resignation in April 1969, also never reached the level of approval of the Latin American presidents. Only a few times did the practically monthly surveys of the IFOP show a positive response of more than 70 percent (a maximum of 74 percent was reached in 1960); most of the time it was more than 50 percent and quite often more than 60 percent. In 1963 it dropped a few times to between 43 and 48 percent and was at 54 percent in May 1968 and at 53 percent at the time of his resignation.[44]

Are Presidential Governments Stable and Parliamentary Cabinets Unstable?

In the vast majority of presidential systems the president appoints his cabinet without congressional input, and the same is true for the dismissal of cabinet members.[45] The "advise and consent" role of the U.S. Senate limits the president's choice, but ultimately the choice belongs to the president and not to Congress. The president might not get the most wanted cabinet member, but he will get someone he wants. In Korea since 1987 the prime minister is proposed by the president and confirmed by the legislature. He then appoints his ministers, but he is not elected by the legislature, nor does he subsequently need its confidence. He remains the president's prime minister. In the Philippines, cabinet nominations are subject to approval by the Congressional Commission on Appointments, consisting of the president of the senate and twelve members of each chamber, elected according to the proportional representation of parties in the chambers.

The power of approval in these cases does not make the legislature in any way responsible for the appointment, but it allows the legislature to frustrate the president. The U.S. "advise and consent" role is the exception rather than the rule. Korea (as of 1987), Nigeria, and the Philippines also deviate from the predominant pattern. Significantly two of these countries have experienced strong U.S. influence. Even so, since only the president has the power of dismissal, the system is closer to "pure" presidentialism than to a semipresidential, semiparliamentary system.

The free choice by a president of his collaborators, the opportunity to dismiss them whenever their advice becomes undesirable, and their incapacity in such a case to return to the parliament with an independent power base is likely to discourage strong-minded, independent men and women from joining a presidential cabinet and making a commitment to politics. In a parliamentary system, those leaving the cabinet might use their position as parliamentarians to question the policies of a prime minister in the party caucus, in legislative committees, and from the benches in the parliament. A president can shield his ministers from criticism much more than a prime minister, whose ministers may have to confront the parliament's questions, interpellations, and censure, when the principle of division of powers is carried to its logical conclusion. Once more, practices and the relative positions of the congress and the presidency in a constitutional system can modify these implicit patterns, just as modern prime ministers and their cabinets are becoming more like presidents and their cabinets in presidential regimes.

It is often assumed that the freedom of presidents to appoint a cabinet without considering the demands of coalition parties or even powerful personalities or factional leaders in their own party assures greater cabinet stability. However, as Jean Blondel writes:

> The U.S. shares a common characteristic with the other Constitutional presidential countries, even though these countries did not normally live continuously under this regime. Ministerial duration is short in America: among Atlantic countries only Finland, Portugal and Greece had a shorter average duration of ministers than the U.S.—which, on the other hand, with ministers lasting an average just over three years, scores only a little more than the bulk of the Latin American countries, and is precisely at almost the same point as Costa Rica. Constitutional presidentialism does therefore lead, even where it has operated effectively and without hindrance, to a low ministerial duration; if the average ministerial longevity is under four years in Argentina, the Dominican Republic, Bolivia, Ecuador, Chile and Peru, it is under three and a half years in Venezuela and scarcely over two years in Colombia both of which had an unbroken period of constitutional presidentialism since the late 1950s. The average duration of ministers in Chile between 1945 and the end of the Frei presidency in 1970 was only one and a half years, although Chile had then an unbroken series of regularly elected constitutional presidents.[46]

Let it be noted that in many parliamentary regimes the prime minister or chancellor is also free to appoint his cabinet, that there is no investiture vote of the cabinet or approval of individual ministers, and that often the prime minister is voted into office first and then proceeds to form his cabinet. However, and this is the difference from a presidential system, the parliament can deny the prime minister investiture or confidence if it disapproves of his cabinet. Certainly in coalition governments the partners have a decisive say in the composition of the cabinet.

It can be argued that the game of "musical chairs" among ministers in some parliamentary cabinet governments, the *cursus honorum* in government offices culminating in ministerial appointment, does not assure experience and competence, but it seems very doubtful that the almost total renewal of government with each new president appointing his men or women is better. The fact that in the United States since 1945—with the exception of Johnson's retention of the cabinet after the assassination of Kennedy—only two cabinet members served under different presidents is striking and probably not exceptional in presidential systems. Besides, most presidential systems do not have highly trained and independent bureaucracies. They must rely on a government of "amateurs" with little time to become acquainted with the machinery of government or with policies in process and their implementation. Moreover, the experience they acquire on the job is not available to their successors.

In addition the generally more collective decision making in parliamentary cabinets provides all the ministers with some familiarity with a wide range of issues, so that when one finally becomes prime minister he or she cannot be ignorant of a series of issues. A state governor who gains the presidency has no reason to be familiar with foreign policy, to give just one example.

The position of ministers in parliamentary governments is quite different from that of ministers or secretaries in presidential regimes. Certain trends, however, are likely to lead toward a degree of convergence between systems that in principle are different. I am thinking of parliamentary systems with highly disciplined parties and a prime minister with an absolute majority or those that follow the model of the *Kanzlerdemokratie,* in which the prime minister is free to select his cabinet without parliamentary approval. All this together with the tendency to personalize power in modern politics (particularly thanks to television) has reduced the sense of collective responsibility and the collegial nature of cabinet government, as well as the individual responsibility of ministers. However, in parliamentary systems when the prime minister is dependent on party coalitions or heads a minority government with parliamentary approval, his relation to the cabinet is likely to be clearly different from that of a president to his cabinet.

Presidents and Vice Presidents

Among the characteristics not essential to a presidential system but found in many presidential systems is the office of vice president.

One of the more complex issues surrounding a vice presidency is the provision for automatic succession in the case of death or inability of the president, which in some cases is complicated by the fact that the automatic successor is elected separately and can represent a different political option, coalition, or party than the president. Or he may have been imposed as the running mate by the presidential candidate without any consideration of his capacity both to exercise executive power and to gain the plebiscitary support the president had at the time of his election. Brazilian history provides an example of the first situation, most recently with the succession to the presidency of Sarney after Neves, and Argentina illustrates the second situation with the succession after Perón of María Estela Martínez de Perón. Presidentialism leads to a personalization of power, but a succession between elections can lead to the highest office someone to whom neither the voters, the party leaders, nor the political elite would, under normal circumstances, have entrusted with that office.

Conflicts between presidents and vice presidents have been frequent. We only have to think of Jânio Quadros and Goulart, Frondizi and Gómez, Alfonsín and Martínez, and most recently Corazón Aquino and Laurel (who went as far as conspiring against President Aquino).

The same rigidity we noted in the fixed terms of presidents continues when an incumbent dies or becomes incapacitated while in office. In the latter case, there is a temptation to hide the incapacity until the end of the term (a temptation that incidentally also appears sometimes in parliamentary democracies). In the case of death or resignation of the president for one or another reason, the vice presidency presumably assures an automatic succession without a vacuum of authority or an interregnum. However, succession by a vice president who completes the term, which has worked relatively smoothly in the recent history of the United States, sometimes poses serious problems. The problems are particularly acute when the constitution allows separate candidacies for president and vice president. Rather than a running mate of the same party and presumably the same political outlook as the presidents, the vice president may have been a candidate of a different party or coalition. In such a case, those who supported the president might feel that the successor does not represent their choice and does not have the popular democratic legitimation necessary for the office. The alternative situation, which today is more likely—that president and vice president have been nominated in agreement—still leaves open the question of the criteria used in nominating the vice president. There are undoubtedly cases in which the vice president has been nominated to balance the ticket and therefore represents a discontinuity. In other cases the incumbent imposes a weak candidate so that the vice president might not represent a potential challenge to his power, and in still others, the incumbent makes a highly personal choice, such as his wife. Nothing in the presidential system assures that the voters or the political leadership of the country, if they had been able to, would have selected the vice president to exercise the powers they were willing to give to the president. The continuity that the automatic succession in presidential systems seems to assure therefore is sometimes more apparent than real. In the absence of a vice president with the right of succession, there is the possibility of a caretaker government until new elections, which are supposed to take place at the earliest possible date. But it is not sure that the serious crisis that might have provoked the need for succession would be the best moment to hold a new presidential election.

The Party System and Presidentialism

Several authors have noted that most stable presidential democracies approach the two-party system, according to the Laakso-Taagepera index,[47] while many stable parliamentary systems are multiparty systems. They also provide convincing arguments that presidencies function better with two-party rather than multiparty systems and describe the tension between multipartyism and presidentialism.[48]

Since with the exception of the United States, Costa Rica, Venezuela, Argentina, Colombia, and in the past Uruguay, most presidential democracies in the Americas (at least nine) are multiparty systems, it can be argued that there is no fit between the institutions and the party system. It could be argued that these countries should or could move toward a two-party system by "political engineering," for example of the electoral laws and other rules, but this seems doubtful. The Brazilian military regime attempted to impose a two-party framework but was forced to give up the idea. The electoral law enacted by Pinochet before leaving power had the same intent. South Korea, with between three and four parties in the legislature and three main contenders in the first free presidential election, has moved toward a two-party system with the fusion in 1990 of the Democratic Justice Party led by Roh Tae Woo, the opposition Reunification Democratic Party (RDP) led by Kim Young Sam, and the New Democratic Republican Party of Kim Jong Pilm (although the latent purpose was to establish a dominant party system like that of Japan).[49] It is questionable that a system in which one of two parties enjoys a large majority and is assured of gaining the presidency guarantees stability. The opposition minority, PPD (Party for Peace and Democracy) led by Kim Dae Jung, will have little chance of sharing or alternating in power. One might ask if a very polarized polity will not frustrate the opposition and contribute to unstable politics as well as opportunities for corruption in the dominant party. The situation in the Republic of Korea (where the DJP and the RDP together won 64.6 percent of the vote in the 1987 presidential election) would have differed from that of the United States, Costa Rica, and Venezuela, where on the average the president's party controls between 45.8 percent (U.S.) and 50.9 percent (Costa Rica) of the seats in the lower chambers. In the December 18, 1992, presidential election, however, Kim Young Sam was elected with 42 percent of the vote. His opponent, Kim Dae Jung, who gained 34 percent, announced his retirement from politics. The billionaire founder of the Hyundai industrial group drew about 16 percent. A two-party system seemed to emerge.

One of the paradoxes of presidential regimes in many Latin American democracies (and the Philippines) is the complaint that parties are weak and lack discipline and that representatives behave in parochial and self-interested ways. I say *paradox* because these characteristics of parties and their representatives make it possible in multiparty systems (in particular) for presidencies to work. A president without a clear majority in a multiparty situation with ideological and disciplined parties would find it difficult to govern, and even more difficult with an opposition majority in the congress. It is the possibility of convincing individual legislators, of producing schisms within the parties, of distributing pork barrels and forming local clientelistic alliances that enables a president to govern and enact his program without a majority. The idea of a more disciplined and "responsible" party system is structurally in conflict, if not incompatible, with pure presidentialism (obviously not with premier presidentialism or with the French semipresidentialism or semi-parliamentarism.)

Presidents have to favor weak parties (although they might wish to have a strong party of their own if it was assured a majority in the congress). The weakness of parties in many Latin American democracies therefore is not unrelated to the presidential system but, rather, a consequence of the system.

One might argue whether parties are essential to functioning democracies, but certainly the history of democratization has been associated with the development of parties and their legitimation. It is also true that nondemocratic regimes have been based on hostility to multipartisin either through establishing a monopoly or a hegemonic "leading role" of a single party, attempting to create other forms of representation, or the outright suspension or outlawing of party activity. In parliamentary democracies even antiparty movements have to transform themselves into parties to gain access to or a share of power, sometimes like the NSDAP (National sozialistische deutsche Arbeiterpartei) to destroy democracy, sometimes to participate in the parliamentary process and ultimately in government coalitions, like a segment of the "Greens" in the Länder of the Federal Republic of Germany. The antiparty stance of some Latin American presidents would be largely fruitless without building a party and searching for support across party lines. In Brazil, presidents have constantly stressed that they are independent from and above party; they have formed governments with ministers recruited from parties other than their own, even when they have made their political career in one party. No leader in a parliamentary system could win power by saying like Janio Quadros: "I have no commitments to the parties that support me—the ideas that I sustain in my campaign are mine alone." Even Hitler constantly emphasized his commitment to the "Movement." When a presidential candidate can say, "Professional politicians don't do anything except perturb Brazilian life," how can we expect the slow and continuous building of democratic parties? Who can be surprised at the constant party switching of Brazilian legislators when presidents switch parties (like Sarney) or disregard their ties to parties that elected them?

Mainwaring in his excellent analysis of the Brazilian case concludes:

> The question is why presidents have opted for supra- and anti-party tactics. In part, the answer may be attributed to the individual styles of the different presi-

dents or to Brazil's anti-organizational political culture. An essential argument here, however, is that the combination of presidentialism, a fragmented multiparty system, and undisciplined parties has made it difficult for presidents to function through party channels and has encouraged anti-party practices. It is not only personalities and political culture, but also political structures that explain why presidents have acted against parties.[50]

Presidentialism with Adaptations

The difficulties generated by the pure model of presidentialism have led in a number of Latin American countries to constitutional norms or political practices, to agreements among politicians or parties, that ignore or profoundly modify the principles of presidentialism. In some cases, as I will show, these practices have contributed to governability and prevented serious crises or the breakdown of democracy. However, in several cases they violate the spirit of presidential government, ignore or frustrate the wishes of the electorate, and have been outright undemocratic (although agreed to by democratically elected politicians) by limiting the choice of the voters. These patterns contribute to weakening the accountability we associate with democracy, particularly the accountability of political parties. They might also contribute to the cynicism of the electorate about parties and politicians, if not to its alienation and radical tendencies away from the mainstream of electoral politics (as in the case of Colombia).

Multipartism or drift toward it in a number of countries with presidential systems can lead to two responses: (1) an exclusionary policy in which the two main parties attempt to prevent the entry of other parties by sharing power and modifying the rules of the game, as in Colombia, or (2) constitutional reforms directed toward "coparticipation" or toward quasi parliamentarism, such as some patterns in Uruguay and Bolivia.

In Uruguay the complex political system has led after redemocratization to practices described by María Ester Mancebo as "from coparticipation to coalition."[51] These practices have contributed to what might be called a "nonpresidential" style of politics. They should not, however, be confused with "coalition government" in parliamentary systems.

Guillermo O'Donnell[52] independently and starting from a very different problem, has noted that Uruguay has a very different style of policy making from Argentina and Brazil. He asks

why the Uruguayan government did not adopt its own Paquete, specially during the euphoria that followed the first stages of the Austral and the Cruzado. Was it because President Sanguinetti and his collaborators were more intelligent, better economists or better informed than their Argentine, Brazilian, and Peruvian counterparts? Armed with this curiosity I went to Uruguay. There I found, with no little surprise, that some high officers of the Executive complained quite bitterly about the various constraints that Congress had imposed on the much higher degrees of freedom they would have liked to have in various matters, including indeed economic policy! It happens that in this case of redemocratization, although far from being the perfect institution that nowhere is, Congress effectively came back to work at the moment of democratic installation. Simply, because of constitutional restrictions and historical embedded practices, the President does not have the power to unilaterally decree things such as the *paquetes* of the neighboring countries. The President of Uruguay, for the validity of many of the policies typically contained in those *paquetes*, must go through Congress. In other words, the elements of secrecy and surprise that seem so fundamental to the *paquetes* are *de facto* eliminated. Furthermore, going through Congress means having to negotiate those policies, not only with parties and legislators, but also with various organized interests. Consequently, against the apparent preferences of some members of the Executive, the economic policies of the Uruguayan government were "condemned" to be incremental, rather inconsistent, and limited to quite limited goals—such as achieving the decent performance we have seen, not the heroic goals which the (first) *paquetes* heralded.

I must say that it was in Uruguay that I really learned about the difference of having or not having, as a network of institutionalized powers that texture the policy making process. Or, in other words, between representative and delegative democracy.

The Uruguayan "National Intonation" and "National Coincidence" were responses to the fact that the party winning the presidency had no majority in the two houses of the congress. In 1984 the Colorados had 41 percent of the vote and 42 percent of the seats, and in 1987 the Blancos had respectively 39 percent and 40 percent. This situation is likely in any multiparty system with an electoral system not favoring the largest party very disproportionately. Presidents Sanguinetti and Lacalle both chose to respond to the situation as a parliamentary party leader would have done by expanding the "parliamentary base" of his government, although the strategies of the two men differed considerably, largely because the political contexts were different (transition and consolidation phases). The difference from a typical parliamentary coalition government was that the cabinet members were not leaders of the parties and that neither of the leaders who were the "addressees" of the "understanding" resigned the right to act as "responsible opposition." In a presidential system they were entitled to do so without causing the fall of the government. Those cabinets naturally did not receive an explicit approval in the congress. In policy making President Sanguinetti had to use his veto power frequently.

Bolivia is another country in which the pure model of presidentialism in practice has been modified in ways that are more congruent with parliamentarism.[53] A presidential system assumes that a candidate or a party aggregates a broad basis of support, preferably a majority of those voting. The *voto útil* should eliminate or weaken minor candidacies. Before the elections the weaker parties should form broad coalitions in order to improve the chances of the candidate closest to their views and ultimately to lead to a two-party format. This has not been the case in a number of countries with a presidential system. Bolivia stands out for its fragmented electoral record in presidential elections, with leading candidates gaining less that 30 percent of the vote. Loyalty to parties and leaders on historical, ideological, class, and regional bases is probably more responsible for this pattern than the provision of a decision by the Congress among the three leading candidates. The resulting stalemates in presidential selection and the impossibility for a president of governing without making alliances are contributing to the frustration and considerable volatility of voters and might in the near future facilitate the emergence of a populist candidate running against the parties. (Such a candidate might in turn be blocked by the parties with strength in the congress).

After the last two elections the candidate with the largest plurality did not become president. In the first of these elections the runner-up Paz Estenssoro of the MNR (Movimiento Nacionalista Revolucionario) was chosen, and in 1988 the third in the running, Paz Zamora of the MIR (Movimiento de Izquierda Revolucionario) won; he had the support of the second-place Banzer. This was on the basis of article 90 of the 1967 constitution, which establishes that:

> If none of the candidates for the presidency or the vice presidency obtains the absolute majority of votes, the Congress will consider the three with the largest number of votes for one or another office and make an election among them. If none obtains a majority of the participating representatives in the first round of voting there will be successive votes among the two having obtained most votes until one obtains an absolute majority in a public and continuous session. The president so elected will have a fixed term of four years without being eligible until four years after the end of his mandate.

In a political situation so basically incongruous with an ideal presidential system, Bolivian politics has been working in many ways as if it were parliamentary—with pacts (like the Pacto por la Democracia), multiparty governments, a congressional "vote of no confidence" leading to the resignation of President Siles Suazo in 1985, but without many of the characteristics of a working parliamentary system. The parties making the system work do not explicitly assume responsibility for their actions, and voters cannot make them accountable at election time. The no-reelection principle leads to a reshuffling of the "coalitions" for or after each presidential election. For example, the ADN (Alianza Democrática Nacional) led by Banzer supported the Pacto por la Democracia and MNR president Paz Estenssoro and his policies in the difficult period of economic reform but, after the 1988 presidential elections, shifted its support to Paz Zamora, the candidate of the MIR leading to the Pacto Patriótico rather than to Sánchez de Lozada of the MNR, who had been the framer of the New Economic Policy (NPE) under Paz Estenssoro. The principle of "least distance" in coalition formation did not work.[54]

In the July 1985 presidential election the leader of the ADN, the former dictator general Banzer, obtained 28.6 percent of the vote. He was closely followed by the historic leader of the MNR, Paz Estensorro, with 26.4 percent, the MIR candidate with 8.9 percent, and the Movimiento Nacionalista Revolucionario de Izquierda (MNRI) candidate with 4.8 percent. Other candidates obtained 18.4 percent, and 12.9 percent of votes were blank or void. Since none of the candidates obtained a majority the election went to the congress, where Paz Estensorro, the second-place candidate, obtained 94 votes from MNR, MIR, MNRI, and PDC members, while Banzer received only 51 votes.

In the 1988 election Gonzalo Sánchez de Lozada of the MNR was ahead with 23.07 percent of the vote; he was followed by Banzer (ADN) with 22.70 percent, Paz Zamora (MIR) with 19.64 percent, and CONDEPA (Conciencia de Patria) with 10.98 percent and IU (Izquierda Unida) with 7.18 percent. The alliance between ADN and MIR gave the presidency to Paz Zamora.

While these last two presidential elections according to article 90 of the constitution were fully congruent with politics in a parliamentary system, they ran counter to the logic of presidentialism. Given the minority vote and the small margins between candidates, however, the "parliamentary" coalition making was not illogical. The system remained presidential because, once elected, the president held office for a full term without depending on the confidence of the congress. Introducing the possibility of a vote of nonconfidence, preferably the constructive vote of no confidence, for a president elected by the congress, would transform the Bolivian system easily into a parliamentary one retaining the possibility of a popular presidential election should any candidate obtain an absolute majority.

The Myths of Presidential Leadership and Leaderless Parliamentary Democracy

One strong argument made in favor of presidentialism is that it provides for strong, personalized leadership. This argument ignores the fact that presidents very often are not strong leaders but compromise candidates. While their office endows them with considerable powers, the congress's obstruction might make their leadership impossible, and in the course of their mandate they might lose their capacity for leadership, as examples in recent Latin American history would show. My argument is that strong leadership can be found in many parliamentary systems.

We do not have to turn to the United Kingdom with its two-party system, which assured the leadership of Churchill and more recently of Margaret Thatcher. In continental multiparty systems Adenauer and De Gasperi were able to shape new democracies, and Willy Brandt with a coalition government managed to shift the policies of West Germany decisively. Nor can we ignore the opportunity for leadership enjoyed by Scandinavian prime ministers such as Branting, Tage Erlanger,[55] and Olaf Palme in Sweden, Gerhardsen in Norway, Kreisky in Austria, and Henri Spaak in Belgium, to mention some social democratic prime ministers. In the new southern European democracies, a parliamentary system made possible the leadership of Adolfo Suárez, Felipe González, and even Calvo Sotelo after a coup attempt in 1981 in Spain, of Karamanlis and Papandreou in Greece, and now the prime ministership, with an absolute majority, of Cavacco Silva in Portugal. These have not been leaderless democracies, but at the same time the failure of Suárez and Calvo Sotelo did not endanger democratic institutions, nor were they endangered when conservatives and communists united to force Papandreou's resignation.

I would argue that there is a certain convergence between parliamentary and presidential systems in the fact that, in many democracies, people increasingly vote for a party leader who can govern. They shift their support to the party that promises to sustain such a leader in power and withdraw it from a party that does not have an appealing leader to head the government. The weakening of ideological loyalties and rigidities, the erosion of "kept electorates" by a more homogenized class structure, the growing independence of voters with higher levels of education, and the use of the *voto útil* against minor parties allow strong leaders to appeal directly to the electorate at the same time as they strengthen the appeal of their party and with it their parliamentary base. In contemporary politics the use of television, which permits a leader to appeal directly to the electorate, reinforces that tendency perhaps even too much. Voters in contemporary parliamentary democracies increasingly vote for a party to assure that its leader forms a government, and they vote against the party whose leader does not enjoy their trust. Personalization of leadership makes contemporary parliamentary systems with leaders who know how to use it more similar to presidential systems but without some of the negative consequences I discussed at length in my analysis of presidentialism.

It puts some limit, however, on the capacity of an individual with no party base to appeal directly to the electorate, as shown by the failure of former president Eanes and his PRD (Democratic Renewal Party) and the difficulties that an attractive leader such as Suárez found due to the lack of a strong party's support. In parliamentary systems, to improvise a leader by means of a personal and mass media appeal such as we are seeing today in Brazil would be impossible. Contemporary parliamentary systems cannot be described as unable to produce leadership and stable governments, but they do this without losing the flexibility that I have highlighted as one of their advantages. In fact, they allow, as the long tenure of prime ministers in a number of parliamentary democracies shows, the possibility of continuity in leadership that the no-reelection principle excludes in many presidential systems.

Personalized, even charismatic, leadership is not incompatible with parliamentary democracy, but such a leader has also to gain the confidence of a party, of a cadre of politicians that will supply him with cabinet members, with leaders of parliamentary committees, and with a constant presence in society through elected officials such as governors and mayors. Such a leader in contrast to one in some presidential systems will not be isolated or surrounded only by his personal loyalist technocrats and friends. He or she will be both a national and a party leader and therefore will have more resources to use in governing effectively. I emphasize once more that this is a probability but that no system, either parliamentary or presidential, can assure capable leadership able to gain the confidence of a party and the nation.

Perhaps one of the main advantages of a parliamentary system is that it provides a much larger pool of potential leaders than a presidential system, though this is not true when, for example, a single party has a hegemonic position due to its majority. In a multiparty system in which leaders of all major parties have a reasonable expectation of becoming prime minister or of playing a leading role in the cabinet, the number of aspirants to leadership positions that will enter parliament is likely to be much larger than in most presidential systems. Moreover, in the parliamentary process potential leaders can gain a certain visibility between elections, unless the media are exceedingly controlled by the government. Different leaders can make their reputations in parliamentary debates, in motions of censorship, votes of no confidence, and other public actions. The parliament is in some ways a nursery for potential leaders. In addition, the parliamentary system does not exclude leaders who have lost power; they are likely to sit on the benches of the opposition waiting for their turn, something that defeated presidential candidates often cannot do. In a parliamentary system the leader or leaders of the opposition can make a position clear to the electorate without having to wait for a presidential campaign, which, in any event, is relatively short. They can become visible and identifiable to the voters long before an election. It is no accident that in presidential systems the candidates often do not come from the legislature but have been governors of states where they had a home base of clientelistic links and where they made a reputation. This circumstance produces the important disadvantage that presidential candidates very often have little experience in foreign policy and macroeconomic problems and very weak ties to the legislatures that will have to support their programs and policies. This is true even for the United States and probably for other federal states like Brazil and Argentina.

Many studies have shown that political careers leading to top cabinet positions and ultimately the prime ministership are a function of a combination of loyalty and competence as well as length of time in parliament. Backbenchers can occasionally attack the party leadership and particularly the prime minister and his government, but biting too often is penalized. Even in those parliamentary systems that retain the principle of freedom of conscience of the MP, members who change party are a small minority, quite in contrast to the recent Brazilian experience (see chapter 8).[56] Although the traitors are welcomed in another party they are distrusted and unlikely to make successful political careers, including, with a few notable exceptions, those who contributed to the disintegration of the UCD in Spain. While the incentive structure in parliamentary systems encourages party discipline and therefore consolidation of party organizations, presidential systems have no such incentives for party loyalty (except where there are well-structured ideological parties). The president can provide personalized incentives to potential supporters, and the success of an individual legislator depends less on the performance of his party in power than on the strength of his more or less clientelistic ties with his constituency. That is why the United States Congress is today still one of the strongest legislatures and one in which individual members have great independence, although other factors, such as the sizable staff and resources that Congress provides to its members and the ideological diversity within the parties, contribute to the same effect.

Presidential systems can have strong parties, but the parties are likely to be ideological rather than government oriented. More often than not presidentialism is associated with weak, fractioned, and clientelistic or personalistic parties. We have only to think of the parties in Brazil, in the Philippines, and more recently in South Korea. Presidentialism might lead to the emergence of leaders, but it is unlikely to lead to party leaders able to govern with sufficient support in the congress, and very often those leaders will turn to nonparty cabinets of experts whose careers depend fully on their competence. In this context, I wonder to what extent the Peronist party can be happy with a cabinet of experts. Those who complain about the weakness of political parties and the poor quality of legislative leadership in some Latin American countries should perhaps look more seriously into the relationship between those conditions and the presidential system.

Presidentialism, Federalism, and Multiethnic Societies

It is sometimes argued that presidentialism is particularly appropriate for federal republics because the presidency can serve as a unifying symbol, especially in the absence of a monarchy, and can represent the nation as a totality in a way a parliament cannot. This argument might sound plausible, and the powerful example of the United States, which combines federalism reflected in an influential senate and a presidency, seems to support it. However, we should not forget the large number of democracies with a federal or quasi-federal structure that have parliamentary government, beginning with a country of the enormous social and cultural heterogeneity and extension of India. The Federal Republic of Germany is another example of combined federalism and parliamentarism, and in fact the Länder and their prime ministers have provided an important pool of candidates to the chancellorship of the republic. Canada and Australia are two other vast federal countries with parliamentary governments. Divergent forms of government account for some of the practical differences between the United States and Canada, particularly their respective party systems.[57] In spite of the strains between Quebec and English-speaking Canada, the parliamentary system probably has contributed to the unity of the country. Switzerland, which is probably the most federal country, not to say confederal, in Europe, has opted for a system that cannot strictly be called parliamentary, given its constitutional conventions, but that also is not presidential. Austria is another federal republic with a parliamentary system, although direct election of the president formally places it in the category of semipresidential or semiparliamentary. In addition, a number of quasi-federal regimes like the Estado de las Autonomías in Spain, the regionalized state in Italy, and the growing federalism in Belgium have developed with parliamentary systems. Certainly in Spain and Belgium the monarchy has served some of the integrative functions attributed to a presidency, and the same can be said about the governor general in the dominions, but the indirectly elected presidents of the Federal Republic of Germany and Italy have often been able to fulfill that same function without the powers normally attributed to a president in a presidential regime.

In some Latin American countries the heavy demographic weight and even greater political weight of some large states with large metropolitan areas would mean that a directly elected president would not be as representative of the whole federation as one in a country whose states were more equilibrated in population and resources. Therefore it would be doubtful to say that presidential systems serve national integration better than parliamentary systems.

One of the negative aspects of Latin American presidentialism has been the use of the power of intervention in the federal states, suspending or displacing authorities and appointing an intervenor with full powers. This practice is not inherent to presidentialism but is rather the result of certain constitutional provisions and their interpretation. Undoubtedly a central government, either a presidential or a parliamentary one, has to have some power to prevent actions by state authorities against the constitution or that represent a threat to public order. As the Argentine history shows, however, it seems dangerous to allow one person to make a decision to intervene without the possibility (except impeachment) of being held accountable by some representative body.[58] This practice has contributed much to the weakness of federalism in a number of Latin American countries. A practice that has weakened federalism in Latin America even more is the appointment of governors by the president. This procedure contradicts any idea of federalism.

The direct election of governors and their unipersonal authority is an indirect consequence, again not necessary but likely, of presidentialism. Such a system creates an inequality of representation because, in the case of multiple competitors for the office, it may deprive the majority of citizens of any chance to participate in the executive of the State, and that executive is in no direct way accountable to the state legislature.

A theme that will become more important in debates about democracy will be how democratic processes either help to solve ethnic, cultural, communal-religious, and linguistic conflicts or exacerbate them.[59] This is not the place to deal seriously with this enormously complex issue. Nor can we provide an answer to the question of presidentialism versus parliamentarism and these conflicts. We are handicapped because presidentialism has prevailed in societies that are relatively integrated ethnically and in societies where the problems mentioned have not yet erupted. For the few cases in which presidentialism has been tried in multiethnic societies—Nigeria and Sri Lanka—the experience has been short lived.

Advocates of presidentialism argue that a president who is elected by a statewide electorate can serve as a symbol of integration in spite of ethnic divisions. The success of such symbolism obviously depends very much on the method of election chosen. A simple plurality in a single election, which might assure hegemony to the largest ethnic group, certainly would not work. The Nigerians have attempted to deal with the problem in their constitution by dividing the country into relatively large, ethnically homogeneous states and requiring that a presidential candidate gain at least 25 percent of the votes in two-thirds of the states of the Nigerian Federation to assure that he does not represent any particular ethnic group or narrow coalition. The candidate must, therefore, seek support all over the country. A union of any two of the three largest groups behind a single candidate would not be sufficient support to reach the required threshold. The distribution formula assumes a territorial concentration of groups—that is, a certain level of homogeneity within areas but heterogeneity among areas. Horowitz discusses the uniqueness of the Nigerian situation and some of the difficulties in applying Nigeria's constitutional provisions elsewhere, specifically in South Africa, as well as the changes needed in the election of the legislature to compliment the election of the president.

One might object that whatever procedure is used in the election, ultimately a unipersonal executive will have to come from one of the ethnic groups and will be perceived as identified with that group. In any conflict in which his group is involved it will be difficult to convince his opponents that he stands above ethnic interests (or to forgo alleging such partisanship). Should this happen and should he fail to solve the problem, the rigidity of the fixed term of office makes it once more difficult to replace the president or to rearrange supporting coalitions. If a president, elected by whatever method, chooses to form a cabinet that neglects or is perceived as neglecting the interests of minorities, the situation cannot be changed (unless the system is premier-presidential or presidential-parliamentary, in which case there are the problems to be discussed).

In a multiethnic society without an absolutely dominant group supporting one party and obtaining an absolute majority, a parliamentary system would offer the possibility of coalition formation and consociational type of agreements, which could provide a flexible response to ethnic conflict. Not only coalition governments but external support for minority prime ministers would provide incentives for negotiation, compromise, and power sharing. Cooptation of leaders of ethnic protest would be possible. Obviously if the political leadership is not committed to the survival of a multiethnic state but to its breakup or to the hegemony of one group by any means, no democratic institutions will be able to function, neither parliamentary nor presidential. Votes then become irrelevant, and clubs rule.

Presidentialism and the Military

One argument used sometimes in favor of presidentialism is that it provides the political system with a personalized leadership that the armed forces can identify with as their supreme commander; it would be more difficult to identify with a prime minister. Such a direct relationship has existed historically between the armed forces and the monarch, and we still find traces of it in European monarchies even after democratization in Europe in the years between wars and today in Spain. Sometimes this relationship has been dangerous to democracy, as in the case of Greece, but when the monarch has been committed to it, as the Spanish king Juan Carlos has been, it can be favorable to the stability of a democracy. Presidents both in presidential and semipresidential systems have been conceived as continuators of the traditional relationship between heads of state and armed forces. This has sometimes meant a strong tendency to elect generals to the presidency, not only in Latin America but in some European countries in the interwar years, such as Finland, Poland, the Weimar Republic with Hindenburg, and Portugal both before and after the Estado Novo.

It is not always clear to what extent such a direct relationship of the armed forces to the president, particularly when he himself is an army officer, has contributed to a weakening of civilian political leadership and political parties. The political practices of the Weimar Republic, in which the high command of the army had direct access to the president without mediation by the cabinet in a semipresidential, semiparliamentary regime, have not been seen by many scholars as contributing to the stability of German democracy. In Portugal similar practices led to a peculiar dyarchy of the parliament and the military, which grew out of a pact between the parties and the MFA (Armed Forces Movement). The initial constitution-making process, which limited the powers of the parliament, and the role of the moderate military in breaking with revolutionary threats gave the armed forces a place not reserved to them in most democratic constitutions. This situation has changed only with recent constitutional reforms. In that context, the directly elected president, himself a military man, had to play an important role.[60] However, it is not assured that a civilian president in a presidential system can play the role of head of the armed forces better than the heads of the military hierarchy subordinated to the minister of defense and through him to the cabinet and the prime minister, as is the case in most democracies.

Undoubtedly, the personalization for a period of time of authority in a president who is both the head of government and the head of state—a symbolic point of reference for the nation when he enjoys widespread legitimacy and support—might be congruent with the value system of a military organization. But in the case of delegitimation and controversy surrounding the president, such a personalized relationship might prompt the military to take unconstitutional actions against the president. A less drastic response would be likely in the case of a less personalized direct and permanent relationship, as in a parliamentary system, where a minister of defense mediates between a prime minister and the armed forces.

The Head of State in Parliamentary Regimes

In analyzing parliamentary regimes—except in biographical and sometimes journalistic writings—political scientists tend to neglect the role of the head of state: monarch, governor general in the British Commonwealth countries, and president in the republics.[61] The role of heads of state is not irrelevant to our main theme because in presidential democracies this role and that of chief executive are not separated. Only if the head of state in parliamentary regimes is assumed to be a decorative figure would the absence of division between these roles in presidentialism be irrelevant. We have already noted some of the tensions generated by confusion of the roles of head of state—the dignified part of the presidential role—and chief executive and often party leader—the object of legitimate controversy and of attack by the opposition.

Without falling into a functionalist teleology—the notion that everything has to have a function, that monarchs and their "successors," the presidents in parliamentary republics, cannot be simply survivals of times past—it seems justified to enquire into these roles. There is evidence that on occasion a king can play an important, perhaps decisive, role, such as that played by King Juan Carlos of Spain at the time of the February 23, 1981, coup attempt. One might object that the king was important on that occasion only because Spanish democracy was not consolidated and the monarchy represented a "backward legitimation" derived from the Franco legacy, but I surmise that something more was at stake. We should not forget that many of the constitutional parliamentary monarchies of Europe survived the crisis of democracy in the twenties and thirties. And if presidents in pure parliamentary republics were irrelevant, it would not make sense for politicians to put so much effort into electing their preferred candidate to the office.

This is not the place to develop a detailed analysis of the roles of heads of state, but we might suggest a few ranging from the apparently trivial to the politically important. A trivial one is the assumption of a large number of "representative" and ceremonial functions in the life of modern states, from receiving credentials of ambassadors to visiting foreign countries to inaugurating meetings and buildings. These activities consume time that, in the case of presidents, is subtracted from governing. Travel abroad for a number of purposes, for which Latin American presidents usually require congressional authorization, is also time consuming. Ceremonial activities of a king or head of state outside of the daily political battles can link the regime to groups that might feel flattered and otherwise alienated, such as intellectuals, artists, and last but not least the military. One advantage is that a nonpartisan figure, if he or she is respected, makes it more difficult for public events to become occasions for delegitimizing protest.

Heads of state, perhaps because they are not pressed by daily business, can also keep informed, maintain contact with a wide range of persons, including the leading politicians, and convey their views privately but with some authority to prime ministers. In fact we know, from the example of Theodor Heuss and Chancellor Adenauer, how such a relationship can develop into one of trust and counsel.[62] No one in a presidential system is institutionally entitled to such a role.

The head of state can play the role of adviser or arbiter by bringing party leaders together and facilitating the flow of information among them. He also can serve as a symbol of national unity in ethnically or culturally divided states; if he had executive functions, this would be difficult to do. This role is one of the important functions of the monarchy in Belgium.

The combination between neutral friend to the parties and their leaders competing for power and dispenser of information and advice is not easy to maintain, and not all heads of state are up to the task. We know little about how that role is performed since discretion surrounds the activities of monarchs and presidents of parliamentary republics. However, differentiating between the roles of head of state and prime minister can be an element favoring compromise, negotiation, and moderation.[63]

Responses to the Critique of Presidentialism

Responses to the implicit critique of presidentialism in my writings have taken four basic directions: (1) admitting the arguments but citing the political culture of Latin America and the weight of tradition; (2) focusing on particular aspects of presidentialism that are not essential to it and are susceptible to reform; (3) favoring semipresidential, semiparliamentary systems; and (4) searching for innovative solutions.

There can be no question of the strength of the presidential tradition in Latin America, but to appeal to tradition could make any innovation impossible. In addition, in many countries the periods of democratic rather than authoritarian presidentialism have been short. Most presidents have been de facto governors deriving power from a coup rather than an election, or from a dubious election. The masses of people by themselves prefer a system they know to something unknown and not understood. It is the task of the elites to explain the earlier failures of presidentialism and their reasons for preferring another system. Even when people acknowledge the failure of presidentialism, as large numbers of Brazilians today do, they will not tend to choose parliamentarism (as Brazilians will be able to do in the 1993 plebiscite) unless their political leaders choose it and advocate it publicly.

The second type of response has much advanced our understanding of presidential systems. There can be no question that specific constitutional or legal reforms (particularly of electoral laws) might improve presidential systems and facilitate governability. I agree with many of them, particularly those related to the impact of the electoral cycle in presidential systems. Others, like a runoff election to avoid, in my view largely mechanically, a president with only minority support, seem more debatable.

The next section discusses, critically, the semipresidential, semiparliamentary regimes.

As to innovative solutions to the problems of presidentialism, I am not enthusiastic, although I confess I have tried to formulate some.

Semipresidential or Semiparliamentary Systems or Bipolar Executive

The success of the Fifth Republic in France has attracted the attention of scholars and politicians and has led to consideration of similar systems as an alternative to both presidentialism and parliamentarism.[64] Such a system has been described in the literature as a bipolar executive, a divided executive, a parliamentary presidential republic, a quasi-parliamentary and a semipresidential government, and most recently by Shugart and Carey as a premier-presidential system, indicating how different those systems can be both in theory and practice.[65] The list of countries that have experimented with or instituted such regimes is fairly long, and all those who write about the regimes, particularly Maurice Duverger, agree that they function very differently.[66] In fact, Arend Lijphart has argued that these systems are not syntheses of parliamentary and presidential systems but rather systems that alternate between presidential and parliamentary phases.[67]

Basically, dual executive systems have a president who is elected by the people either directly or indirectly, rather than nominated by the parliament, and a prime minister who needs the confidence of parliament. Other characteristics not always found but often associated with dual executive systems are: the president appoints the prime minister, although he needs the support of the parliament, and the president can dissolve the parliament. This is a significant break with the principle of separation of powers. In presidential systems we find this power only in the 1980 Pinochet constitution of Chile, in Paraguay (which has no history of democratic government), in Uruguay (where it exists only in very special cases and has never been invoked), and in the 1979 Peruvian pseudoparliamentary constitution. In dual executive systems, to dissolve the parliament the president needs the agreement— the countersignature—of the prime minister, but since the president names the prime minister, he is likely to find someone who will support dissolution. It was this combination of presidential power to dissolve the Reichstag and freedom to appoint a chancellor who would countersign the dissolution that led, at the end of the Weimar Republic, to the fateful elections in which the Nazis gained strength and finally, in the semifree March 1933 election, a majority. Sometimes the president can bypass parliament by claiming emergency powers and calling for a referendum. Powers assigned to the president and the prime minister vary appreciably, both legally and even more in practice, but in contrast to the monarch or the pres-

ident in parliamentary systems, the president in these systems is not a symbolic figure but enjoys potential if not actual power to affect policies and the governmental
process.

These systems have emerged under very special and unique circumstances in
quite different countries.[68] Attention is mainly focused on the Fifth Republic, and
it is often forgotten that one of the first democracies that experimented with this
model was the Weimar Republic. It is surprising to find little attention paid to the
way that democracy operated when dual executive systems are discussed today. Arguments for the introduction of such a system were first formulated by Max Weber.
Hugo Preuss, the drafter of the Weimar constitution, followed Weber, with some
differences in emphasis. Dual executive systems used today are not very different
from those formulated in Weimar Germany.[69] Another outstanding example of
such a regime is that of Finland, while three other cases—Austria after 1929, Iceland, and Ireland—have worked fundamentally as parliamentary systems even
though they have some of the characteristics of semipresidential systems, by my
definition.[70] More recently Portugal, influenced by the French model, has attempted to introduce such a system,[71] and semipresidential systems have been discussed in Latin America in the course of recent transitions, although they have not
been institutionalized in constitutional reforms.[72] Some elements of the Weimar
experience were also influential in shaping the Spanish constitution of 1931. The
contrast between Weimar and the Fifth Republic already tells us that the relationship between this type of system and the stability of democracy is not unambigu-
ous. In all cases in which such a system has been introduced, particular historical
circumstances contributed decisively to its enactment. It should not be forgotten
that all European democracies in 1918 were constitutional monarchies, with the exception of Switzerland and France. At that point, the French Third Republic with
its *régime d'assemblée* was not an attractive model, and therefore Germany, after
abolishing the monarchy, turned to political innovation. Originally the aim of Max
Weber and others was to establish a parliamentary monarchy after the British
model. The impossibility of doing so and certain characteristics of the German
party system, the federal character of the state, and concerns about leadership in
Germany's difficult international position led to a directly elected president without abandoning the parliamentary tradition already established. A strong leader
was wanted for the new democracy, but full presidentialism with separation of
powers, as in the United States, was not considered.

The 1919 German constitution, approved in Weimar, established a semipresidential, semiparliamentary system. The president was popularly elected for a seven-
year term and could be reelected. He appointed and dismissed the chancellor, who
selected the cabinet, although the Kanzler needed the confidence of parliament.
With the signature of the chancellor, the president could dissolve the Reichstag.
Should the chancellor refuse, the president could dismiss him and appoint another
who would dissolve the Reichstag and call a new election, governing in the interim.

Naturally as long as the Reichstag was able to produce a majority supporting a government, it was not dissolved, but without a majority there was the possibility of presidential cabinets and short-lived governments, leading to repeated elections in the hope of producing a Reichstag majority. In addition the president had direct command of the armed forces and was able to give *"unmittelbare Befehle."* He also had the wide powers of article 48 in emergency situations. All these powers played an important role in the demise of the Weimar democracy.

In Finland, where many on the right wanted to establish a constitutional monarchy, the impossibility of doing so and the fear of hegemony of the left, which was distrusted, led to the peculiar compromise that has lasted until today.[73]

In many cases, as in France in 1958–62, a major factor in introducing a dual executive government was distrust of political parties, although the functioning of such a system ultimately depends on parties and the relationship between the president and the parties and the party system. The idea of a neutral power arbitrating between the parties or above them was very appealing in countries where polarization between parties made parliamentarism difficult, as was the case in Austria's constitutional reform of 1929, which was practically abandoned in 1931.

As Bartolini[74] has shown in great detail, dual executive systems have been introduced in countries that achieved their independence from another country or from a dominating power and sought a symbol of the new nation. This was to some extent the case in Finland but more particularly in Ireland and Iceland after independence. Popular legitimation was wanted to give the president in a new democracy or new state some of the dignity of the disappeared monarch.

The circumstances that led to a dual executive system in Portugal are more complex because of the uncertainties of a transition to democracy via military coup. The possibility of having a general as president to arbitrate between the legislature, representing political parties, and the Council of the Revolution, representing first the Movement of Armed Forces (MFA) and later the armed forces, is a feature of the Portuguese system that imitates the French model. Later constitutional reforms (1982) and a change in the party system (particularly when the government has majority support) has led to an increased parliamentarization of the system.[75]

The particular crisis of the Fourth Republic, brought to a head by the Algerian war and the coup of May 13, 1953, as well as the unique historical role of Charles de Gaulle led to the Fifth Republic. It could even be argued that in France and in Portugal one of the considerations for introducing a bipolar system was to assure subordination of the army to a president who had particular legitimacy with the armed forces, as was the case with Charles de Gaulle and with President Eanes.[76]

A formalistic legal and constitutional analysis of these regimes in our view does not reveal the entire truth and is even misleading. Even an analysis of actual party constellations in the assembly and of the president's support is not sufficient. The underlying and conflicting conceptions of the political system that often have led to the introduction of bipolar regimes, and the ambiguities and compromises resulting from them, explain the lack of consensus in the interpretation of constitutional roles and the partisan alignments supporting the powers of the president or the assembly and the prime minister that are reflected in the debates of constitutional lawyers and that can become critically important in a crisis of the regime. Advocates of bipolar regimes should give more serious attention to the complex (and well-studied) Weimar experience.

The systems that can broadly be classified as dual executive show many significant differences in powers attributed to the president by the constitution. These powers do not always coincide with actual powers exercised at least at some stages. As Duverger[77] notes in his discussion of seven cases, in three of them the president plays an important role, in the fourth he could play an important role, and in the other three his role is weak; in none of the cases is the strength of the presidency a reflection of the formal constitutional powers given it. In addition, analysis of Weimar by Kaltefleiter[78] and others shows how the same institution worked very differently under different circumstances and more specifically different relationships between the president and the party system. The same can be said for the Fifth Republic, although the fact that the president has lacked a majority in the parliament for only a short period (1986–88) makes the pattern more consistent.

As with all political institutions, it is impossible to analyze the performance of a bipolar regime independently of the larger political system, most specifically the party system and the complex historical situation. In fact, I suspect that this is truer of bipolar regimes than of other types of government. It would be a simplification to attribute the stability of the Fifth Republic in France to the introduction of a new constitution because simultaneously an important change was introduced in the electoral system with a shift from proportional representation to a two-round majority system (1958–86). After the return to proportional representation in 1986, a threshold for representation was introduced. The strong electoral system, to use the terminology of Sartori, combined with a presidential system and its institutionalization under the very personal leadership of de Gaulle, produced a fundamental change in the party system and with it the political system. It is impossible to separate the impact of the constitutional change from the impact of the change in electoral system, but let us not forget that Michel Debré, the mastermind of the Fifth Republic's constitution, had written that "the electoral procedure is a more serious question than the separation of powers" and that, in contrast to Weimar, Finland, and Austria, France initially abandoned proportional representation.

We should not forget either that the final consolidation of the Fifth Republic coincided with the historic crisis of communism, the minor ally and potential competitor with the Socialist party. In addition, once France overcame the final decolonization crisis under the leadership of de Gaulle, the republic has faced no comparable crisis. In comparing the Fourth and Fifth Republics it is only fair to remember these facts and the European context after World War II, with the threat of a potentially disloyal communist opposition and the principled opposition of the

Gaullist RPF (Rassemblement du Peuple Français) to the institutions of the Fourth Republic.

The literature on these regimes leads to the conclusion that the system can work approximating either a presidential model or a parliamentary one with a president who exercises influence but not power. This depends only in part on the institutional design and the intention of those introducing the system and much more on the party constellation in each situation. Raymond Aron in 1981 wrote, "The president of the republic is the supreme authority as long as he has a majority in the national assembly, but must abandon the reality of power to the prime minister if ever a party other than his own has a majority in the assembly".[79] This is what happened in France in 1986, in Portugal after 1982, and for significant periods in Finland. In no case has the system worked as half-presidential and half-parliamentary, with the president and the prime minister jointly heading the government. The Fifth Republic instead of semipresidential has most often been presidential and only occasionally parliamentary. Duverger reaches the same conclusion: that the Fifth Republic is not a synthesis of parliamentary and presidential systems but an alternation between presidential and parliamentary phases. Those who defend the distinctiveness of the two types of regime can argue, however, that the parliamentary mode of a bipolar system (the majority supporting the prime minister is different from the majority that elected the president) does not work fully like a parliamentary system because constitutionally the president has powers that are specific to him and because tasks may be functionally divided.

Sartori criticizes Duverger, noting that in the case of cohabitation the system does not turn strictly parliamentary because a popularly elected president retains certain powers and an autonomous legitimacy. The presidency adapts to the circumstances but does not transform itself. The problem is: will it adapt itself or embark on a conflictual course, particularly if a dissolution and new elections confirm the duality?[80]

It could be argued that the system can work as a purely presidential system with the parliament totally secondary. This would be the case when a fractionalized and ineffective parliament is incapable of supporting a prime minister. In such a situation, the prime minister would be only an alter ego of the president tolerated by the parliament. To some extent that was the situation of Brüning. As that example shows, the system then would depend on the absence of strain between the prime minister and the president, something unlikely when the president and his entourage, as in the case of Hindenburg, have an agenda that is in conflict with that of the prime minister. The system in that case does not assure government stability.

I would argue that as much or more than a pure presidential system, a dual executive system depends on the personality and abilities of the president. At the same time, the responsibility becomes diffuse and additional conflicts are possible and even likely, creating situations in which a fixed term of office compounds the problem.

It is important to analyze in some detail the situations in which the system has worked well to a considerable extent independently of the personality of the president. Kaltefleiter in his detailed analysis of the presidencies of Ebert and of Hindenburg in his first term and the commentators on the Fifth Republic have highlighted the conditions under which this has been the case. Incidentally, it is important to remember that neither Ebert nor de Gaulle were popularly elected when they first assumed their presidencies. Ebert was chosen by the legislature in an indirect election. Their initial success therefore was not due to a plebiscitary popular election that produced the leadership that Max Weber had in mind. Kaltefleiter's conclusion is that the influence of the president is primarily the consequence of support by his party and not of his office. The system does not eliminate the problems of the party system; on the contrary the party system controls the success of the system. Optimally, the president is also the leader of his party and that party has a majority in the parliament. This has been the fortunate circumstance in which de Gaulle, Pompidou, and to a lesser extent Scharf in Austria and more recently Mitterand have found themselves. One could argue that President de Gaulle was able to generate that kind of party support, but it is doubtful whether his success was due to his personal appeal in a crisis situation or to the office he held, and how much it has to be attributed to the change in the electoral system. Bipolar systems have also worked well with a president who has considerable influence on his party, as was the case with Scharf in Austria, and with a president who does not have great influence on the parties, but a structured party system is able to provide a parliament that supports the government, as has been the case with other presidents in Austria.

The situation is very different with unstructured party systems, polarized multipartism, and great party fractionalization. In such a context, a president who is also the leader of an important party, such as Ebert in his first presidency and Kekkonen in Finland, can use his position to bring the party to work with others and provide relatively stable government. However, the case of Ebert shows that such a policy is likely to erode the power of the president within his party, since inevitably his positions will not be those of a party leader. He might still exercise considerable influence on his party, as Ebert did during his second presidency and as most Finish presidents have; in this case he might govern jointly with a prime minister. The situation becomes much more difficult for a president who has no great influence in his party or any party and has to support policies with which he disagrees or else undermine the parliamentary government. In such situations when the party system is weak, even expressing an opinion that coincides with the opposition contributes to a growing crisis. The case of Alcalá-Zamora in Spain in the thirties illustrates these problems well. Presumably such a situation could be resolved by dissolving the parliament, as the constitution theoretically permits, in order to produce a majority supporting a prime minister compatible with the president. However that solution would not work if the electorate returned to power the party or coalition supporting the prime minister. In that case, the president might very well be forced to resign or grudgingly abdicate power. The incompatibility between the president with considerable powers and a parliament in which a party or parties not acceptable to him are in the majority can lead to a serious impasse generating a crisis of the political system.

Kaltefleiter refers to the situation of a stalemated, fractionalized party system that is unable to produce a government, in which case the reserve powers of the president become decisive. But the system does not become purely presidential; at most it is a constitutional dictatorship using emergency powers. Such a situation, as the second presidency of Hindenburg shows, has built-in elements of extraordinary instability because there is no real division of powers and the president cannot govern without the support of a legislature, which, however, is unable to provide support for him. The situation ends up being similar to the worst of the true presidential systems with an ineffective and rebellious congress.

In the case of Weimar, the possibility of relying on the powers of the president contributed to a disastrous outcome. It made it easier for the parties to abdicate their responsibility to provide a parliamentary government and led to the parliament's toleration of Brüning, to the successive presidential cabinets when Hindenburg withdrew support from Brüning, and then to the constant search for a majority for the presidentially appointed chancellors. Successive elections in a period of economic and political crisis allowed the Nazis to become the strongest party in the parliament and finally led Hindenburg to appoint Hitler chancellor in the hope that he and his allies would be able to obtain a majority, which they finally got in the semifree election of March 1933.[81]

It would require a careful analysis to discover advantages of a bipolar system under the most favorable conditions, which as I have said are that (1) the president is the leader of, or a highly influential figure in, one of the major parties and (2) the party can form a coalition with an absolute majority in a parliamentary government that is able to work with the president. What are the advantages over a purely parliamentary government? They are difficult to define without entering into more details than space permits here, but presumably a bipolar system allows the president to change the prime minister and to change policies without creating a crisis in the system or even within the party that forms the government. This has been the case of Mitterand with changes in the direction of a socialist party in the parliament from interventionism to a more liberal policy. It is hard to say if such a change could have been generated within the party in the parliament in the absence of a president and therefore of the party's interest in holding together for the purpose of winning the presidency again. Some would argue that another advantage of a bipolar system is that responsibility for failure can be pushed onto the prime minister, leaving the president untouched. However, this possibility does not contribute to the emergence of responsible and cohesive parties. Some proponents emphasize that a dual executive allows the prime minister to assume a more powerful role whenever the president is unable to exercise his role effectively. This idea assumes that the president does not cling to his power and that he has no right of dissolution to use against a prime minister supported by the party that has withdrawn confidence from him.

Suleiman, in chapter 5 herein, notes that instability and inefficiency develop even when the president and the prime minister are supported by the same party or party coalition. Inevitably the president has his own staff and can develop policies that are at odds with those of his prime minister. Moreover, members of the cabinet with direct access to the president might bypass the prime minister and turn to the president to overrule the decisions of the prime minister, who then is in an embarrassing situation. The result inevitably is a lot of politicking and intrigues that may delay decision making and lead to contradictory policies due to the struggle between the president and the prime minister. The French experience under Mitterand shows that the system does not assure maximal efficacy.

In conclusion, it can be argued that a bipolar system might work, but not necessarily as its promoters intended. It can work when it becomes de facto a parliamentary system, as it has done in Ireland, Iceland, and Austria in the Second Republic, or when the party or parties supporting the president and those with a majority in the chamber are the same, and exceptionally when a very adroit politician realizes that he must permit a prime minister with majority support in the parliament to exercise power. However, bipolarity is probably not an effective system for overcoming the problems of a polarized or fractionalized party system, unless it is combined with other important circumstances, such as the electoral changes under the Fifth Republic, the historical crisis of the French Communist party, or the exceptional leadership qualities of Charles de Gaulle in the first years of the Fifth Republic. In the face of a weak or ineffective party system, contrary to what some of its proponents hoped, it is only an apparent therapy, to use the expression of Kaltefleiter.[82] It cannot overcome the weaknesses of a party system.

The other implicit danger of an authoritarian interpretation of the powers of the president is exemplified by the way in which Carl Schmitt shifted the interpretation of the Weimar constitution. He used his notion of the *Hüter der Verfassung* (the guardian of the constitution)[83] to create the image of a leader who was above and against the parties, which ultimately led to the Führerstaat's breaking with the democratic liberal tradition. Such a danger cannot be excluded when the presidency is occupied by a populist leader who personalizes power or by a military man who can use his military constituency to consolidate his power against the legislature.

In view of some of the experiences with this type of system it seems dubious to argue that in and by itself it can generate democratic stability.[84] Some of the conditions favorable to the success of a bipolar system are to some extent the same as those that assure stable parliamentary government, namely, a parliament in which the parties are able to give support to a prime minister but with the additional condition that the prime minister can work well with the president.

Excursus: The President in the Spanish Republic, 1931–1936

The Spanish Republic (1931–36) has not been included in the analysis of semi-presidential, semiparliamentary regimes for the obvious reason that the president was not popularly elected but indirectly elected by the parliament and elected members of an electoral college. However title V of the 1931 constitution granted him powers that exceeded those of presidents in parliamentary democracies.[85] The most important was that the prime minister had to have the *double confidence* of the president and the unicameral chamber. The presidential confidence was strengthened by the fact that nonconfidence motions required an absolute majority of the chamber. Only the president could appoint and dismiss the prime minister, which meant that he could veto political leaders he considered unsuitable regardless of their strength in the chamber, but the parliament also had the power to deny its support to the president's appointee. In addition, the president had the power to dissolve the legislature twice during his mandate and to call for new elections, a faculty of which Niceto Alcalá-Zamora made use in 1933 and 1936. He also presided over cabinet meetings and intervened in them. On the other hand, the parliament convened after the second dissolution could decide whether the dissolution was necessary, and a negative vote by a majority of the legislature would lead to the president's removal (article 81). This article was applied in 1936 although the dissolution of the rightist legislature led to one dominated by the Popular Front.

It would be too complex and long to discuss the way in which President Alcalá-Zamora conceived his office, the ambiguities of the constitution, the decisions Alcalá-Zamora made, his clashes with the main party leaders, his conflicts with Prime Minister Lerroux, the presidential veto of Gil Robles (the leader of the CEDA [Confederación Española de Derechas Autónomas], the largest party in the 1933–36 legislature), the presidential government of 1935 that dissolved the Cortes, the attempt to form a center bloc led by Alcalá-Zamora in the February 1936 election, and his ouster by the Popular Front–dominated parliament on April 3, 1936. Although there is considerable debate[86] on how much the presidential component of the constitution and the personality of Alcalá-Zamora contributed to the crisis of the republic and ultimately to the civil war, there can be no doubt that the *double confidence* model contributed to the instability of the republic. To the extent that it fits into the model of premier-presidentialism, the Spanish system of these years does not support the hopes some scholars and politicians have for that type of regime.[87] It at least shows that such a model depends enormously on the personality of the incumbent (an unpredictable factor) and that it cannot serve to overcome the problems derived from a polarized multiparty situation. Significantly the immovability of a president who exercised the power to veto possible parliamentary governments and who might dissolve parliament led to discussion among the military (at the end of 1935) of intervention, and Gil Robles, the leader of the CEDA, might have acquiesced in such plans if there had been consensus, particularly if Franco, the most prestigious general, had been ready to support them.

Alcalá-Zamora during the Constituent Assembly debates already noted the ambiguities of the text. He asked: shall the president use the *Gaceta* (publication containing laws and decrees) or just wear a tailcoat? Shall he lay cornerstones or be stoned?[88]

The Dual Executive and the Military

A constitutional and political problem connected with the dual executive model that deserves considerable attention is the question of who has authority over the armed forces, the president or his prime minister. The question is particularly relevant because most democratic constitutions, even in parliamentary systems, in continuity with the traditional conception of the monarch as supreme commander of the armed forces view the president as the symbolic head of the military. There can be no question that an elected president in a pure presidential system is the head of the armed forces, even though the actual military policy making is delegated to the secretary of defense, who might or might not be a civilian and whom the president appoints freely. In a pure parliamentary system, the appointment of the defense minister or the ministers of the armed forces falls to the prime minister, who forms the entire cabinet. In fact, the exigencies of modern warfare have led to the appointment of a minister of defense rather than ministers of the three branches of the armed forces in order to assure better coordination among them. This innovation has been desired not only by civilians but by the most competent military professionals to reduce interservice rivalries and lack of coordination. One of the symbols of the supremacy of the constitutionally legitimated political authority in many democracies has been selection of a civilian minister of defense from the political leadership. This solution has not always been considered undesirable by the military because a politician can more efficiently represent the interests of the armed forces to the political leadership than one of their peers with less political skill.

A dual executive system is likely to have at least three major actors and very often four: the president, the prime minister, the minister of defense, and generally a joint chief of staff who has the immediate command of the forces. The hierarchical line that is so central to military thinking acquires a new complexity. Will the president act through the minister of defense? Or will the minister of defense establish a direct relationship with the president bypassing the prime minister and reporting directly to the president, who makes decisions without necessarily informing and obtaining the consent of the prime minister?

Such a direct, simple hierarchical relationship would be welcomed by the military. It would symbolize the distinctiveness of the military sphere and the withdrawal of military politics from broader political considerations and control by the parliament. Such a pattern would be even more likely if the minister of defense were a military person whose loyalty would not be to a political team at the head of the government but to a president–commander in chief "above parties." A president who sees himself as a representative of the nation and above parties is not unlikely to find a personal relationship with his minister of defense and through him with the armed forces, and to some extent to realize his function of moderating political conflicts and thereby consolidating the regime. In so doing, he, unwittingly perhaps, exempts the military from civilian political control.

Such a pattern is likely to lead to greater stability in the office of the minister of defense if he has the support of the armed forces' top leadership, while, in turn, his position in the cabinet might be reinforced by the trust of the president and the head of the military establishment. It was not an accident that in the Weimar Republic between 1919 and 1933 there were twenty cabinets and only four ministers of defense.[89] Once a personal relationship is established between the president and the minister of defense and the heads of the military establishment, the president is likely to see any interference in that relationship by the prime minister as undesirable and to jealously guard the autonomy of the military establishment. Such patterns would be especially congenial to a president with a military background. Such presidents have sometimes been elected in democracies where subordination of the military was a major issue or where the military could represent itself as above parties, as in the case of Hindenburg, Mannerheim in Finland, Eanes in Portugal, and last but not least de Gaulle. All of those presidents in dual executive systems enjoyed a special relationship with the armed forces.

Let us assume a situation in which the prime minister represents a different party or party coalition than the president and is able to impose his choice for the ministry of defense over the preferences of the president. Suppose that the defense minister enters into conflict with the high command of the armed forces. Is it not likely in such a situation that the top levels of the military establishment, finding the president more sympathetic to their point of view, would make use of their special relationship with the president to approach him in his capacity as commander in chief, bypassing the prime minister and the minister of defense? Such a situation would place the prime minister and his minister of defense in a very difficult position should the president attempt to use his reserve powers to propose or veto military policies and appointments.[90]

The system, therefore, involves a latent political and even constitutional crisis. Let me note that even in a constitutional monarchy like Spain, where the powers of the king are very well defined and the political responsibility for leading the country is clearly in the hands of the prime minister and his cabinet, including the minister of defense, this issue has been quite delicate. At some point the military has turned to the king directly, bypassing the political leadership. How much more would this be the case in the situation of a dual executive? The constitution for such a regime should define clearly the legal status of each executive so that their positions would not have to be resolved in a crisis situation by their respective power bases, leaving it to the military establishment to choose which of the two democratically legitimated authorities is most favorable to its interests. The dual executive model has room for constitutional ambiguities regarding one of the central issues of many democracies: the subordination of the military to the democratically elected authorities and hopefully to civilian supremacy.

Why Are Semipresidential, Semiparliamentary Solutions Attractive?

In view of these considerations we might ask ourselves why this system of dual executive, semipresidential or semiparliamentary government, or premier-presidentialism is attractive to many democrats confronted with the crisis and failures of presidentialism and unwilling to consider parliamentarism.[91] Undoubtedly, the apparent success of the Fifth Republic has generated much of the interest in this type of system, but some other cases, particularly the Weimar Republic and the elements of a mixed system, though not strictly speaking semipresidential, of the Spanish Republic in 1931–36, have been insufficiently considered. In the Latin American context, with its strong tradition of presidentialism, the introduction of a mixed system is perhaps to many an indirect, even surreptitious, way to move toward parliamentarism, assuming that parliamentary practices could be introduced while retaining the symbols of presidentialism. The mixed system is, therefore, the result of an unwillingness to dare to make a radical change in constitutional tradition. My own opinion is that the negative experience that many countries have had with presidential regimes offers an extraordinary opportunity for constitutional innovation, but this is not the consensus of politicians and constitutionalists in Latin America, although some voices have come out clearly in favor of parliamentarism.

To know better the difficulties and weaknesses of the dual executive model, let us look a little bit closer at the conditions under which such a system can be transformed into a parliamentary system, which is the aim of some of those advocating it, even when they might not confess it publicly. After all, the examples of Ireland, Iceland, and Austria show that such a development can take place. I have to confess that I do not see this as an easy political development, but I would not exclude the possibility of using the dual executive model as a transitional system that ultimately would become a parliamentary system. Such a process would require a number of conditions that, while not impossible, in my view are somewhat unlikely. They are the following: the major parties would agree on electing the president by consensus, and the president would not be strongly identified with any party and would not be eager to exercise his powers. Essentially it would involve the choice of a personality with high prestige who would be acceptable to almost everybody except those on the extremes of the political spectrum and who would be ready to act as a neutral arbitrator under extreme circumstances but who would have no ambition to exercise power. I do not think it is always easy to find a person satisfying these requirements. Besides, such an agreement or tacit understanding among the parties would not be enforceable; a major party could break it by supporting a strong candidate. With such an understanding, all the leaders of major parties, the men and women with ambition to govern the country, would run for seats in the congress and be ready to search for a majority in the legislature in order to form a government in which they could act as powerful parliamentary prime ministers, respecting the symbolic status and the influence of the president. This would be a true semiparliamentary system under the cover of a semipresidential constitution. I wonder if in Latin America the parties and the leaders with ambition to govern would be willing to forsake a competition for the presidency and to compete for power in parliament in order to gain a vote of confidence.

Even if such a "gentlemen's" agreement is reached, no one can assume that it would become an unwritten rule. Besides, an outsider, a populist candidate, could always denounce such a pact. Perhaps a suggestion of a Bolivian politician could initiate the change: require that a presidential candidate "above parties" be nominated by two-thirds of the members of the congress. Such a majority would not agree to nominate anyone with ambition to govern. But the voters would still have to legitimize that choice.

If the presidency is occupied by a powerful personality, a leader of a major party, the system is not likely to move into the parliamentary mold. If the president has support in the congress, the system is likely to remain presidential, that is, a system with implications already discussed.

Presidentialism with the "Cover" of a Presidential Prime Minister

In view of some discussions about introducing parliamentary components in presidential systems in Latin America, it is important to stress that a prime minister who heads a cabinet and directs an administration, is freely appointed and dismissed by the president, and does not need the confidence of parliament is not to be confused with the semipresidential, semiparliamentary constitutional model. Creating such an office is only a form of delegating presidential powers, which might allow the president to avoid some criticism and to displace it onto the prime minister. However, the powers of such a prime minister and his ministers would not be very different from those of secretaries in the cabinets of presidential regimes, who are given considerable autonomy to run their departments, or from the autonomy of a national security adviser who makes important decisions that are presumably reviewed by the president. In such a system, the president continues to be the only and ultimate decision maker and legitimator of decisions made by others.

The possibility that such a prime minister and his ministers might be members of the legislature does not change the situation. In fact, in some parliamentary systems ministerial office is incompatible with membership in parliament. The possibility that these officers might be subject to questions or interpellations by the parliament does not change the matter either, although it gives more power to the legislature. After all, the members of the United States Cabinet constantly appear before Congress. Only the possibility of a vote of censure obliging the president to dismiss a minister represents a true shift of power to parliament. However, as long as the president is free to appoint a successor to a dismissed minister who does not need the confidence of the chamber, the system is still basically presidential. It would be a system, however, in which the legislative majority would have the capacity to frustrate presidential policy, indirectly to veto his decisions without making the chamber and the parties of the majority responsible, particularly when the president has no power of dissolution.

The presidential power of dissolution would violate the assumptions of the separation of powers and further encourage presidential absolutism because the president's mandate would not be affected by the adverse response of the electorate until the next presidential election.[92] In fact, if the electorate were to give its support to the same party or party constellation, the president would be seriously weakened and the conflict between the president and the legislature would become even more visible and acute. Only if the president then allows the prime minister to govern will the system become semiparliamentary. His refusal to do so would probably create a serious constitutional crisis.

A presidential cabinet that might be overthrown by the legislature, without the capacity to impose its own choice as prime minister, combined with a president who lacks the power of dissolution, would be an unviable solution and less stable than separation of powers in a presidential system or the model of dual confidence of most semipresidential, semiparliamentary systems.

Such an institutional arrangement is a formula for permanent, sometimes cumulative conflict between the two powers, with no resolution. The president survives but is frustrated and sometimes increasingly stalemated, but the legislature cannot change the president's political course if he is not ready to seek a compromise.

One example of pseudoparliamentarism is provided by the Peruvian constitution of 1979. The president names the prime minister to head the cabinet, and both jointly name the ministers, but the parliament can censure the cabinet or individual ministers by simple majority vote. If the chamber votes no confidence in three cabinets, the president can dissolve the chamber, although only once per term and not during the last year of a term. The president can be weakened, and a process of confrontation put into motion, but the president remains in office for his fixed term and can continue to appoint ministers.

One of the ways in which the congress can weaken or frustrate a president without assuming responsibility for making policy (except negatively) is by censuring members of presidential cabinets and forcing their dismissal. Some legislatures have this power. The regime continues being presidential (contrary to the opinion of Shugart and Carey) because the president appoints successors to the dismissed ministers, but he cannot threaten the legislature with dissolution. This is a formula for permanent, sometimes cumulative, conflict between the two powers with no resolution. The president survives but is frustrated, and the same is true for the opposition majority in the legislature, which cannot change his political course if he is not ready to seek a compromise.

Presidentialism, Parliamentarism, and Democratic Stability

My analysis of the problematic implications of presidentialism for democracy should not be read as implying that no presidential democracy can be stable. But the odds in many societies are not favorable. It should not be read either as arguing that parliamentary democracies always assure stability, but they provide greater flexibility in the process of transition to and consolidation of democracy. Nor does this analysis indicate that any type of parliamentary regime will do. In fact, the analysis is incomplete without a discussion of the type of parliamentary regime and its particular institutional arrangements, including electoral laws, that could best achieve democratic stability.

All regimes depend, however, on the willingness of society and all major social forces and institutions to contribute to their stability. They depend also on the consensus to give legitimacy to authority acquired by democratic processes, at least for the time between elections and within the limits of the constitution. Ultimately, all regimes depend on the capacity of political leaders to govern, to inspire trust, to have a sense of the limits of their power, and to achieve a minimum of consensus. Our argument has been that these qualities are even more important in a presidential regime, where they are more difficult to achieve in such circumstances. A dependency on the qualities of a political leader, which the leader at any particular moment might or might not have, involves greater risks. My aim here has been to revive a debate on the role of alternative democratic institutions in building stable democracies.

Parliamentarism and Party System

One of the main arguments made against parliamentary systems is that they require relatively disciplined parties, a level of party loyalty, a capacity of parties to work together, and the absence or isolation of antisystem parties. There can be no question that political parties play a central role in a parliamentary system, while in a presidential system the personal leadership and charisma of a presidential candidate can presumably overcome or ignore a fractionalized and unstructured party system.[93] Let us say that party systems in parliamentary regimes have been extremely varied, ranging from two-party systems to polarized multiparty systems, and that probably the type of party system is related more to the electoral law than to whether the regime is parliamentary or presidential. It is argued that a presidential system tends toward a two-party system, but the evidence is inconclusive, particularly when we think of the case of Chile and the multiparty system in Finland, and even in France today. South Korea after its return to democracy might also be cited, although the fusion of parties could be seen as a move toward a two-party format (if it were not a search for hegemony). Although the March 1992 congressional elections confirmed the multiparty system, the presidential election of December 18, 1992, in which Kim Young Sam received 42 percent of the vote, his opponent Kim Dae Jung, 34 percent, and the outsider (the president of Hyundai), 16 percent seems to conform to the two-party format that is congenial to presidentialism.

Given the congruence of two-party systems with presidentialism, one would assume that in countries with a two-party tradition the restoration of democracy or the continuity of democratic politics should have consolidated bipartism. This, however, is not always the case: in Colombia the leftist Alianza Democrática M-19 could obtain 12.5 percent of the vote in the April 1990 presidential election and 26.8 percent of the vote in the December 1990 election to the constituent assembly. In Uruguay the recent gains by the Frente Amplio, including the mayoralty of Montevideo, have broken the two-party format. In addition party fragmentation in Brazil and Peru is greater than in the past. Multipartism is probably here to stay in Latin America, with the exceptions of Costa Rica, Venezuela, and Argentina. In cases such as Chile it is well structured and institutionalized; in others, such as Brazil, it is highly unorganized and volatile. There is no sign that the party systems are accommodating to a presidential institutional format.

The argument is made that the absence of disciplined parties, the narrow, localist interests represented by the parties or by individual deputies, and the instability of party loyalties in many Latin American countries are obstacles to the introduction of parliamentarism. The question is to what extent this kind of party system and type of parties in Latin American congresses are results of a presidential system with a weak congress, sometimes reinforced by proportional representation electoral systems. I would argue that since parties are not responsible and accountable for government stability and policy, because those are the tasks of the president, they are likely to concentrate their efforts on opposing, criticizing, and perhaps fiscalizing the executive, but not to give it support, respond to its policy initiatives, or assume responsibility for them. It is only natural that once a president is elected, parties are likely to turn to their distinctive partisan agendas in the congressional elections and, even if they were part of the president's electoral coalition, assert their distinctiveness by criticizing the president. It is also natural that, not having responsibility for national policy, they would turn to the representation of special interests, localized interests, and clientelistic networks in their constituencies. There is no reason for them to care about the success of a president from a different party or to support unpopular policies because there is no reward for doing so and, in fact, a great likelihood of being penalized. There are no incentives for party responsibility and party discipline. In fact, often a president has to turn to pork barrel and clientelistic policies to neutralize the opposition.

I would therefore argue that some of the negative characteristics of parties in some Latin American countries, both their unstructured and their undisciplined character as well as their ideological rigidity in such cases as Chile, have been reinforced by the presidential system. On the other hand, I believe, parliamentarism could change these characteristics, although perhaps not without other institutional changes. New and different incentives for parties and their leaders would, naturally, not produce change in political practices overnight.

Governing in Parliamentary Regimes

Institutions lead the same actors to behave differently; they provide incentives or disincentives for certain behavioral patterns. My assumption is that parliamentarism would impose on parties and leaders patterns encouraging greater responsibility for governance, greater accountability (except under conditions of extreme fractionalization), and at the same time the need to cooperate and compromise (except when one party gains an absolute majority). Parliamentarism also allows changes in leadership without a regime crisis and continuity without the fears associated with *continuismo* in presidential systems.

In parliamentary systems governments can demand from parties (either their own if it had a majority or those in a coalition) support in votes of confidence, threatening them otherwise with resignation in the case of lack of support and ultimately with dissolution of the legislature. The role of each party and even of each deputy would be clear to the voters, who are unlikely to sanction destructive actions by parties. The party that fails to support its prime minister would have to pay a price. In the Spanish experience in recent years, an undisciplined, faction-ridden party (the UCD) was severely punished by the electorate. In fact, one of the main reasons for the UCD's and the Communists' loss of support in 1982 was the internal squabbling perceived by the electorate, while the fact that the PSOE was able to overcome its internal tensions and to appear as a united party capable of governing gave it its victory in 1982, 1986, and 1989.[94] Logically the self-interest of parties and legislators in the majority is to assure their leader or leaders in a coalition success and stability in power. They do not always do so, but they are likely to pay a price, except perhaps where the alternative is antisystem parties or parties perceived as antisystem, as was the case in the Fourth Republic and in Italy after World War II. I would argue that there are even some dangers in party cohesion and discipline, particularly when a single party has an absolute majority. Unity might stifle internal democracy and debate, as has been the case in majority parties like the PSOE in Spain, PASOK in Greece, and the British Conservatives under the leadership of Margaret Thatcher.

Even though the self-interest of parties and their parliamentary members may be a major factor in assuring that parties perform their main function in a parliamentary democracy, modern parliamentary systems have introduced additional mechanisms to reduce the dangers of party fractionalization and government instability, which critics sometimes associate with parliamentarism.

Fractionalization of the party system is largely a function of the social structure, but a strong electoral system can reduce it considerably. Undoubtedly, single-member constituencies, in which a plurality of votes assures election, are likely to reduce the number of parties represented in the parliament, except where ethnic or linguistic minorities have an assured representation in areas in which they are numerically dominant. Such a system, however, might have the danger of polarization in societies deeply divided between Left and Right. When coalitions are allowed, the premium won by the largest plurality in polarized societies can lead to coalitions in which extremist parties condition and weaken more moderate parties. The system also might exclude from representation the minorities in ethnic linguistic areas, giving an impression of total consensus on nationalist separatist tendencies. It is no accident, therefore, that a number of Western democracies turned to proportional representation after World War I.

Proportional representation, however, does not need to be a totally weak electoral system that assures seats to minority ideological or interest-group parties and thus contributes to government instability, as in the Weimar Republic. Some systems of proportional representation and electoral devices can reduce fractionalization. Proportional representation does not have to lead to situations like those in the Netherlands and Israel, where 1 percent of the vote assures one seat. A number of parliamentary democracies have introduced a minimum threshold for representation: a certain percentage of votes, as in the Federal Republic of Germany, or a certain number of districts won, or a combination. That device presents some difficulties in multiethnic, multilingual societies such as Spain and therefore cannot always be used. Sometimes it is even inequitable; the Fifth Republic requires a 12 percent threshold. Some proportional representation systems, such as the d'Hondt system used in Spain, Greece, and Chile (1925–73), particularly in districts with few members assure a disproportionate representation to major parties and contribute to what in Spain is called the *voto útil*, that is, the tendency of voters to support parties that have a prospect of providing the government with a leader.

The argument is made that in parliamentary systems very often coalition governments are needed because no party is likely to have an absolute majority. It should be clear from the European experience that coalition governments can be stable and that, once party discipline is strongly enforced, they might allow for more democratic representation and debate than some majority governments. They may also facilitate alternation when two major parties have large and stable electorates, as is the case in Germany, where the FDP acts as a balance wheel between the Social Democrats and the Christian Democrats. However, I have to admit that government instability has been one of the strong arguments against parliamentarism and in favor of presidentialism. In making that argument, it has been forgotten that there is considerable cabinet instability in presidential systems and that in multiparty systems presidential cabinets are very often also coalition governments, although they have the disadvantage that the ministers are selected as individuals who do not necessarily commit their parties to support their policies. The image of assembly government overthrowing at whim governments associated with the Third and Fourth Republics and with Italian democracy in recent decades is not the rule in parliamentary systems, even in Latin countries. Since 1977 Spain has had only three prime ministers, in spite of considerable cabinet instability under Suárez during the period that preceded his fall. Besides, the negative image associated with cabinet instability should be corrected; it has been argued that under the Fourth Republic cabinet instability contributed indirectly to the capacity of the system to make some major decisions.[95] On the other hand, instability is often more apparent than real because the same persons occupy the prime ministership for a long time, although discontinuously, and many of the ministers stay in office after cabinet changes; even the parties occupying certain ministries are the same over a prolonged period. There is much more continuity than is apparent when we look at figures on the duration of cabinets and frequency of crises.

The experience of government instability in the Weimar Republic led the Bonn lawmakers to introduce an important constitutional innovation: the constructive vote of nonconfidence of article 67, which was repeated in article 113 of the Spanish constitution of 1978. This innovation has been discussed in proposals of constitutional reform in Portugal.[96] Let me quote the German *Grundgesetz:*

ARTICLE 67

1. The Bundestag can express its lack of confidence in the Federal Chancellor only by electing a successor with a majority of its members and by requesting the Federal President to dismiss the Federal Chancellor. The Federal President must comply with the request and appoint the person elected.

2. Forty-eight hours must elapse between the motion and the election.

ARTICLE 68

If a motion of the Federal Chancellor for a vote of confidence is not assented to by the majority of members of the Bundestag, the Federal President may, upon the proposal of the Federal Chancellor dissolve the Bundestag within 21 days. The right to dissolve shall lapse as soon as the Bundestag with the majority of its members elects another federal chancellor.

This constitutional device gives the prime minister in parliamentary systems a strong position; he or she cannot be overthrown by a purely negative majority, as happened in the Weimar Republic when Nazis and Communists made stable government impossible but were unable to provide an alternative one. In fact, the device has been criticized for the rigidity it introduces by making alternation in government more difficult.

It should be clear by now that the combination of some electoral law reforms modifying extreme proportional representation and the device of the constructive vote of nonconfidence can very much reduce government instability in parliamentary systems. It allows at the same time, a change of prime ministers without provoking a constitutional crisis or turning to such extreme measures as impeachment of a president. In parliamentary democracies, leadership crises lead to government crises and not, as in presidential systems, to regime crises.[97]

One possible advantage of parliamentarism is that the leaders of the parties who aspire to govern have an opportunity to become familiar with the issues in committees and in the major debates and to interact with each other. It has become impossible to aspire to govern a country without having been involved in the day-to-day business of politics, of legislating, debating the budget, confronting the government or the opposition. In that process leaders can emerge in the parties, a shadow cabinet might develop, and the public can slowly become familiar with the leader of the opposition before the electoral period when that leader makes a bid for the support of a party in order to gain the prime ministership. Although some people might dislike professional politicians, modern states are too complex to be governed by amateurs. The parliament can be a school, a nursery, for leaders. Members of parliament share a great deal of experiences, personal relations, and party links that can make negotiation, consensus, and accommodation between government and opposition possible when their roles are reversed.

Parliamentary Government: Prime Ministerial Government

One is tempted to characterize some of the modern parliamentary systems as prime ministerial or chancellor (*Kanzler*) regimes.[98] As opposed to the classical *régime d'assemblée* of the Third and even the Fourth French Republics, they are based on granting the prime minister the power to "determine and be responsible for general policy guidelines" (to use the words of article 65 of the German *Grundgesetz*). The chancellor in addition is given the power to appoint and dismiss the ministers, who conduct the affairs of their departments within the chancellor's policy guidelines. The position of the chancellor depends on the strength of the parties—his own and those entering into the governing coalition—but in principle he is more than a *primus inter pares*. In addition, he has a direct relationship to the electorate because the parties enter the campaign under a leader whom they propose to make a prime minister and ask for support to achieve that goal. The chancellor, as leader of the winning party, personalizes the campaign. This is not true, however, in all parliamentary systems.

Some analysts have suggested that the "prime minister" or "presidente de gobierno" in Kanzler democracy represents a certain convergence with the personalization of powers in presidentialism. This is only partly true, because ultimately the prime minister needs the confidence and support of his or her party (if it has a majority in the parliament) and, in the case of a coalition government, of his or her coalition partners. In the case of minority governments, the prime minister needs the support of parties that, without being in the government, support its policies or tolerate it. Even in the privileged position of the prime ministership, continuous attention is necessary to maintain that support, and therefore we can still speak of parliamentary government, or perhaps, to be more exact, of party-parliamentary government.

The Difficult Transition from Presidentialism to Parliamentarism

In the process of constitutional innovation in countries that traditionally have had a presidential constitution, or where an authoritarian regime enacted such a constitution, the transition to democracy takes place through the free election of a new president, presumably under the old constitution, for either a normal or a reduced mandate. This situation differs fundamentally from the one in which many Western European democracies found themselves at the moment of transition. In Western Europe, the first election after a dictatorship was for a legislature, whether constituent or not, that was free to create the new institutions without having to delegitimize a democratically elected president. The Spanish Cortes elected in 1977 as the result of the Law for Political Reform, which facilitated the transition, was in principle free to discuss any constitutional form. It even debated for symbolic reasons, though without any viability or meaning for the political process, whether Spain should be a monarchy (as the popular referendum on the Law for Political Reform had already decided in December 1976).

It is debatable if a constituent assembly or a legislature that, without being elected for that purpose, undertakes the task of making new constitutional laws or amendments can ignore the existence of a democratically elected president. This imposes a new and complex issue, the collaboration between the congress and the president. However, it seems reasonable to think that a president who has been elected as a symbol of democratic renewal will collaborate with the congress in making the new political institutions and will put his weight and prestige behind a new constitution (particularly if he cannot be reelected). The new president would not be required to relinquish power until after the approval of the new constitution according to proper procedures. And if the president makes a commitment to defend the new constitution, he or she would not be required to relinquish office until the end of a term. Let us not forget that parliamentary systems have as head of state either a monarch or a president who, generally, is elected not by the people but by a representative electoral college. A popularly elected president in such a situation, as defender and supporter of the new constitution, would be fully entitled to exhaust his or her mandate to perform the functions assigned to the presidency in the new constitution. This would be particularly true for a president elected with the support of all those wishing a transition to a fully democratic political system. Such a solution would also have the advantage of assuring a formal and symbolic continuity with past legality, while breaking with the authoritarian legacy in what is incompatible with a new democratic regime. It could then be a valuable component of what in Spain was the *reforma-pactada ruptura-pactada*. The president elected according to the existing constitutional norms before democracy would be part of the process of *reforma*, and the new constitution and the new parliamentarily supported government, part of the *ruptura* with a past that contributed to the breakdown or was the product of authoritarian imposition, as in Chile.

Conclusion

This analysis has focused on some of the structural problems inherent in presidentialism: the simultaneous democratic legitimacy of president and congress, the likelihood of conflict, the absence of obvious mechanisms to resolve it, the zero-sum character of presidential elections, the majoritarian implication that can lead to a disproportionality leaving more than 60 percent of voters without representation, the potential polarization, the rigidity of fixed terms and no-reelection rules normally associated with presidentialism, among others. It also has discussed some of the implications of presidentialism for the political culture, the party system, and the recruitment of congressional elites. Let me stress that not all of these consequences obtain in each and every case. I only argue that they are likely. Much more research is needed to prove them systematically, even though examples of these patterns come easily to mind and are documented in some of the contributions to this volume. In fact, Alfred Stepan and Cindy Skach in chapter 4 carry out the counterfactual analysis, with all of its difficulties, of what would have happened if a number of democracies had been parliamentary rather than presidential in serious crises and (as I have already done for Spain in 1977) what might have happened to some of the parliamentary democracies should they have had presidential constitutions.

I have also discussed the great variety and ambiguous character of the so-called semipresidential or semiparliamentary systems of dual executive, which have also been called premier parliamentarism and presidential parliamentarism. Those systems, as commentators have noted often, function either as presidential or as parliamentary, and can lead to conflict situations or stalemate unless the president shows extraordinary political skills and savoir faire in the case of a parliamentary majority different from the one that sustained him in his election. In fact, in the case of the Weimar Republic and the Spanish Republic in the thirties, the dual executive system led to solutions of dubious constitutionality and contributed decisively to undermining democratic institutions. I have also highlighted the particularly disquieting consequences of these systems for the relationship with the armed forces.

Finally, I have analyzed briefly some of the main objections to parliamentarism, noting how under certain circumstances they might be justified[99] but also how contemporary parliamentary democracies have overcome some of the dysfunctional consequences of extreme parliamentarism and its fractionalized party systems. I have also discussed at some length how parliamentary systems in contemporary politics can lead to the emergence of strong national and party leadership capable of governing with sufficient support under critical conditions.

There can be no question that neither parliamentarism nor presidentialism, nor a mixed system, is able to handle successfully intractable problems such as those faced today by Lebanon, Cyprus, and probably societies involved in civil war or in the problems of some African countries. Nor would I question that there are degenerate forms of both presidentialism and parliamentarism; some cases come easily to mind. I only argue that presidentialism seems to involve greater risk for stable democratic politics than contemporary parliamentarism.

Political engineers, like engineers who build bridges, should plan for the most unfavorable conditions, although we might hope they will never materialize. Doing so may be considered wasteful when the additional costs are counted, which in the case of political institution building are the costs of innovation, of challenging tradition. As the builders of bridges can never assure that the bridges will not collapse under some extreme circumstance, no constitution maker can assure that the institutions he creates will survive all challenges and dangers and assure a consolidated democracy. However, the accumulated evidence of the past in presidential systems, particularly in Latin America and Asia, and the success of contemporary parliamentary democracies in Western Europe show odds that seem to favor parliamentary institutions.

Innovation is not necessarily good, but to cling to the institutions of the past when they have failed too often and to choose not to innovate is to miss a historical opportunity. Perhaps as a citizen of Spain, where political leaders could reach a consensus to dare to create new institutions that have led to a consolidated democratic parliamentary regime, I am biased in my preferences. I think, however, that the intelligent use of historical opportunity after many failures and dictatorships is evidence that innovation is possible and can be successful. No one in Spain between 1975 and 1978 could have been sure that the experiment would be successful. However, the experience of Spain and other European democracies, particularly the German Republic, shows that innovative leadership and thoughtful constitution making can greatly help to generate the conditions for a stable democracy.

In the early stages of the Spanish transition to democracy, Adolfo Suárez, who was not yet the prime minister who would lead it, in a speech conveying openness to change, quoted a poem by a "great Spanish writer." Let me also close with the lines of Antonio Machado:

> ¡Que importa un día! Está el ayer alerto
> al mañana, mañana al infinito
> hombres de España, ni el pasado ha muerto
> ni está el mañana—ni el ayer—escrito.

[What does one day matter! Yesterday is alert to tomorrow, tomorrow to infinity. People of Spain, neither has the past died nor is tomorrow—or yesterday—written.—My translation]

Appendix

Some Considerations on Quantitative Analyses of the Stability of
Parliamentary and Presidential Democracies

Although my analysis of the difference for democratic consolidation, institutionalization, and performance between presidentialism and parliamentarism was not originally based on a systematic comparison of the records of countries with one or another type of regime, several authors have provided evidence for the greater or lesser likelihood of stability and breakdown in both types. A systematic and quantitative comparison, given the problem of defining the historical period to be covered, the countries to be included, and the large number of variables that might or might not be held constant, presents enormous methodological problems.

Scott Mainwaring and Matthew Shugart[100] list 24 countries with 30 years of uninterrupted democracy between 1959 and 1989 (including India, despite the period of emergency powers). Of those 24 countries, 18 have parliamentary regimes, 3 are presidential (the United States, Costa Rica, and Venezuela), 2 are semipresidential (Finland and France), and 1 has a unique form of government (Switzerland).

Alfred Stepan and Cindy Skach[101] have focused on the 86 countries that became independent between 1945 and 1979. Among them 15 were democratic for 10 consecutive years. Stepan and Skach count 32 countries that were parliamentary the first year of independence, of which 15 were continuous democracies between 1980 and 1989. The exclusion of microstates would reduce the number of democracies (Dominica, Kiribati, Nauru, St. Lucia, and St. Vincent) but also the number of nondemocratic states (Gambia, Grenada, Mauritius, Seychelles, Tuvalu). This would mean that of 22 remaining newly independent states with a parliamentary government the first year, 10 would be continuous democracies between 1980 and 1989, and none with another type of regime in the first year.

Matthew Shugart and John M. Carey[102] have taken a different approach by listing 48 countries that had by 1990 held at least two democratic elections without breakdown. Among them they list 27 pure parliamentary democracies (strangely they do not include India), 12 presidential regimes, and 9 other types (5 premier-presidential, 2 president-parliamentary, and 2 assembly independent, using their typology of regimes). Since they classify, formally correctly, Austria and Iceland as premier-presidential, but these states function in fact as parliamentary, I would count them as parliamentary, increasing the number of parliamentary democracies to 29 and decreasing premier-presidential regimes to 3. If we isolate their 23 "third world countries" (among them Argentina, Uruguay, Turkey, together with Senegal, Botswana, and Papua New Guinea), 9 are parliamentary, 11 presidential (all Latin American except Senegal), and 3 "other" types.

Their inclusion of the "not newly independent countries," particularly the presidential or modified presidential regimes in Latin America, reduces the difference found in the Stepan-Skach analysis. The fact that fewer of the microstates (which were disproportionately democratic) are not included also affects the comparison.

Shugart and Carey rightly point out that by 1991, 11 "third world countries" with presidential regimes by their criterion were "democratic," to which one could add 3 with modified presidential systems, compared to 9 parliamentary (10 if we add India). The recent return to democracy of Latin American countries (including the somewhat dubious cases of El Salvador, Guatemala, and perhaps Honduras) explains the difference between the 9 or 10 parliamentary democracies (with at least two democratic elections without breakdown) and the [14] "presidential" democracies among the 48 countries (49 with India) considered.

However, Shugart and Carey's questioning of a relationship between regime type and democratic stability is based on an analysis of the breakdowns of democratic regimes in the twentieth century. They list a total of 40 cases of breakdown—some countries experiencing more than one—22 of parliamentary systems, 12 of presidential systems, and 6 of "other types" (1 premier-presidential [Austria] and 5 presidential-parliamentary, among which they include the Weimar Republic, Ecuador [1962], Peru [1968], Korea [1961], and Sri Lanka [1982]).

According to their data, breakdowns affected 7 parliamentary democracies (all in Europe) before World War II, 2 mixed systems (Germany and Austria), and only 1 presidential democracy (Argentina). The breakdown of European democracies is well documented, but there is considerable ambiguity about when and for how long Latin American countries could or could not be considered democratic and if and when they broke down. This explains why only Argentina is included in that period.

If we consider the period after World War II, Shugart and Carey list 14 cases of breakdown of parliamentary democracies, rightly excluding the transition from the Fourth to the Fifth Republic as a case of reequilibration and cases in which no consecutive elections were held before the breakdown, in order to eliminate newly independent countries that held a first election under the watchful eye of a departing colonial power or as a demonstration for foreign consumption. Only 1 of these 14 breakdowns happened in Europe (in Greece). The 14 breakdowns of parliamentary regimes contrast with 12 breakdowns of presidential systems and 4 of systems they call "presidential parliamentary." (The listing however omits multiple breakdowns in the same country; to have included these might have increased the number of Latin American breakdowns).

These figures would support the thesis that the type of regime makes little difference, or even that parliamentary regimes are more vulnerable than pure presidential ones. However, more information is needed either to prove or disprove such a conclusion. To begin with, how many democracies, parliamentary and presidential, were there before World War II? Latin America included 17 countries, all of them presidential—except for short interludes—before 1945. How many were by any reasonable standard democracies? How many, besides Argentina, experienced a breakdown?

When we turn to interwar Europe[103] we are dealing overwhelmingly with parliamentary democracies, except for a few semipresidential regimes: Germany and Finland and, depending on the criteria used, Austria, Ireland, and even the Spanish Republic. Of a total of 28 countries (including Turkey and Russia), 25 (or at least 22) were parliamentary. The total included 12 stable democracies and ¹ countries that experienced a breakdown or a failure of democratic consolidation. Of the 2 truly semipresidential regimes, 1, the Weimar Republic, experienced a breakdown.

In that context of 15 "old states" (excluding empires) that did not experience major border changes, 9 were stable parliamentary democracies. Of the 8 new states, 5 suffered a breakdown. Democracy did not consolidate or survive in the 5 defeated empires—Russia, Turkey, Austria, Hungary, and Germany—irrespective of regime type.

Parliamentarism in interwar Europe, in contrast to postwar Europe (with the exception of Greece), did not assure democratic development or stability. Perhaps, among other factors, a learning process took place in a number of countries, and the constitutions introduced innovations contributing to postwar stability. After the war, of 14 European democracies, only 1 experienced a breakdown. I am obviously not counting countries in the Soviet orbit like Czechoslovakia (1948) or Hungary.

In that same period, of the democratic presidential regimes in states that had gained independence before 1945—whose number is more difficult to ascertain—only the United States and Costa Rica did not experience a breakdown. The number of breakdowns is certainly more than 1 if we count only Argentina, Chile, Brazil, Uruguay, Peru, Colombia, and Venezuela, leaving out more dubious presidential democracies.

The post–World War II weak parliamentary regimes, according to Shugart and Carey, are, in Asia: Burma, Pakistan (1954–77); Singapore (1972); Thailand (1976); Turkey (1980); and Sri Lanka (1970s). There are also 1 in Oceania (Fiji, 1988); 4 in Africa: Kenya (1969); Nigeria (1966); Sierra Leone (1967); and Somalia (1969); and 2 in America: Guyana (1974–78) and Surinam (1975). That makes weak parliamentary regimes in 12 countries. If we add Greece to them we have a total of 13 breakdowns and 13 (if we count Malta) stable European and 13 stable non-European (including Commonwealth countries but no microstates) parliamentary democracies. Therefore we have 13 breakdowns compared to 26 more or less stable, strictly speaking parliamentary democracies (not counting the Fourth Republic in France). This means 13 breakdowns in 39 countries.

Of the total of presidential regimes in the same period we have the United States, Costa Rica (since 1953), and Venezuela (since 1958) that have not experienced a breakdown. But at least 10 other countries (Argentina, Bolivia, Brazil, Chile, Colombia, and Uruguay, plus Ecuador and Peru, both classified by Shugart and Carey as presidential-parliamentary) experienced the demise of democracy. And that is to ignore the more dubiously democratic presidential regimes in Latin

America and the Philippines (1972); Korea (1972); and 2 presidential-parliamentary regimes (Korea, 1961, and Sri Lanka, 1982). This means that in a minimum of 11 countries (ignoring repeated breakdowns and the type of presidentialism) democracy broke down, compared to 3 fully stable presidential republics.

In summary, we have in post–World War II 13 breakdowns in 39 parliamentary democracies (defined by the criteria of Shugart and Carey, plus India); and at least 10 breakdowns among 13 presidential democracies (with some dubious cases deliberately excluded).[104]

The fact that, of those 10 countries experiencing breakdowns since 1945, at the time of writing 9 are democracies shows that democratization is possible in countries with a presidential tradition and that these 9 countries are presidential democracies. Perhaps the societies and their leadership in those presidential democracies have learned from past failures, and we might find in the future presidential systems as stable as parliamentary democracies are in Europe. However, some of the troubles in several presidential democracies in recent times—Peru, Philippines, Venezuela, Haiti, Brazil—do not argue well for those democracies. Certainly factors other than the type of regime account for difficulties, but it is not unreasonable to argue that presidentialism compounds the difficulties for reasons that are congruent with our analysis.

Notes

In making final revisions of this chapter for publication I find myself in a difficult and even embarrassing situation. My essay has been circulating in different versions since 1984, translated in Argentina, Chile, Brazil, and Italy, and widely discussed, especially in Poland. I published a shortened version, translated into Hungarian and Mongolian, in the *Journal of Democracy*. Circulation has led to a number of critical comments, a debate with my critics, and frequent friendly exchanges with colleagues. Scholars agreeing with my arguments have developed them further and provided empirical proof of them. Discussions of constitutional reform (in some of which I have participated) have taken the issues raised by my essay into account.

The question is: how much should I take all this discussion into account here? My inclination is not to enter into a careful analysis of all the arguments and evidence presented. I feel that it would not be fully fair to my critics not to publish the original text to which they responded, but at some points I refer to their critiques to clarify my own argument and in footnotes to some of the contributions to the debate. I also include additional sections not part of the original paper.

I want to thank the Wissenschaftskolleg zu Berlin, whose fellowship (1990–91) made possible work on this essay, and Rocío de Terán for her continuous assistance, Terry Schutz for her careful editing, and Terry Miller for typing and retyping of the manuscript.

1. My approach would be misunderstood if it were read as strictly institutional and even more as a legal-constitutionalist perspective. I take into account those aspects, although perhaps less than other recent writings such as Matthew Soberg Shugart and John M. Carey, *Presidents and Assemblies: Constitutional Design and Electoral Dynamics* (Cambridge: Cambridge UP, 1992), which provides for a more systematic analysis of the powers of presidents.

My focus is on the political logic of presidential systems and some of its likely consequences on the selection of leadership, popular expectations, style of leadership, and articulation of conflicts. Some of the empirical evidence is found in the chapters of this volume, and it is our hope that our analysis will generate more and systematic evidence of those aspects that cannot be found in or directly derived from the institutional norms.

2. F. A. Hermens, *Democracy or Anarchy: A Study of Proportional Representation* (Notre Dame, Ind.: Notre Dame UP, 1941); Maurice Duverger, *Political Parties: Their Organization and Activity* (1951; New York: Wiley, 1954); Stein Rokkan, "Elections: Electoral Systems," *International Encyclopedia of the Social Sciences* (New York: Crowell-Collier-Macmillan, 1968); Dieter Nohlen, *Wahlsysteme der Welt* (Munich: Piper, 1978); Douglas Rae, *The Political Consequences of Electoral Laws* (New Haven: Yale UP, 1967); R. S. Katz, *A Theory of Parties and Electoral Systems* (Baltimore: Johns Hopkins UP, 1980); Rein Taagepera and Matthew Soberg Shugart, *Seats and Votes: The Effects and Determinants of Electoral Systems* (New Haven: Yale UP, 1989); B. Grofman and A. Lijphart, eds., *Electoral Laws and Their Political Consequences* (New York: Agathon, 1986); Arend Lijphart and B. Grofman, eds., *Choosing an Electoral System: Issues and Alternatives* (New York: Praeger, 1984); and Giovanni Sartori, "The Influence of Electoral Systems: Faulty Laws or Faulty Method," in Grofman and Lijphart, *Electoral Laws and Their Political Consequences*, pp. 43–68.

3. Werner Kaltefleiter, *Die Funktionen des Staatsoberhauptes in der parlamentarischen Demokratie* (Cologne: Westdeutscher Verlag, 1970); and Stefano Bartolini, "Sistema partitico ed elezione diretta del capo dello stato in Europa," *Rivista italiana di scienza politica* 2 (1984):209–22.

4. Shugart and Carey, *Presidents and Assemblies;* Waldino Cleto Suárez, "El poder ejecutivo en América Latina. Su capacidad operativa bajo regímenes presidencialistas de gobierno," *Revista de estudios políticos* (nueva época) 29 (Sept.-Oct. 1982): 109–44. Richard Moulin, *Le présidentialisme et la classification des régimes politiques* (Paris: Librairie Générale de Droit et de Jurisprudence, 1978), is a work of scholarship in the classical legal tradition, rich in references to the constitutional texts and the academic commentaries with a wealth of information on the variety of presidential systems, the relations between executive and legislature, the role of cabinets, impeachment, party systems and presidentialism, and so forth, in the United States and other presidential regimes, particularly the constitutional history of Chile. It also includes an extensive bibliography. Only the equal treatment of the constitutions of democracies and nondemocratic regimes is disturbing.

5. G. Bingham Powell, Jr., *Contemporary Democracies: Participation, Stability, and Violence* (Cambridge: Harvard UP, 1982), and Arend Lijphart, *Democracies; Pattern of Majoritarian and Consensus Government in Twenty-one Countries* (New Haven: Yale UP, 1984).

6. The neglect until very recently by social scientists of presidentialism outside the United States is reflected in the facts that the *Presidential Studies Quarterly* from 1977 to 1992 (vols. 7 to 22) published only 3 articles on the subject; that the *Legislative Studies Quarterly* between 1976 and 1992 published none; that *International Political Science Abstracts* between 1975 and 1991 lists 141 articles on Latin America, 96 on countries outside the United States and Latin America, and 23 on general topics on the executive or the presidency.

7. Scott Mainwaring, "Presidentialism in Latin America: A Review Essay," *Latin American Research Review* 25, no. 1 (1990): 157–79, is an excellent summary of the literature and debates in Latin America. See also Arturo Valenzuela, *The Breakdown of Democratic Regimes: Chile* (Baltimore: Johns Hopkins UP, 1978). Another important survey article is: Mario D. Serrafero, "Presidencialismo y reforma política en América Latina," *Revista del Centro de Estudios Constitucionales*, Madrid, Jan.–Apr. 1991, pp. 195–233.

8. Mainwaring, "Presidentialism in Latin America."

9. Juan J. Linz, *Crisis, Breakdown and Reequilibration,* vol. 1 of *The Breakdown of Democratic Regimes,* edited by J. Linz and Alfred Stepan (Baltimore: Johns Hopkins UP, 1978); see "Excursus on Presidential and Parliamentary Democracies," pp. 71–74. It would be absurd to argue that presidents need to be elected on a first-past-the-post basis. I agree with Donald L. Horowitz, *A Democratic South Africa? Constitutional Engineering in a Divided Society* (Berkeley: U California P, 1991), that this view is an "untenable assumption about the way presidents are inevitably elected" (p. 20). He attributes such an assumption to me, but all I have done is to discuss the way in which presidents have been and are most often elected—either by a plurality in one round or in a runoff election. He rightly points out that in Nigeria in 1979 and 1983 and in Sri Lanka in 1978 and 1988 a different method of election was used, but it does not seem to me reasonable to base an analysis of presidential politics on those two cases (and a total of four elections at the time of his and my writings) rather than on the cumulative experience in Latin American republics and a few other cases.

10. The important essay by Anthony King, "Executives," in *Handbook of Political Science,* edited by Fred I. Greenstein and Nelson Polsby, vol. 5 of *Governmental Institutions and Processes* (Reading, Mass.: Addison-Wesley, 1975), pp. 173–256, limits itself to a comparison of the United States and the United Kingdom, with no reference to presidentialism outside the United States.

11. In view of the constant clamor for "strong" presidents, the popular hopes linked with "strong" presidents in many countries with presidental regimes, Shugart and Carey's finding that systems rating high in powers of the president in law making and cabinet formation have been more prone to crises is significant.

Ultimately, from its historical origins on, a separation of powers has been conceived to generate "weak" government, "checks and balances" (which can turn into "stalemates," divided responsibility, distrust between powers), just the opposite of "strong" power and leadership. No surprise that the terms of presidents who wanted to be "strong"—Vargas, Allende, Marcos, Goulart, Alán García, Aristide—ended in one or another kind of disaster. We know too little about the role of the presidency in Georgia to tell if Gamsakhurdia should be in that list, but it would not be surprising if some of the new presidents of former Soviet Union republics might not run the same fate.

See the collection of essays by Carlos S. Nino, Gabriel Banzat, Marcelo Alegre and Marcela Rodríguez, Roberto Gargozelle, Silvino Alvarez and Robert Pablo-Saba, and Jorge Albert Barraguirre, *Presidencialismo y estabilidad democrática en la Argentina* (Buenos Aires: Centro de Estudios Institucionales, 1991), esp. Carlos S. Nino, "El presidencialismo y la justificación, estabilidad y eficiencia de la democracia," pp. 11–27.

12. Klaus von Beyme, *Die parlamentarischen Regierungssysteme in Europa* (Munich: R. Piper, 1970), is a monumental comparative study of parliamentary regimes.

13. This analysis does not include pluripersonal presidentialism because of its atypical character, the unique circumstances that have led to its establishment, and last but not least its lack of success. For a discussion of plural presidencies, see Shugart and Carey, *Presidents and Assemblies,* pp. 94–105.

Advocates of collegial presidencies should keep in mind the experiences in Roman history and the analysis of George Simmel on the size of groups and decision making in addition to the contemporary failures.

14. The majority runoff has been advocated to avoid election by a small plurality, which is possible in a multiparty election, and to assure election by a majority. The system, however, as Shugart and Carey have noted, has several not so desirable consequences. First it en-

courages a larger number of candidates in the first run, discouraging the coalescence of op-posing forces, so that those who place first and second can attract the support in the runoff of those who failed and those who failed can enhance their bargaining position with one of the two candidates in the runoff. The first candidates in this case obtain a lower percentage of votes compared to elections by pure plurality. The second consequence is that the out-come depends on first-round contingencies. Let us remember that in 1989 some Brazilians feared a runoff between Lula and Brizola, the two leftist candidates, if the Right had divided its vote more than it did. To these I would add that in the runoff, the winner might receive a vote out of proportion to his original electoral appeal that might not, however, represent real support for him but contribute to his sense of being "elected by the people." The presi-dential majority in this case is as or more "artificial" than a parliamentary majority for a prime minister heading a coalition, but it generates very different expectations.

15. Fred W. Riggs, "The Survival of Presidentialism in America: Para-constitutional Prac-tices," *International Political Science Review* 9, no. 4 (1988): 247–78, is an excellent analysis of "American exceptionalism." For European responses to American presidentialism, see Klaus von Beyme, *America as a Model. The Impact of American Democracy in the World* (Aldershot, U.K.: Gower, 1987), chap. 2, "The Presidential System of Government," pp. 33–76.

16. Committee on Political Parties of the American Political Science Association, *Toward a More Responsible Two-Party System* (New York: Rinehart, 1950).

17. Shugart and Carey, *Presidents and Assemblies*, chap. 6, pp. 106–49.

18. President Fernando Collor of Brazil when, after introducing his stabilization plan on television without previous consultation, he encountered congressional resistance, he threatened congress with mobilizing the masses: "There is no doubt that I have an intimate deep relation with the poor masses" and that congress "must respect me because I am the center of power." Commenting on this, one of his strongest supporters, former finance min-ister and then senator Roberto Campos lamented: "This is juridical butchery, which lashes confidence in the Collor plan." See *Latin American Regional Reports: Brazil Report* (RB-90-04), 3 May 1990, p. 6, and "Mounting Criticism of Authoritarian Governments Novo Brasil Plan," ibid. (RB-90-05), 7 June 1990, pp. 1–3, Campos quote on p. 31.

President Collor could not, with his electoral constituency, make threats against con-gress creditable in the way that Goulart (or Allende) could by mobilizing masses in the Petrobras Stadium. For an analysis of the Brazilian crisis in 1964, which was also a crisis of relations between president and congress, and the possible constitutional reform that might have allowed Goulart's reelection, see Thomas E. Skidmore, *Politics in Brazil, 1930–1964: An Experiment in Democracy* (New York: Oxford UP, 1967).

Alfred Stepan, ed., *Authoritarian Brazil* (New Haven: Yale UP, 1973), and "Political Lead-ership and Regime Breakdown: Brazil," in Linz and Stepan, *Breakdown of Democratic Re-gimes*, pp. 119–37, esp. pp. 120–33.

It should be noted that this sense of the "superiority" of the democratic mandate of pres-idents is found not only in Latin America but in other presidential democracies. For exam-ple, de Gaulle on December 17, 1969, in a speech disclosed: that the head of state has his ori-gin in "la confiance profonde de la Nation" and not in "un arrangement momentané entre professionnels de l'astuce" (*Le monde*, 19 Dec. 1965) quoted by Moulin, *Le présidentialisme et la classification des régimes politiques*, p. 27.

19. Karl Marx, "The Eighteenth Brumaire of Louis Bonaparte," in *December 2, 1851. Con-temporary Writings on the Coup d'Etat of Louis Napoleon*, edited by John B. Halsted (Garden City, N.Y.: Doubleday, 1992), pp. 152–53.

20. Mattei Dogan, ed., *Pathways to Power, Selecting Rulers in Pluralist Democracies*

(Boulder: Westview, 1989), chap. 10, "Irremovable Leaders and Ministerial Instability in European Democracies," pp. 239–75.

21. The case of María Estela Martínez de Perón, vice president who acceded to the presidency after the death of her husband in July 1974 and was ousted by the March 1976 coup, is a prime example of difficulties caused by the rigidity of presidentialism. Faced with the total failure of her government in November 1975, her opponents wanted to start her impeachment. Then anticipated elections were announced for the end of 1976, but they would not presumably lead to a transfer of power. After a reorganization of the cabinet in August 1975, Christmas brought a mass resignation of cabinet members and December 29 a new demand for impeachment. Mrs. Perón's health was questioned in an effort to apply rules of incapacity. In February 1976 impeachment was again initiated and approved by the lower house but blocked in the senate. After another reorganization of the cabinet, a meeting of party leaders on March 12 was unable to come to a solution. After a coup on March 29, Mrs. Perón was ousted, imprisoned, and tried by the military regime. For a detailed analysis of this crisis, see Mario Daniel Serrafero, "El presidencialismo en el sistema político argentino" (Ph.D. diss., Universidad Complutense—Instituto Universitario Ortega y Gasset, Madrid, 1992), pp. 265–79. This thesis is an outstanding monograph on the Argentinian presidency. Unfortunately, I have not been able to incorporate many of its findings into my analysis.

At the time of writing, the crises in Venezuela involving President Carlos Andrés Pérez and in Brazil involving President Fernando Collor are further examples of the rigidity of presidentialism.

22. On the vulnerability of a single-person election to the influence of mass media, see the excellent article by Giovanni Sartori, "Video-Power," *Government and Opposition*, Winter 1989, pp. 39–53. See also Thomas E. Skidmore, ed., *Television, Politics, and the Transition to Democracy in Latin America* (Washington, D.C.: Woodrow Wilson Center Press, 1993).

23. Shugart and Carey, *Presidents and Assemblies*, pp. 87–91.

24. Adam Przeworski, *Democracy and the Market. Political and Economic Reforms in Eastern Europe and Latin America* (Cambridge: Cambridge UP, 1991), pp. 34–35.

25. Donald Horowitz, "Comparing Democratic Systems," *Journal of Democracy* 1, no. 4 (1990): 73–79, and my response on pp. 84–91. Scott Mainwaring and Matthew S. Shugart, "Juan Linz, Presidentialism and Democracy: A Critical Appraisal," in *Politics, Society and Democracy: Latin America*, edited by Arturo Valenzuela (Boulder: Westview Press, 1994).

26. Mainwaring, "Presidentialism in Latin America," has dealt extensively with the responses to the tensions between presidents and congresses in Latin America and the immobility derived from it (particularly with multipartism), pp. 167–71.

27. Quoted by Russell H. Fitzgibbon, "Continuismo in Central America and the Caribbean," in *The Evolution of Latin American Government, A Book of Readings*, edited by Asher N. Christensen (New York: Henry Holt, 1951), pp. 430–45, esp. p. 436.

28. Sung-joo Han, "South Korea: Politics in Transition" in *Politics in Developing Countries*, edited by Larry Diamond, Juan J. Linz, and Seymour Martin Lipset (Boulder: Lynne Rienner, 1990), pp. 313–50, esp. p. 321 on the mobilization against the constitutional revision that permitted a third-term presidency of Park Chung Hee in 1969. The constitutional amendment achieved by referendum provoked heavy student agitation and can be considered to have been a turning point in the government's ability to maintain the electoral support necessary to keep the president in office. Many who held a reasonably favorable attitude toward Park and high regard for his achievements were disappointed by the tampering with the constitution (p. 325).

29. Juan J. Linz, "Il fattore tempo nei mutamenti de regime," *Teoría política* 2, no. 1 (1986): 3–47.

30. Albert O. Hirschman, *Journeys toward Progress: Studies of Economic Policy-Making in Latin America* (Garden City, N.Y.: Doubleday, 1965), pp. 313–16 about "la rage de vouloir conclure."

31. Daniel Levine, "Venezuela: The Nature, Sources and Prospects of Democracy," in *Democracy in Developing Countries*, pp. 247–89, esp. pp. 256–60; and *Conflict and Political Change in Venezuela* (Princeton: Princeton UP, 1973). See also Jonathan Hartlyn, *The Politics of Coalition Rule in Colombia* (Cambridge: Cambridge UP, 1988).

32. It is significant that Robert A. Dahl, "A Bipartisan Administration," *New York Times*, 14 Nov. 1973, suggested that, during the period between Nixon's resignation and the election of a new president, a coalition government including Democrats and Republicans be created. Cited by A. Lijphart, *Democracy in Plural Societies* (New Haven: Yale UP, 1977), pp. 28–29.

33. On the method of presidential elections see Shugart and Carey, *Presidents and Assemblies*: pp. 208–25, particularly table 10.1, p. 211, which also gives the median percentage of votes for the two highest-scoring candidates. Dieter Nohlen, ed., *Handbuch der Wahldaten Lateinamerikas und der Karibik* (Opladen: Leske & Budrich, 1993), is the most complete source on election legislation, returns in presidential and congressional elections, names of parties and elected presidents for all the countries south of the Rio Grande and the Caribbean.

34. The bibliography on the Spanish transition to democracy and the first election is too extensive to list here. For references see my article "Innovative Leadership in the Spanish Transition," in *Innovative Leadership in International Politics*, edited by Gabriel Sheffer (Albany: State U New York P, 1993).

35. Comments of Prime Minister Felipe González at meeting organized by the Fundación Ortega y Gasset, Toledo, Spain, May 1984.

36. Walter Bagehot, *The English Constitution* (London: World Classics, 1955 [1887]).

37. Scott Mainwaring, "The Dilemmas of Multiparty Presidential Democracy: The Case of Brazil" (Kellogg Institute Working Paper 174, University of Notre Dame, 1992).

38. *New York Times*, 26 Feb. 1992, p. 52.

39. On the parties and party systems, see Scott Mainwaring and Timothy Scully, eds., *Building Democratic Institutions: Parties and Party Systems in Latin America* (Stanford: Stanford UP, forthcoming). Guillermo O'Donnell, "Delegative Democracy" (paper prepared for the meeting of the East-South System Transformations Project, Budapest, Dec. 1990), characterizes a "new animal"—a subtype of existing democracy, which in my view has much in common with many presidential systems, as I characterize them. O'Donnell does not, as I would, link those characteristics with presidentialism, although the empirical bases for his theoretical analysis are basically the Latin American presidential systems.

40. Peru in recent elections is an extreme example. While Fernando Belaúnde of Acción Popular (AP) in 1980 gained 45.4 percent of the vote and the candidate of the Partido Aprista Peruano (PAP) got 27.4 percent, in 1985 Alán García (PAP) gained 53.1 percent and the AP candidate ran fourth with 7.3 percent. In 1990 in the first round Mario Vargas Llosa, the candidate of the coalition Frente Democrático (FREDEMO) was running ahead with 32.6 percent of the vote. Alberto Fujimori (Cambio 90) followed him with 29.1 percent, and the PAP candidate, Luis Alva Castro, ran third with 26.6 percent. In the runoff Fujimori obtained 62.5 percent and Vargas Llosa 37.5 percent. In the election to the lower house the same year, PAP was ahead with 29.4 percent of the seats, followed by Cambio 90 with 17.8 percent and AP

with 14.4 percent, showing the disjunction between presidential and legislative votes. Subsequently in the constitutional crisis in which Fujimori unconstitutionally dissolved the congress in the *autogolpe* of April 5, 1992, he justified his action in the following terms:

> Today we feel that something prevents us from continuing to advance on the road to national reconstruction and progress in our fatherland. And the people of Peru know the cause of this stalemate. They know that it is none other than institutional disintegration. The chaos and corruption, the lack of identification with the great national interests of some of our basic institutions, such as the legislature and the judiciary, impede the government's development.

Alberto Fujimori claimed in the same manifesto: "I insist that as a citizen elected by large national majorities, I am moved only by the wish to achieve the prosperity and greatness of the Peruvian nation."

On the crisis of Peruvian democracy and the *autogolpe* of President Alberto Fujimori on April 5, 1992, see Eduardo Ferrero Costa, ed., *Proceso de returno a la institucionalidad democrática en Perú* (Lima: Centro Peruano de Estudios Internacionales, 1992).

41. Edgardo Catterberg, *Argentina Confronts Politics, Political Culture and Public Opinion in the Argentine Transition to Democracy* (Boulder: Lynne Rienner, 1991), p. 91; Apoyo, *Alán García, Vargas Llosa y la consolidación de la democracia en Perú* (paper presented at the Conference of the World Association for Public Opinion Research (WAPOR): Public Opinion and the Consolidation of Democracy in Latin America, Caracas, Jan. 1990).

42. Carlos Huneeus, *La Unión de Centro Democrático y la transición a la democracia en España* (Madrid: Centro Investigaciones Sociológicas, Siglo 21, 1985), p. 313.

43. Erich Peter Neumann and Elisabeth Noelle, *Statistics on Adenauer. Portrait of a Statesman* (Allensbach: Verlag für Demoskopie, 1962), pp. 40–44.

44. IFOP (Institut Français d'Opinion Publique), *Les français et de Gaulle*, presented by Jean Charlot (Paris: Plon, 1971), pp. 194–208.

45. Shugart and Carey, *Presidents and Assemblies*, pp. 106–30, esp. pp. 106–11, on the "appointment game" in the United States and other systems requiring legislative confirmation.

46. Jean Blondel, *Government Ministers in the Contemporary World* (Beverly Hills: Sage, 1985), pp. 122–25, 127, 129–34, 156–59, quote from p. 123.

47. Markku Laakso and Rein Taagepera, "Effective Number of Parties: A Measure with Application to Western Europe," *Comparative Political Studies* 12 (1979): 3–27. Alfred Stepan and Cindy Skach, in a paper prepared for the Third Meeting of the East-South System Transformations Project, 4–7 Jan. 1992, Toledo, Spain (updated in chapter 4 of this volume), have calculated the Laakso-Taagepera index for the "effective number of parties for forty-two consolidated democracies in the world between 1979 and 1989." Excluding the unique case of Switzerland there were thirty-one pure parliamentary democracies in this universe, six semipresidential democracies, and four pure presidential democracies. Of the thirty-one pure parliamentary systems, ten had between 3 and 7 effective partie. Of the six semipresidential systems, four had between 3 and 5. However, no pure presidential democracy had more than 2.5 effective political parties. The small cell of long-standing presidential systems with 3.0 or more effective parties is probably one of the reasons why there are so few continuous democracies with 3 or more parties (pp. 9–10). However, Chile between 1932 and 1973 was an exception; it was a presidential democracy lasting twenty-five years or more with more than 3.0 effective parties.

48. Scott Mainwaring, "Presidentialism, Multipartism, and Democracy. The Difficult Combination," *Comparative Political Studies* 26, no. 2 (1993): 198–228.

49. The political complexity of the move toward a two-party format in what was a four-party system by the founding of the Democratic Liberal party (DLP) by the former DJP, RDP, and NDRP is analyzed by Sung-joo Han, "The Korean Experiment," *Journal of Democracy* 2, no. 2 (1991): 92–104.

50. Mainwaring, "Dilemmas of Multiparty Presidential Democracy," p. 29.

51. María Ester Mancebo, "From Coparticipation to Coalition: The Problems of Presidentialism in the Uruguayan Case, 1984–1990" (paper presented at the 15th World Congress of the International Political Science Association, July 1991, Buenos Aires); Romeo Pérez Antón, "El parlamentarismo en la tradición uruguaya," *Cuadernos del CLAEH* (Centro Latino Americano de Economía Humana), 2d ser., yr. 14 (1989, no. 1): 107–33.

52. O'Donnell, "Delegative Democracy."

53. Eduardo Gamarra, "Political Stability, Democratization and the Bolivian National Congress" (Ph.D. diss., University of Pittsburgh, 1987); Laurence Whitehead, "Bolivia's Failed Democratization 1977–1980," in *Transitions from Authoritarian Rule, Latin America,* edited by Guillermo O'Donnell, Philippe C. Schmitter, and Laurence Whitehead (Baltimore: Johns Hopkins UP, 1986), pp. 49–71.

54. René Antonio Mayorga, "Bolivia: Democracia como gobernabilidad?" in *Estrategias para el desarrollo de la democracia en Perú y América Latina,* edited by Julio Cotler (Lima: Instituto de Estudios Peruanos—Fundación Friedrich Naumann, 1990), pp. 159–93; and *¿De la anomía política al orden democrático?* (La Paz: CEBEM [Centro Boliviano de Estudios Multidisciplinarios], 1991), pp. 216–75; Eduardo A. Gamarra and James M. Malloy, "The Patrimonial Dynamics of Party Politics in Bolivia," in Scott Mainwaring and Timothy Scully, eds., *Building Democratic Institutions,* forthcoming. Relevant discussions of the Bolivian political system by Eduardo Gamarra, René A. Mayorga, Jorge Lazarte, and others are in René Antonio Mayorga, ed., *Democracia y gobernabilidad en América latina* (Caracas: Editorial Nueva Sociedad, 1992).

55. The Swedish social democratic leader headed the government from 1946 to 1969, leading his party and maintaining an ideological identity while searching for consensus among political actors. See Olaf Ruin, *Tage Erlander* (Pittsburg: Pittsburg UP, 1990).

56. On the weakness of party identification and loyalty in Brazil, see Scott Mainwaring, "Politicians, Parties and Electoral Systems: Brazil in Comparative Perspective," *Comparative Politics,* Oct. 1991, pp. 21–43; and "Brazilian Party Underdevelopment in Comparative Perspective" (Kellogg Institute Working Paper 134, University of Notre Dame, 1990), pp. 21–25, 26–29.

57. Seymour M. Lipset, *Continental Divide: The Values and Institutions of the United States and Canada* (New York: Routledge, 1990).

58. Ana María Mustapic, "Conflictos institucionales durante el primer gobierno Radical: 1916–1926," *Desarrollo económico* 24, no. 93 (1984): 85–108.

59. Donald L. Horowitz, *A Democratic South Africa?*

60. One example of the potential for conflict between the president and the prime minister and his minister of defense was the case of Portugal at the time of the constitutional revision in the early eighties. When the deputies decided that the president would appoint the military officials nominated by the government (art. 136 of the 1982 text), the law based on that text was vetoed and sent back to the assembly by the president. See José Durão Barroso, "Les Conflits entre le président portugais et la majorité parlementaire de 1979 à 1983," in *Les régimes semi-présidentiels,* edited by M. Duverger (Paris: Presses Universitaires de France, 1986), pp. 237–55.

61. On the role of the head of state—monarch or president—in parliamentary regimes,

see Kaltefleiter, *Die Funktionen des Staatsoberhauptes in der parlamentarischen Demokratie,* particularly the extended discussion of the role of the king or queen in the United Kingdom. The role of King Juan Carlos of Spain, both in the transition to democracy (1975–77) and during the coup attempt in 1981, was unique. However it has to be stressed that until after the 1977 election and formally until the enactment of the 1978 constitution, he was not a constitutional monarch in a democratic parliamentary monarchy. Therefore his role as *motor del cambio, piloto del cambio, garantizador del cambio* (motor, pilot, or guarantor of the transition), according to different interpretations of his role, though of undeniable importance, does not fit into our analysis of working parliamentary systems. Although also an exception, his role in the traumatic hours following the sequester of the entire government and legislature on February 23, 1981, shows the importance of the division of roles and of the "reserve" powers of a legitimate and popular head of state. On the role of the king, see Charles T. Powell, *El piloto del cambio: El rey, la monarquía y la transición a la democracia* (Barcelona: Planeta, 1991); Vicente Palacio Atard, *Juan Carlos I y el advenimiento de la democracia* (Madrid: Espasa Calpe, Colección Austral, 1989); Joel Podolny, "The Role of Juan Carlos I in the Consolidation of the Parliamentary Monarchy," in *Politics, Society and Democracy in Spain,* edited by Richard Gunther (Boulder: Westview Press, 1992), pp. 88–112. On the constitutional status of the king, see Manuel Aragón, "La monarquía parlamentaria," in *La constitución española de 1978,* edited by A. Predieri and Eduardo García de Enterría (Madrid: Civitas, 1980), p. 414.

   Spaniards today widely agree with the statement: "Without the presence and the actions of the King the transition to democracy would not have been possible." In 1983, 64 percent, and in 1985, 67 percent, agreed; respectively 19 percent and 18 percent, more or less, disagreed, and 18 percent and 15 percent had no opinion. In 1983, 86 percent agreed that "the King, in stopping the coup of the 23rd of February has gained the respect of Spanish democrats," and between 80 and 89 percent agreed with the statement: "The King has been able to gain the affection of Spaniards including those who did not see the monarchy with favor," with only 6–8 percent disagreeing.

   62. An interesting document on the relation between a powerful chancellor and a highly respected and intelligent president of the republic in a parliamentary regime is: *Theodor Heuss–Konrad Adenauer: "Unserem Vaterland Zugute" der Briefwechsel 1948–1963,* edited by Rudolf Morsey and Hans Peter Schwarz with the collaboration of Hans Peter Mensing (Berlin: Siedler, 1989).

   63. The logical possibility of a prime minister who is elected directly but is not head of state cannot be excluded, but it has not existed in practice. This solution has been proposed in Holland, where the monarchy would be retained, and in Israel.

   64. When I wrote this essay I used the term *semipresidential* because it was the most frequently used term for the kind of government in question, particularly in the United States, where it became known through the writings of Maurice Duverger. Shugart and Carey prefer "premier-presidentialism" to describe this type of regime and offer good arguments in favor of that designation. Perhaps the expression, *dual executive systems,* would be adequate. Since my original text has been translated into several languages, I will continue to use *semipresidential.*

   65. Regarding semipresidential or semiparliamentary (or dual executive) systems, apart from the works of Kaltefleiter and Bartolini already cited (and their sources), see Humberto Nogueira Alcalá, *El régimen semipresidencial. ¿Una nueva forma de gobierno democrático?* (Santiago: Andante, 1986).

   66. Maurice Duverger, *Echec au roi* (Paris: Albin Michel, 1978); "A New Political System

Model: Semipresidential Government," *European Journal of Political Research* 8 (1980): 165–87; Michel Debré, "The Constitution of 1958: Its Raison d'Etre and How It Evolved," in *The Fifth Republic at Twenty,* edited by William G. Andrews and Stanley Hoffman (New York: State U New York P, 1980); Ezra Suleiman, "Presidential Government in France," in *Presidents and Prime Ministers,* edited by Richard Rose and Ezra Suleiman (Washington, D.C.: American Enterprise Institute, 1980), pp. 93–138.

67. On the "majoritarian" character of presidentialism, see Arend Lijphart, chap. 2 herein. On Lijphart, see the discussion in Shugart and Carey, *Presidents and Assemblies,* pp. 20–21.

68. Maurice Duverger, ed., *Les régimes semi-présidentiels* (Paris: Presses Universitaires de France, 1988) with essays on Portugal, Finland, France, and the Weimar republic and discussions of the papers presented.

69. For the presidency in the Weimar Republic and its origins, see Kaltefleiter, *Die Funktionen des Staatsoberhauptes,* chap. 4, pp. 130–44, with reference to the writings of Max Weber and Hugo Preuss and legal commentaries on the constitution. Regarding the functioning of the system, see the excellent analysis on pp. 153–67.

70. On Ireland see Basil Chubb, *The Constitution and Constitutional Change in Ireland* (Dublin: Institute for Public Administration, 1978), chap. 2.

71. Horst Müller, "Parlamentarismus—Diskussion in der Weimar Republik. Die Frage des 'besonderen' Weges zum parlamentarischen Regierungssystem," in *Demokratie und Diktatur. Geist und Gestalt Politischer Herrschaft in Deutschland und Europa, Festschrift für Karl Dietrich Bracher,* edited by Manfred Funke et al. (Düsseldorf: Droste, 1987), pp. 140–57. The Portuguese regime of the 1976 constitution and its successive reforms has not been incorporated into many discussions of semipresidential regimes, even though it is an extremely relevant case, Luis Salgado de Matos, "L'expérience portugaise," in Duverger, *Les régimes semi-présidentiels,* pp. 55–83, includes an interesting analysis of the voting patterns in the election of President Eanes in 1976 and 1980 (see maps on pp. 66–67) that shows radical shifts in support depending on the coalitions supporting Eanes and the larger political context. In the same volume, see Barroso, "Les conflits entre le président portugais et la majorité parlementaire." Kenneth R. Maxwell and Scott C. Monje, eds., *Portugal: The Constitution and the Consolidation of Democracy,* (New York: Camões Center, Columbia University, special report no. 2, 1991) includes comments by social scientists and politicians on the 1976 constitution and its subsequent reform.

72. Consejo para la Consolidación de la Democracia, *Reforma constitucional. Dictamen preliminar del* (Buenos Aires: EUDEBA, 1986) includes the text of the proposal and accompanying documents. The *consejo* was created by President Alfonsín in December 1985. It worked under the leadership of Professor Carlos S. Nino and submitted its report to the president on March 13, 1986.

73. In the case of Finland, there is no great clarity on the respective responsibilities of president and prime minister, although there are "reserve domains" of presidential authority. Article 33 of the constitution establishes that "the president shall determine the relations of Finland with foreign powers," which was so important in postwar relations with the Soviet Union. Otherwise the president has acted as an arbiter in crisis situations and in forming governments in a multiparty system requiring coalitions among a wide spectrum of parties. Kekkonen excluded the Conservatives in order to maintain the "red-green alliance." Perhaps more than other semipresidential-semiparliamentary regimes, the Finnish, which has a "division of labor" and multiparty coalition politics, seems to fit the concept of a "dual executive" and not to oscillate between presidential and parliamentary modes of governing.

See David Arter, "Government in Finland: A 'Semipresidential System'?" *Parliamentary Affairs* 38 (1985): 477–95; Jaakko Nonsiainen, "Bureaucratic Tradition: Semi-presidential Rule and Parliamentary Government; The Case of Finland," *European Journal of Political Research* 16 (1988): 221–49; and the reference to the Finnish case in Kaltefleiter, *Die Funktionen des Staatsoberhauptes*, pp. 167–73 and passim, and in Shugart and Carey, *Presidents and Assemblies*, pp. 61–63. See also Bartolini, "Sistema partitico ed elezione diretta del capo dello stato in Europa."

74. Bartolini, "Sistema partitico ed elezione diretta del capo dello stato in Europa."

75. The shift toward a more parliamentary system in Portugal is reflected in the constitutional reform of 1982. Article 193 of the 1976 constitution stipulated that the government was politically responsible to the president of the republic and the parliament. The new article 193 does not specify the type of responsibility, and article 194 states that the prime minister is responsible to the Assembleia da Répública, in the realm of political responsibility of the government, although article 198.2 grants the president of the republic the exceptional power of dismissing the government should it be necessary to assure the normal functioning of democratic institutions.

76. On the other hand, the fear of a military president led framers of the 1931 constitution of the Spanish Republic to make ineligible for the presidency anyone active in the military or in the reserves and anyone retired from the military for less than ten years.

77. Duverger, "A New Political System Model."

78. Kaltefleiter, *Die Funktionen des Staatsoberhauptes*, pp. 153–67.

79. Raymond Aron, "Alternation in Government in the Industrialized Countries," *Government and Opposition* 17, no. 1 (1981): 3–21.

80. Giovanni Sartori, *Seconda Repubblica? Si, ma bene*. (Milan: Rizzoli, 1992).

81. See Rainer Lepsius, "From Fragmented Party Democracy to Government by Emergency Decree," in Linz and Stepan, *Breakdown of Democratic Regimes*, esp. pp. 34–39, 45–50; Eberhard Jäckel, "Der Machtantritt Hitlers—Versuch einer geschichtlichen Erklärung," in *1933 Wie die Republik der Diktatur erlag*, edited by Volker Rittberger (Stuttgart: Kohlhammer, 1983), pp. 123–39.

82. Kaltefleiter, *Die Funktionen des Staatoberhauptes*, pp. 183–97, esp. p. 197.

83. In 1929 Carl Schmitt, one of the leading political scientists and constitutionalists of Germany, published in the *Archiv des öffentlichen Rechts* (Neue Folge) 16: 161–237, an article titled "Der Hüter der Verfassung" and in 1931 a pamphlet under the same title, in *Beiträge zum öffentlichen Recht der Gegenwart*, Heft 1 (Tübingen), offering an authoritarian antipluralistic and plebiscitary interpretation of the Weimar constitution.

84. Regarding the stability of parliamentary semipresidential regimes in Europe between the two world wars, see Linz, *Crisis, Breakdown and Reequilibration*, pp. 74–75. Of the seventeen countries analyzed before the depression, apart from Portugal, Yugoslavia, and Spain (1918–23), Germany had the greatest instability with 210 days average duration of cabinet, followed by the Third Republic in France with 239 days, Italy (1917–22) with 260, Austria with 267, and Finland with 294. After the depression, Spain with 101 days average duration, France with 165, Austria with 149, Germany with 258, Finland with 592, Estonia with 260, and Belgium with 285 are the countries with the most unstable governments of the fourteen countries that are included. Note that two of the systems with a dual executive are among the most unstable countries. In two of the countries with high government instability and a parliamentary regime democracy survived until World War II. See also Ekkart Zimmermann, "Government Stability in Six European Countries during the World Economic Crisis of the 1930s: Some Preliminary Considerations," *European Journal of Political Research* 15 (1987): 23–52.

85. Nicolás Pérez Serrano, *La constitución española* (9 Dec. 1931) (Madrid: Editorial Revista de Derecho Privado, 1932), pp. 244–74; see articles 75, 81, and 87. See Antonio Bar, *El presidente del gobierno en España: Encuadre constitucional y práctica política* (Madrid: Editorial Civitas, 1983), pp. 121–28, for a study of "rationalized parliamentarism" and the role of the president of the Second Republic.

He was elected by the members of the Cortes, a unicameral legislature, and an equal number of electors (who were directly elected by the people) for a term of six years and could not be reelected. However, the first president was elected by the legislature on December 10, 1931.

The system of dual confidence was derived from article 75: "The President of the Republic appoints and dismisses freely the president of the government, and, at his proposal the ministers. He shall dismiss them necessarily in the case that the Cortes should explicitly deny them their confidence."

86. On the working of the Spanish constitution of 1931 and the presidency, see: Joaquín Tomás Villarroya, "Presidente de la República y Gobierno: Sus Relaciones," *Revista de estudios políticos* (nueva época) 31–32 (Jan.–Apr. 1983): 71–90 (which quotes leading politicians on the "dual confidence"), and "La prerrogativa presidencial durante la Segunda República: Mediatización, *Revista de estudios políticos* 16 (1980): pp. 59–87; Stanley G. Payne, *Spain's First Democracy: The Second Republic, 1931–1936* (Madison: U Wisconsin P, 1993), describes in detail the working of the system. On the removal of the president, see Joaquín Tomás Villarroya, *La destitución de Alcalá-Zamora*, (Valencia: Fundación Universitaria, San Pablo, CEU, 1988). For the position of Niceto Alcalá-Zamora see his *Los defectos de la Constitución de 1931 y tres años de experiencia constitucional* (Madrid: Civitas, 1981, first published 1936) and *Memorias. Segundo texto de mis memorias* (Barcelona: Planeta, 1977). Javier Tusell, "Niceto Alcalá-Zamora y una crisis política en el segundo bienio Republicano," *Hispania* 33 (1973): 401–16.

87. If it did not compound confusion the system could be described as "semi-premier-presidential" because half the electors of the president were to be popularly elected (although the first president, like Ebert and de Gaulle, was elected by the legislature).

88. *Diario de Sesiones de las Cortes Constituyentes*, 3 Nov. 1931, p. 2092.

89. Karl Dietrich Bracher, *Die Auflösung der Weimarer Republik* (Stuttgart: Ring-Verlag, 1957), chap. 9 about the Reichswehr, pp. 229–84; see pp. 249–53 for articles 53 and 54 of the constitution, which required the double confidence of the Reichstag and the president for the minister of defense.

90. There is also the possibility, though it is less likely, that the top military leadership might turn to congressional leaders to oppose the president.

91. There is likely to be more experimenting with mixed formulas in view of the growing dissatisfaction with pure presidentialism and the distrust of pure parliamentarism (which not all forms of parliamentarism merit, probably), or the unwillingness to break with the tradition of presidentialism. In addition to the "premier-presidential" (semiparliamentary, semipresidential) systems we discuss, Giovanni Sartori has developed another type in "Le riforme istituzionali—Tra buone e cattive," *Rivista italiana di scienza politica* 21 (3 Dec. 1991): 375–408, with commentary by Angelo Pianebianco (pp. 409–18) and Stefano Passigli (pp. 419–40) and a rejoinder by Sartori (pp. 441–46). Also in Sartori, *Seconda Repubblica?*

The resistance to parliamentarism (in any version) and the difficulty of making the French type of semipresidential, semiparliamentary system work in view of the "plebiscitary culture" surrounding presidentialism in Latin America has led to the search for other hybrid solutions. One submitted by a working group of Bolivian political scientists and constitutionalists in collaboration with several foreign scholars (including me) to a political commission charged with making constitutional reforms might be dubbed "parliamentarized presidentialism." It does not abandon the presidentialist principle of direct popular election of a president but tries to reduce the risks and costs of "minority" presidencies. It also attempts to deal with the "rigidity" of the presidential mandate and the risk of ingovernability by making possible a constructive vote of nonconfidence in the case of minority presidents and a return of power to the electorate in case of total impasse by a qualified congressional majority, with both presidential and parliamentary elections. The project is based on the Bolivian tradition of parliamentary election of the president in the absence of a majority vote for any candidate.

The proposal starts with presidentialism as a point of departure. In fact, it retains a pure presidentialism (except that it allows for "political" rather than just criminal impeachment, *juicio político*) with one condition: that the majority of the people elect a president. Otherwise the equal democratic legitimacy of the congress enters into play; this body elects a president, choosing between the two candidates with the most popular votes the one who can form the strongest parliamentary coalition. However, the president so elected, by a minority of the electorate *and* a majority of the congress, is subject to a constructive vote of no confidence, which assures his succession by a president with majority support in the congress. In a sense the system is also an alternative parliamentarism, as Sartori's is an alternative presidentialism. The difference is that one case attempts to correct the impasses generated by presidentialism and the other, those of extreme, assembly-type parliamentarism.

92. In pure presidential systems the president cannot dissolve the assembly. There are, however, the exceptions of Paraguay (never tested under democratic conditions) and Chile in the authoritarian 1980 constitution. In Uruguay and Peru dissolution can be invoked after the congress has censored cabinet ministers or even the entire cabinet for political reasons (in the case of Peru, this must happen three times) with additional restrictions.

The possibility of dissolution by a president who stays in office may not resolve but exacerbate the conflict between the congress and the president. The electorate might return a congress that is hostile to the president, and the stalemate might be prolonged. Only if dissolution leads to the election of a new congress and a simultaneous presidential election might this risk be reduced; the voters then would have a chance to side with the president or with the opposition.

93. The preference for presidentialism and even mixed forms of semipresidential systems is often based on hostility to political parties, if not to democratic pluralism. It is not surprising that conservatives not fully reconciled to the transition to democracy in Germany (the DVP and DNVP), the Finnish conservatives, and more recently "reconstructed" communist parties or leaders in the former USSR and Mongolia should have favored a president who is presumably above parties. In addition, in a recently unified country like Germany, there was the hope of finding a "substitute" Kaiser in a federal republic or, in countries like Finland, Ireland, and Iceland, a symbol of the new national independence.

94. On this point see: Linz, "Change and Continuity in the Nature of Contemporary Democracies," in *Reexamining Democracy, Essays in Honor of Seymour Martin Lipset*, edited by Gary Marks and Larry Diamond (Newbury Park, Calif.: Sage, 1992), pp. 182–207, esp. pp. 188–90 and the studies quoted there.

95. Philip Williams, *Politics in Post-War France. Parties and the Constitution in the Fourth Republic* (London: Longmans, Green, 1954), p. 399.

96. In relation to the constructive vote of censure, see Bar, *El presidente del gobierno en España*, with reference to the works of the German and Spanish constitutionalists. Guilherme d'Oliveira Martins, Dieter Nohlen, José Juan González Encinar, António Vitorino,

José Magalhães, and Jorge Sampaio, *A revisão constitucional e a moção de censura construc-tiva* (Lisbon: Fundação Friedrich Ebert, 1988) includes chapters about the Bonn constitu-tion and the 1978 Spanish constitution, with bibliographical references. On the use of the constructive vote of no confidence in Germany, see Lewis J. Edinger, *West German Politics* (New York: Columbia UP, 1986), p. 247.

97. The way in which parliamentary governments in Europe actually work is enor-mously varied, particularly in the formation of cabinets and their relation to the parliament. This is not the place to discuss that rich and complex experience; I refer the reader to the monumental work of Klaus von Beyme, *Die parlementarischen Regierungssysteme in Europa*, pt. 2, pp. 499–900.

98. Chapter 3 of this volume, by Giovanni Sartori, rightly argues against pure parlia-mentarism, the *gouvernement d'assemblée*, in which the parliament governs and the execu-tive—the prime minister and his cabinet— has no authority and is unprotected against quickly shifting majorities in the assembly that cannot be made accountable.

He argues for an impure solution that he sometimes calls semiparliamentary, which side-steps the principle of the sovereignty of parliament. My argument in favor of premier-parlia-mentarism, like the British or the German Kanzlerdemokratie, coincides with his, but we dif-fer in the characterization of those regimes. In my view they are parliamentary because the election of the prime minister or Kanzler is made by the parties in the parliament and con-tinuance in office ultimately depends on the parliament, where one wins a vote of confidence, fails to provide an alternative government, or even fears dissolution and the need to confront the electorate. Modern, rationalized parliamentary systems do not eliminate the role of par-ties or of parliamentarians but limit the arbitrary, irresponsible, excessive use of parliamen-tary power. However, the executive has to pay attention to the parliament, to his or her party or the supporters of a coalition, and therefore is not "independent" and "unaccountable" for the whole legislative period. The democratically elected "unequals" above whom or among whom he or she governs have a share in power and are potentially accountable for their use of it.

99. The Israeli parliamentary system is generally considered as a "bad" case of parlia-mentarism, with its highly fractionalized party system (largely a result of the electoral law), the difficulty of forming coalitions and their instability, the stalemate due to the concessions made in forming coalitions, and other problems. Reforms short of moving to a pure presi-dential system have been proposed, including the direct election of the prime minister. See the "Conclusion, Directions for Reform" in Ehud Sprinzak and Larry Diamond, *Israel: Democracy under Stress* (Boulder: Lynne Rienner, 1993).

100. Scott Mainwaring and Matthew Shugart, "Juan Linz, Presidentialism and Democ-racy," in *Politics, Society, and Democracy: Latin America. Essays in Honor of Juan J. Linz* (Boulder: Westview Press, 1994).

101. Alfred Stepan and Cindy Skach, "Meta-Institutional Frameworks and Democratic Consolidation" (paper prepared for the Third Meeting of the East-South System Transfor-mations Project, 4–7 Jan. 1992, Toledo, Spain).

102. Shugart and Carey, *Presidents and Assemblies*, pp. 40–41.

103. Juan J. Linz, "La crisis de las democracias," in *Europa en crisis 1919–1939*, edited by Mercedes Cabrera, Santos Juliá, and Pablo Martín Aceña (Madrid: Editorial Pablo Iglesias, 1991), pp. 231–80; see table 1, p. 235.

104. Tatu Vanhanen, "Institutional Strategies and Democratization" (paper presented at the 15th World Congress of the International Political Science Association, July 1991, Buenos Aires).

Part II
Theoretical Perspectives
and the Semipresidential
Case of France

2

AREND LIJPHART

Presidentialism and Majoritarian Democracy: Theoretical Observations

THE PURPOSE of this chapter is to establish the theoretical link between two sets of contrasting types of democracy: presidential versus parliamentary democracy on the one hand, and majoritarian versus consensus democracy on the other. In my book *Democracies* (1984), a comparative study of the twenty-one countries that have had uninterrupted democratic government since approximately the end of the Second World War,[1] I dealt with both, but my main focus was on the contrast between the majoritarian and consensus models of democracy. Moreover, my discussion of the presidential-parliamentary contrast was not sufficiently integrated with my comparison of majoritarian and consensus democracy.[2] In particular, I defined presidentialism and parliamentarism in terms of two contrasting characteristics, ignoring a crucial third distinction, and I linked the presidential-parliamentary contrast to only one of the differences between majoritarian and consensus democracy, ignoring its impact on several other relevant distinctions. This chapter offers me a welcome opportunity to correct these deficiencies and to establish the overall connection between the presidential-parliamentary and majoritarian-consensus contrasts.[3]

My analysis entails a critique of presidential government but on different grounds than Juan J. Linz, Arturo Valenzuela, and others in this volume. I especially do not address the rigidity and immobilism that presidentialism introduces in the political process, although I hasten to say that I am in full agreement that these are its most serious weaknesses. My criticism in this chapter focuses on an additional weakness of the presidential form of government: its strong inclination toward majoritarian democracy, especially in the many countries where, because a natural consensus is lacking, a consensual instead of a majoritarian form of democracy is needed. These countries include not only those with deep ethnic, racial, and

religious cleavages but also those with intense *political* differences stemming from
a recent history of civil war or military dictatorship, huge socioeconomic inequalities, and so on. Moreover, in democratizing and redemocratizing countries undemocratic forces must be reassured and reconciled, and they must be persuaded not
only to give up power but also not to insist on "reserved domains" of undemocratic power within the new, otherwise democratic, regime. Consensus democracy,
which is characterized by sharing, limiting, and dispersing power, is much more
likely to achieve this objective than straight majority rule. As Philippe C. Schmitter
has suggested, consensus democracy means "defensive" democracy, which is much
less threatening to cultural-ethnic and political minorities than "aggressive" majority rule.[4]

I deal with my topic in three steps. First, I define presidentialism in terms of
three essential characteristics. Second, I show that, especially as a result of its third
characteristic, presidentialism has a strong tendency to make democracy majoritarian. Third, I examine the various nonessential characteristics of presidentialism—features that are not distinctive to, although frequently present in, presidential forms of government and their impact on the degree of majoritarianism or
consensus.

Presidential Democracy: Three Essential Elements

In *Democracies* (Lijphart 1984, 68–69), I define presidential and parliamentary
regimes in terms of two crucial differences. First, in parliamentary democracies,
the head of the government—who may have different official titles such as prime
minister, premier, chancellor, minister-president, and (in Ireland) *taoiseach* —and
his or her cabinet are dependent on the legislature's confidence and can be dismissed from office by a legislative vote of no confidence or censure. In presidential
systems, the head of government—invariably called president—is elected for a
fixed, constitutionally prescribed term and in normal circumstances cannot be
forced by the legislature to resign (although it may be possible to remove a president by the highly unusual and exceptional process of impeachment). The second
crucial difference is that presidential heads of government are popularly elected, either directly or via an electoral college, and that prime ministers are selected by the
legislatures. I use the general term "selected" advisedly because the process of selection can range widely from formal election to informal interparty bargaining in
the legislature.[5]

Several eminent political scientists (Verney 1959, 17–56; Kaltefleiter 1970;
Duchacek 1973, 175–91; Steffani 1979; Powell 1982, 55–57) have argued that, in addition to the above two crucial differences, there are several other important distinctions. For instance, presidents cannot simultaneously be members of the legislature, whereas prime ministers (and the other ministers in their cabinets) usually
are; and presidents are both heads of government and heads of state, whereas prime

ministers are mere heads of government. There are two problems with these additional distinctions. One is that there are serious empirical exceptions; for example, Dutch and Norwegian legislators have to resign their legislative seats when they join the cabinet, but this does not affect the basically parliamentary pattern of government in these countries in any significant way. Second, even when there are no exceptions, as in the case of presidents being the heads of both state and government, this attribute cannot be argued to be logically necessary. This does not mean that these differences are unimportant. I try to show later on that they affect the balance of power between the executive and the legislature—and hence the degree of majoritarianism or consensus—but, in my view, they cannot be regarded as criteria for *defining* presidentialism and parliamentarism.

I have come to the conclusion, however, that a third essential difference must be stated and that this difference accounts for much of the majoritarian proclivity of presidential democracy: the president is a one-person executive, whereas the prime minister and the cabinet form a collective executive body. Within parliamentary systems, the prime minister's position in the cabinet can vary from preeminence to virtual equality with the other ministers, but there is always a relatively high degree of collegiality in decision making. In contrast, the members of presidential cabinets are mere advisers and subordinates of the president.

The three dichotomous criteria I use yield not only the pure presidential and parliamentary types but six additional types of democracy, as shown in figure 2.1. As the typology shows, there are very few democracies that combine presidential and parliamentary characteristics, and three of the potential "mixed" types have no empirical examples at all. The vast majority of democracies fit the pure parliamentary or presidential types.

It is also worth emphasizing that most empirical cases can be classified in the typology without difficulty or ambiguity, including the cases of Switzerland and Uruguay, which are extremely awkward to classify without using the distinction between one-person and collegial executives. The Swiss Federal Council is a seven-member coequal executive elected by the legislature for a fixed term of office. The Uruguayan *colegiado*, which operated from 1952 to 1967, was a Swiss-inspired, nine-member body, also serving for a fixed term but popularly elected. Cyprus during its first few years of independence was ruled by a directly elected duumvirate (a Greek Cypriot president and a Turkish Cypriot vice president with virtually equal powers) and therefore fits the same type. These characteristics make Switzerland more parliamentary than presidential and Uruguay under the *colegiado* system as well as Cyprus in the early 1960s more presidential than parliamentary, although none of these three cases conform to the pure parliamentary or presidential type.

The cell in the top righthand corner has only a single occupant: Lebanon has a "presidential" system except that the president is elected by parliament instead of the voters.[6] A nondemocratic example of this form of government is South Africa under its 1983 constitution: the president is elected by an electoral college that is in

	Collegial executive		One-person executive	
	Dependent on legislative confidence	Not dependent on legislative confidence	Dependent on legislative confidence	Not dependent on legislative confidence
Executive selected by legislature	*Pure Parliamentarism:* Most West European democracies Australia Canada France (1986–88) India Israel Jamaica Japan Malaysia New Zealand Turkey Nigeria (1960–66)	Switzerland	No empirical examples A	Lebanon
Executive selected by voters	No empirical examples B	Cyprus (1960–63) Uruguay (1952–67)	No empirical examples C	*Pure Presidentialism:* Most Latin American democracies Cyprus France (5th Republic except 1986–88) Nigeria (1979–83) Philippines South Korea United States

Fig. 2 1. A Typology of Parliamentary, Presidential, and Mixed Forms of Democracy, with Some Empirical Examples

turn elected by the three houses of parliament. I do *not* include in this category presidential systems like the United States and Chile, where the legislature has a role in the election of the president if the popular (or electoral college) vote fails to yield a majority winner. The strong Chilean tradition is that the legislature simply ratifies the plurality winner, and in the United States there is almost always a majority winner. The Bolivian case is more problematic; the legislature awarded the presidency to the runner-up instead of the plurality winner in 1985 and to the third-place finisher in 1989. Even here, however, the legislature's powers of selection are severely constrained by the preceding direct popular election.

That three of the types are empty cells in figure 2.1 is not surprising because the logic of the system of legislative confidence militates against them. Type A would be a strong form of *Kanzlerdemokratie:* a parliamentary system except that the prime minister's relationship to the cabinet resembles that of a president and his or her cabinet. On paper, the West German constitution appears to call for such a system, but since the chancellor needs the Bundestag's continuing confidence, the negotiation of a collegial coalition cabinet takes place prior to the formal election of the chancellor by the Bundestag. Types B and C are problematic because a legislative vote of no confidence in a popularly elected executive would be seen as defiance of the popular will and of democratic legitimacy. The only democratically acceptable form of types B and C would be one in which a legislative vote of no confidence in the executive would be matched by the executive's right to dissolve the legislature, and where either action would trigger new elections of both legislature and executive. The C form of such a system resembles Lloyd N. Cutler's (1980) well-known proposal.

The only empirical cases that appear to be difficult to classify are those with both a popularly elected president and a parliamentary prime minister. Here the key question is: who is the *real* head of government—president or prime minister? And this question is usually not hard to answer. In Austria, Iceland, and Ireland, the presidents are weak in spite of their popular election; these systems are unambiguously parliamentary. But what about the so-called semipresidential (or semiparliamentary) Fifth Republic? Raymond Aron wrote in 1981 (p. 8): "The President of the Republic is the supreme authority [that is, the true head of government] as long as he has a majority in the National Assembly; but he must abandon the reality of power to the prime minister if ever a party other than his own has a majority in the Assembly." This is exactly what happened in 1986: Premier Jacques Chirac became the head of government and President François Mitterrand was reduced to merely a special role in foreign policy. The Finnish and post-1982 Portuguese systems resemble the 1986–88 pattern in France and should therefore also be classified as parliamentary.

It may be possible to design a true half-presidential and half-parliamentary system—perhaps by specifying in the constitution that the president and prime minister jointly head the government—but there are no actual examples of such intermediate regimes. In particular, the Fifth Republic is, instead of semipresidential, usually presidential and only occasionally parliamentary. Maurice Duverger (1980, 186) correctly anticipating the shift to parliamentarism in 1986 and back to presidentialism in 1988—as prescient as Aron—concludes that the Fifth Republic is not "a *synthesis* of the parliamentary and presidential system" but an "*alternation* between presidential and parliamentary phases" (emphasis in original).[7]

Presidentialism between Majoritarian and Consensus Democracy

In *Democracies,* I fail to resolve the question of whether presidentialism is conducive to majoritarianism or consensus. On the one hand, I argue that the formal *separation* of powers between the executive and the legislature in presidential regimes contributes to a *balance* of power between these branches of government—one of the characteristics of consensus democracy. But later on, I characterize the

presidential French Fifth Republic as having a "high degree of executive dominance" (Lijphart 1984, 24–25, 33–34, 82–83, 212). The main problem is that I focus
on the impact of presidentialism on only one of the eight traits that distinguish majoritarian from consensus democracy. These traits, which cluster along two dimensions, are:

Executives-parties dimension

   1. One-party cabinets versus broad coalitions
   2. Executive dominance versus executive-legislative balance
   3. Two-party versus multiparty systems
   4. Unidimensional versus multidimensional party systems
   5. Plurality elections versus proportional representation

Federal-unitary dimension

   6. Unitary and centralized versus federal and decentralized government
   7. Unicameral legislatures versus strong bicameralism
   8. Unwritten versus written and rigid constitutions

For each trait in the list, the majoritarian characteristic (e.g., one-party cabinets) is
listed first and the corresponding consensual characteristic (e.g., broad coalitions)
second. I argue that the five characteristics of the first dimension, having
to do with executive power and political parties, are affected by presidentialism—
mainly in the direction of promoting majoritarian rule. (On the other hand, presidentialism does not appear to have significant consequences for the characteristics
of the second, federal-unitary, dimension, and I therefore do not discuss these differences between the majoritarian and consensus models.)

I still believe that separating the executive from the legislative power helps to
balance these powers. This is the result of the paradox of the requirement of parliamentary confidence. In theory, it makes the executive subservient to the legislature,
but in practice it means that, on every important vote, legislators must cast their
votes not only on the merits of the particular issue but also on keeping the cabinet
in office: the fact that most legislators do not want to upset the cabinet too frequently gives the cabinet very strong leverage over the process of legislation. In
presidential systems, the legislature can deal with bills on their merits without the
fear of causing a cabinet crisis—and hence also without being "blackmailed" by the
executive into accepting its proposals. Consequently, in a hypothetical ceteris
paribus situation, separation of power entails greater legislative independence and
a more balanced executive-legislative relationship.

But all other factors are by no means equal, and they can easily negate the effect
of separation of power. In France, for instance, the president's power to dissolve
the National Assembly and the many constitutional provisions curtailing the legislature's prerogatives produce executive dominance in spite of the separation of

power. Similarly, Latin American presidents are usually regarded as dominant, although as Scott Mainwaring (1990) has forcefully argued, this appraisal is exaggerated and it applies only to some of the presidential systems in Latin America. I return to some of the "other factors" in the next section.

When we look at the other characteristics of the executive and of the party and electoral systems on which majoritarian and consensus systems differ—those numbered 1, 3, 4, and 5 in the list—presidentialism invariably entails greater majoritarianism and fewer chances for consensual politics. The first characteristic concerns the concentration of executive power, and it ranges from one-party majority governments to grand coalitions of all significant parties; intermediate forms are minimal winning coalitions (that is, coalitions of two or more parties that together have majority support) and oversized (larger than minimal winning) coalitions that do not include all major parties. Presidentialism entails the concentration of executive power at the extreme majoritarian end of the range: power is concentrated not just in one *party* but in one *person*.

For this reason, it is extremely difficult to introduce executive power sharing in presidential systems. In my book *Democracy in Plural Societies*, I concluded that "while consociational democracy is not incompatible with presidentialism, . . . a better institutional framework is offered by . . . parliamentary systems" (Lijphart 1977, 224). This could be stated more strongly: presidentialism is inimical to the kind of consociational compromises and pacts that may be necessary in the process of democratization and during periods of crisis, whereas the collegial nature of parliamentary executives makes them conducive to such pacts. Moreover, as Linz (1987, 34; see also Hartlyn 1988) points out, when consociational arrangements are squeezed into a presidential system—for instance, by the pact that included, *inter alia*, equal legislative representation and alternation in the presidency by the two major parties in Colombia from 1958 to 1974—the voters' freedom of choice is constrained to a much greater extent than by consociational methods in parliamentary systems.

As far as the party system is concerned, the fact that the presidency is the biggest political prize to be won and that only the largest parties have a chance to win it represents an impulse away from multipartism and in the direction of a two-party system. One generally accepted explanation of the American two-party system—which, with virtually no third parties at all, is the world's most exclusive two-party system—is the winner-take-all nature of presidential elections. In Latin America, the same mechanism appears to operate even when legislative elections are conducted under proportional representation. As Matthew S. Shugart (1988; see also Nilson 1983) has pointed out, this is especially the case when the presidential election is decided by plurality rather than by majority (which may require a runoff election) and, more importantly, when the legislative election is held at the same time or shortly after the presidential election. In France, under a two-ballot majority system for both presidential and legislative elections, the multiparty system has been maintained but in a two-bloc or bipolar format and with considerably fewer parties than in the parliamentary Third Republic, which used the same electoral system. Duverger (1986, 81–82) asks "why the same electoral system coincided with a dozen parties in the Third Republic but ended up with only four [parties in a two-bloc format] in the Fifth Republic." His main explanation is "the direct popular election of the president, which has transformed the political regime."

There is one important countervailing factor. While presidential systems discourage multipartism, they also discourage cohesive parties. In parliamentary systems, reasonably disciplined and cohesive parties are required because they have to support cabinets in office; in presidential systems, this requirement does not apply, and parties can afford to be much laxer with regard to internal party unity. This means that, ceteris paribus, a party system with, say, two or three parties in a presidential democracy would have to be considered less majoritarian than a parliamentary party system with the same number of parties.

The number of parties is closely related to the dimensionality of the party system, that is, the number of issue dimensions that are salient in the party system (Taagepera and Grofman 1985). In two-party systems, only one issue dimension—usually the socioeconomic or left-right dimension—tends to dominate. In multiparty systems, one or more additional dimensions—religious, cultural-ethnic, urban-rural, foreign policy, and so on—is probably present. Consequently, the pressures toward a two-party system exerted by presidentialism are also likely to make the left-right dimension dominant and to squeeze out all other issue dimensions—which may be quite important to political and other minorities.

Finally, presidentialism has a strong effect on the proportionality of the electoral outcome. The fact that a presidential election involves the election of one person means that proportional representation cannot be used; the only possibilities are the plurality and majority methods. And plurality-majority methods (applied in single-member districts) yield increasingly disproportional results as the size of the body to be elected decreases—reaching a peak of disproportionality in the case of the election of one person. The most widely used measure of disproportionality is John Loosemore and Victor J. Hanby's (1971): the percentage by which the overrepresented party or parties are overrepresented (which is, of course, the same as the total percentage of underrepresentation). In proportional representation systems, the Loosemore-Hanby index averages about 5 percent and rarely exceeds 10 percent. It tends to be considerably higher in legislative elections by plurality or majority: between 10 and 20 percent. In Western countries during the 1945–85 period, I found the highest average disproportionality in the French Fifth Republic: almost 21 percent (Lijphart 1988b). The all-or-nothing nature of presidential elections raises the disproportionality to much higher levels: about 46 percent in the 1988 French and American presidential elections, about 59 percent in the Dominican Republic in 1986, and about 63 percent in the 1970 Chilean election won by Salvador Allende.

The argument in this section can be summarized as follows: while the separation of power exerts some pressure toward consensus democracy, the popular election of the president and the concentration of executive power in one person are strong influences in the direction of majoritarianism. The corollary of separation of power—the fixed presidential term of office—does not affect the majoritarian or consensual character of democracy, except that one could argue that unusually long terms of office, such as the six-year and seven-year terms in Argentina and France respectively, accentuate the power concentration and disproportionality features of presidentialism.

Nonessential but Frequent Attributes of Presidentialism and Their Consequences

So far, I have examined the effects of presidentialism on majoritarianism exclusively in terms of the three essential characteristics of presidentialism. Let me now turn to the additional characteristics of presidentialism formulated by other scholars. I do not regard these as essential, but they are frequent attributes of presidentialism, and they may have important effects on the majoritarian or consensual nature of the system. These attributes of presidentialism are often primarily based on the American example (and on its contrast with the British example of parliamentary government). The American case is just one example of presidentialism, but it has had considerable influence abroad, especially in Latin America (Friedrich 1967; Von Beyme 1987). For this reason, the following six characteristics of presidentialism are based on the American model, but I also use the French Fifth Republic and two Latin American countries with long democratic records—Costa Rica and Venezuela—as examples:

1. *The president does not have the power to dissolve the legislature.*[8] This common characteristic of presidentialism reduces the power of the president and increases that of the legislature—making for a more balanced relationship between the two and hence for a more consensus-oriented system. When, exceptionally, the president does have the right of dissolution, as in France, presidential power is greatly enhanced and the regime becomes much more majoritarian.

2. *The president has a veto power over legislation, and the presidential veto can be overridden only by extraordinary legislative majorities.* This kind of veto strengthens presidential power a great deal. Unless the legislature contains large antipresidential majorities, the veto makes the president the equivalent of a third chamber of the legislature. This is what William H. Riker (1984, 109) means when he speaks of "the tricameral legislature found in the United States." Not all presidents have veto powers that can only be negated by extraordinary majorities. The Venezuelan president's veto, for instance, can in the final analysis be overridden by a simple majority (unless the Supreme Court agrees with the president that the bill is unconstitutional). The French president, who is very strong in other respects, also

appears to be weak in this regard; however, the veto is irrelevant in the French case because France operates as a presidential system only when the president has majority support in the legislature.

3. *The president can appoint the members of the cabinet without legislative interference.* In spite of the "advice and consent" provision in the United States Constitution, the president has virtually complete control over the composition of his or her cabinet. The same is true in France and, with slight qualifications, in most Latin American countries; in Costa Rica and Venezuela, cabinet ministers can be censured and thereby removed by congressional action, but two-thirds majorities are required.

4. *The president is not only the head of government but also the head of state.* It is conceivable that a presidential head of government would *not* simultaneously be the head of state: such a system has been proposed in the Netherlands, where the monarch would continue to be the head of state, and in Israel, where a separate ceremonial head of state would be maintained. But in practice, there are no exceptions to the rule that in presidential systems the two functions are combined in one person. It obviously enhances the president's stature very considerably.

5. *The president can serve no more than two elected terms of office.* This provision, which clearly decreases presidential power, is absent from the French constitution, but more stringent provisions apply in Costa Rica, where reelection is completely prohibited, and in Venezuela, where presidents cannot serve two terms in immediate succession; in these two countries, presidents become "lame ducks" immediately after being elected. While this kind of rule is important as a limit on the president's power, it is even more important as a symptom of the widely perceived danger of too much, even dictatorial, presidential power. It is significant that, while such limitations are common in presidential systems, there is not a single example of a similar limit on a prime minister's tenure in parliamentary systems. Moreover, as Harry Kantor (1977, 23–24) points out, limits on reelection "are infractions upon true democracy, which demands that voters be allowed to vote for whomever they choose." I would add that they also conflict with the democratic assumption that the opportunity to be reelected is a strong incentive for elected officials to remain responsive to the voters' wishes.

6. *The president cannot simultaneously be a member of the legislature.* This contrasts with parliamentary systems, where the prime minister and the other ministers are usually, but not always, members of parliament. However, when ministers are not members of the legislature, as in the Netherlands and Norway, they can still participate in parliamentary debates and still have to submit to questions and interpellations. The physical distance between president and legislature, combined with the

president's dignity as head of state and his or her usual residence in a presidential palace, adds to the "imperial" atmosphere of the presidency and hence to majoritarianism.

When we add up the tendencies of these six features for the American case, we find four that tend toward majoritarianism and only two that tend in a consensual direction. Compared with this 4–2 score, the score for France is 5–0, with one nonapplicable item (as explained above, the question of the veto is irrelevant in the French case). Like the United States, Costa Rica also has a 4–2 overall score favoring majoritarianism. Venezuela is the only case with an even 3–3 score. But this unweighted addition makes little sense; for instance, the power to dissolve the legislature is obviously much more important than the incompatibility of executive and legislative offices. Moreover, the above six characteristics do not exhaust a president's potential powers vis-à-vis the legislature; in particular, emergency powers and powers of appointment (of provincial or state governors, supreme court justices, and other officials) would have to be considered in order to complete the picture. Nevertheless, the above examples make clear that the nonessential but frequent features of presidentialism lead, on average, in the same direction as its essential attributes: toward majoritarian democracy.

Conclusions. Paradoxes of Presidential Power

My overall conclusion can be summarized in three words: presidentialism spells majoritarianism. But this conclusion raises several difficult and paradoxical questions. First, majoritarianism means the concentration of political power in the hands of the majority, and if the presidency is the repository of this power, it means a very powerful president; in other words, the logic of presidentialism is that it implies very strong, perhaps even overbearing, presidents. This logic conflicts with the empirical reality of presidentialism in the United States and also, as Mainwaring (1990) has pointed out, in most of the *democratic* presidential regimes in Latin America. How can we explain this paradox?

One explanation is that presidentialism spells not only concentration of (especially executive) power but, by definition, also separation of power; if the separate legislative branch is effectively organized, particularly by a specialized and well-staffed committee structure, separation of power can mean an approximate balance of power between president and legislature and a presidency that is less than all-powerful. This reasoning applies well to the exceptional American case of presidentialism. Fred W. Riggs (1988, 260–66) calls the committee structure of the U.S. Congress one of the "para-constitutional practices" that accounts for the survival and success of presidential government in the United States; other factors of this kind are the "indiscipline" of the American parties—which, as I have emphasized earlier, is generally a mitigating influence on majoritarianism—and the federal division of power. The second explanation, which applies to most of the Latin American cases, is that the fear of omnipotent presidents has produced strong efforts to limit presidential power, especially the denial of immediate reelection. Kantor (1977, 23) has pointed out that "all of the countries" in Latin America, even those that are not democratic, "have constitutions which prescribe all kinds of limitations upon the powers of the president."

The paradox becomes even more puzzling when we consider that the empirical reality is frequently not just that of merely moderate presidential power but of *too little* presidential power and presidents who feel stalemated, powerless, and as a result, deeply frustrated. This description fits the situations of all too many Latin American presidents. Mainwaring (1990, 162) argues that "under democratic conditions, most Latin American presidents have had trouble accomplishing their agendas. They have held most of the power to initiate policy, but they have found it hard to get support to implement policy. If my analysis is correct, it points to a significant *weakness* in democratic presidencies." Deadlock and presidential weakness in the United States are also the chief complaints of the Committee on the Constitutional System (see Robinson 1985). A possible explanation of why American presidents have not felt as frustrated by their lack of power as their Latin American colleagues is that the United States is a major player on the world scene and that foreign policy has provided American presidents with a sufficiently satisfying outlet for their political energies; the general pattern is that, during their terms of office, they tend to direct more and more of their attention and energy toward foreign policy issues.

It is not immediately clear, however, why a situation of balanced presidential and legislative power should produce deadlock and frustration instead of consensus. It seems to me that the problem of what Linz (1987, 26) calls "dual democratic legitimacy"—the fact that both president and legislature can claim democratic legitimation—is only part of the answer. The same problem potentially arises with regard to bicameral systems, consisting of directly elected houses with different partisan compositions, and also with regard to the federal division of powers. Indeed, all of the characteristics of consensus democracy may be seen as attempts to prevent a *single* "democratic legitimacy," which would necessarily be a single concentration of power.

As I see it, the real problem is not so much that both president and legislature can claim democratic legitimacy but that everyone—including the president, the public at large, and even political scientists—feels that the president's claim is much stronger than the legislature's. One indicator of this is that we have great difficulty envisaging a system in which the legislature has the power to dismiss a popularly elected president, but that we can readily conceive of a president's power to dissolve the legislature—in spite of the fact that, after all, the legislature is also popularly elected. President Charles de Gaulle's grandiose statement (cited by Suleiman, chapter 5) is an extreme example of the claim of superior democratic legitimacy: "The indivisible authority of the state is entirely given to the president by the people who elected him. There exists no other authority, neither ministerial, nor civil, nor military, nor judicial that is not conferred or maintained by him." A less extreme version of this claim in the United States is the reminder that the president (together with the vice president) is the only official elected by the whole people—a fact that supposedly gives the president a unique democratic legitimacy. Like de Gaulle's claim, this interpretation conveniently forgets that the Congress is also popularly elected and that, *as a collective body,* it is also elected by the whole people—indeed with larger majorities than are usually garnered by successful presidential candidates. Consequently, although a president's lack of decisive power should induce him or her toward seeking consensus and compromise, the feeling of superior democratic legitimacy may make the president righteously unwilling and psychologically unable to compromise.

If this line of reasoning is correct, presidentialism is inferior to parliamentarism regardless of whether the president is strong or weak. In the first instance, the system will tend to be too majoritarian; in the second case, majoritarianism is not replaced by consensus but by conflict, frustration, and stalemate.

Notes

This article is a revised version of a paper presented at the research symposium, "Presidential or Parliamentary Democracy: Does It Make a Difference?" Latin American Studies Program, Georgetown University, Washington, D.C., 14–16 May 1989. I am grateful to John Carey for his research assistance and his many excellent substantive suggestions.

1. Because I treated the French Fourth (parliamentary) and Fifth (presidential) Republics as separate cases, I had twenty-one democratic countries but twenty-two cases of democracy.

2. One reason for the relative neglect of presidentialism in *Democracies* is that my universe of twenty-two democratic regimes contained only one clear case of presidential government (the United States) and two more ambiguous cases (the French Fifth Republic and Finland). In retrospect, I think that I applied my criterion of uninterrupted democratic rule too strictly and that I should also have included India and Costa Rica among my long-term democracies; the latter would have provided a fourth case of presidentialism. G. Bingham Powell's (1982) comparative study of democracies paid more attention to presidentialism at least partly because Powell had seven cases of it in his universe as a result of his less demanding time frame (a minimum of five years of democracy during the eighteen-year period from 1958 to 1976). Powell's presidential democracies were Venezuela, Chile, Uruguay, and the Philippines, in addition to the United States, France, and Costa Rica. He did not regard Finland as presidential (pp. 60–61); as I discuss later, this is now also my view.

3. Lijphart (1988a) is an earlier, much briefer, attempt to do the same thing.

4. Schmitter, comments at the conference on "Transformation and Transition in Chile, 1982–1989," Center for Iberian and Latin American Studies, University of California, San Diego, 13–14 Mar. 1989.

5. In *Democracies,* I express these differences in terms of characteristics of the respective "chief executives" (Lijphart 1984, 70). I now think the term "head of government" is preferable.

6. Lebanon also has a prime minister with whom the president shares some of his power,

but until the 1989 Taif Accord, which increased the prime minister's powers, the president was clearly more powerful and could be regarded as the real head of government. The Lebanese system has, of course, not functioned normally since the outbreak of civil war in 1975.

7. Since the French model cannot be regarded as intermediate between presidentialism and parliamentarism but is instead a model of alternating systems—an alternation based on shifts in the mood of the electorate that have nothing to do with preferences for one system or the other—it appears to be difficult to argue that this model is a good compromise between the two. However, a strong counterargument (suggested to me by John Carey) is that the French system of alternation can be seen as a solution to one of the basic problems of presidentialism: the possibility of a president opposed by a hostile legislative majority, which is likely to lead to immobilism and stalemate. If this problem occurs in France, it is resolved by the simple temporary shift to a parliamentary arrangement. In other words, France can be said to be able to enjoy the advantages of presidentialism most of the time without suffering this one serious disadvantage. In this special sense, the French model can be argued to be not just a reasonable compromise but one that combines the best of both worlds.

8. Prime ministers sometimes do not have this power either (e.g., Norway) or have it only under special circumstances (e.g., West Germany).

References

Aron, Raymond. 1981. "Alternation in Government in the Industrialized Countries." *Government and Opposition* 17, no. 1: 3–21.

Cutler, Lloyd N. 1980. "To Form a Government." *Foreign Affairs* 59, no. 1: 126–43.

Duchacek, Ivo D. 1973. *Power Maps: Comparative Politics of Constitutions.* Santa Barbara, Calif.: ABC-Clio Press.

Duverger, Maurice. 1980. "A New Political System Model: Semi-Presidential Government." *European Journal of Political Research* 8, no. 2: 165–87.

———. 1986. "Duverger's Law: Forty Years Later." In *Electoral Laws and Their Political Consequences,* edited by Bernard Grofman and Arend Lijphart, pp. 69–84. New York: Agathon Press.

Friedrich, Carl J. 1967. *The Impact of American Constitutionalism Abroad.* Boston: Boston UP.

Hartlyn, Jonathan. 1988. *The Politics of Coalition Rule in Colombia.* Cambridge: Cambridge UP.

Kaltefleiter, Werner. 1970. *Die Funktionen des Staatsoberhauptes in der parlamentarischen Demokratie.* Cologne: Westdeutscher Verlag.

Kantor, Harry. 1977. "Efforts Made by Various Latin American Countries to Limit the Power of the President." In *Presidential Power in Latin American Politics,* edited by Thomas V. DiBacco, pp. 21–32. New York: Praeger.

Lijphart, Arend. 1977. *Democracy in Plural Societies: A Comparative Exploration.* New Haven: Yale UP.

———. 1984. *Democracies: Patterns of Majoritarian and Consensus Government in Twenty-one Countries.* New Haven: Yale UP.

———. 1988a. "Democratización y modelos alternativos de democracia." *Opciones,* no. 14: 29–42.

———. 1988b. "The Political Consequences of Electoral Laws, 1945–85: A Critique, Re-Analysis, and Update of Rae's Classic Study." Paper presented at the World Congress of the International Political Science Association, Washington, D.C.

Linz, Juan J. 1987. "Democracy, Presidential or Parliamentary: Does It Make a Difference?" Paper presented at the Annual Meeting of the American Political Science Association, Chicago.

Loosemore, John, and Victor J. Hanby. 1971. "The Theoretical Limits of Maximum Distortion: Some Analytic Expressions for Electoral Systems." *British Journal of Political Science* 1, no. 4: 467–77.

Mainwaring, Scott. 1990. "Presidentialism in Latin America." *Latin American Research Review* 25, no. 1: 157–79.

Nilson, Sten Sparre. 1983. "Elections Presidential and Parliamentary: Contrasts and Connections." *West European Politics* 6, no. 1: 111–24.

Powell, G. Bingham, Jr. 1982. *Contemporary Democracies: Participation, Stability, and Violence.* Cambridge: Harvard University Press.

Riggs, Fred W. 1988. "The Survival of Presidentialism in America: Para-Constitutional Practices." *International Political Science Review* 9, no. 4: 247–78.

Riker, William H. 1984. "Electoral Systems and Constitutional Restraints." In *Choosing an Electoral System: Issues and Alternatives,* edited by Arend Lijphart and Bernard Grofman, pp. 103–10. New York: Praeger.

Robinson, Donald L., ed. 1985. *Reforming American Government: The Bicentennial Papers of the Committee on the Constitutional System.* Boulder: Westview.

Shugart, Matthew S. 1988. "Duverger's Rule and Presidentialism: The Effects of the Timing of Elections." Paper presented at the Annual Meeting of the American Political Science Association, Washington, D.C.

Steffani, Winfried. 1979. *Parlamentarische und präsidentielle Demokratie: Strukturelle Aspekte westlicher Demokratien.* Opladen: Westdeutscher Verlag.

Taagepera, Rein, and Bernard Grofman. 1985. "Rethinking Duverger's Law: Predicting the Effective Number of Parties in Plurality and PR Systems—Parties Minus Issues Equals One." *European Journal of Political Research* 13, no. 4: 341–52.

Verney, Douglas V. 1959. *The Analysis of Political Systems.* London: Routledge & Kegan Paul.

Von Beyme, Klaus. 1987. *America as a Model: The Impact of American Democracy in the World.* New York: St. Martin's Press.

3

GIOVANNI SARTORI

Neither Presidentialism nor Parliamentarism

PRESIDENTIAL AND PARLIAMENTARY systems are generally defined by mutual exclusion. But an obscurity cannot illuminate another obscurity. To be sure, a presidential system is nonparliamentary, and conversely, a parliamentary system is nonpresidential. However, division of real world cases between these two classes yields both incongruous bedfellows and dubious inclusions.

Presidentialism is generally defined by one or more of three criteria. First, the head of state is popularly elected (directly or indirectly) for a fixed time span; second, the parliament can neither appoint nor remove the government; third, the head of state is also the head of government. The first criterion—direct or quasi-direct popular election—performs very poorly on substantive grounds. It brings together, for example, Austria, Iceland, and Ireland with Portugal, France, and the United States.[1] However, despite popular election the presidents of Austria, Iceland, and Ireland count for little or nothing; and all the above-mentioned cases but one (the United States) fail to pass the "presidential tests" set forth by the other two criteria. The second criterion performs far better than the first; yet it may apply to both presidential and semipresidential systems and thus requires the underpinning of the third criterion.

Our three criteria thus appear to be joint criteria. That is to say, a system is presidential if, and only if, the head of state (president) (1) receives office by popular election, (2) during his preestablished tenure cannot be discharged by parliamentary vote, and (3) heads the government or governments, which he appoints. When all these conditions are met, then we doubtlessly have a "pure" presidential system.

Since these are defining criteria that establish what "presidentialism" includes and excludes, let us make sure that they are understood. The first criterion allows for two possibilities: direct or quasi-direct popular election of a president. How open-ended is that? Quasi-direct elections occur in the United States and in countries such as Argentina and, formerly, Chile (until Allende), whose president is elected by the parliament when no candidate receives an absolute majority of the popular vote. Since the established practice in such cases is to elect the candidate who has obtained a relative majority of the popular vote, this kind of indirect election is in practice the same as a direct one. Bolivia practices instead a parliamentary choosing among the three front runners (in both 1985 and 1989, it picked the second one) and therefore represents a case of dubious quasi-direct election. On the other hand, Finland's election definitely is not quasi-direct: the elected presidential electoral college is the true president-maker in that its freedom of choice is unrestricted. The cutoff point is, then, whether the intermediary bodies (electoral colleges or parliaments) are allowed choices of their own. If the intermediary body performs like a rubber stamp, then the difference between direct and indirect popular election is immaterial; if it can make choices, then the criterion is violated. Similar considerations apply to the third criterion, namely, that the head of state is the head of government or that the president heads the cabinet that he appoints. Here, too, a range of variation is permitted up to the point at which a president and a prime minister enjoy a dual authority.

On these criteria we come up, today, with some thirty presidential countries, mostly concentrated in Latin America. With the sole exception of the United States, all presidential systems have been intermittent. At present the best performer is Costa Rica, "unbroken" since 1949. The second best performer is Venezuela, which has been continuous since 1958 but has recently been endangered by two attempted coups. Peru returned to civilian government in 1979 but is again, at this writing, under nonconstitutional rule. Most other Latin American countries (notably Argentina, Uruguay, Brazil, Chile) reestablished presidential democracies only in the 1980s.[2] And while the last South American bastion of dictatorship—Paraguay—fell in 1989, quite a number of countries in the area still qualify as "unstable," that is, "highly vulnerable to breakdown overthrow"[3]: for example, Ecuador, Bolivia, Honduras, Guatemala, and the Dominican Republic.[4] In other areas, the Philippines is again, since 1986, presidential with little to display in achievement.[5] All in all, then, the record of the presidentially governed countries is—aside from the United States—quite dismal and prompts us to wonder whether their political problem might not be presidentialism itself.

Does it follow that, if presidentialism is to be dismissed, the "good alternative" is parliamentarism? No—it does not follow. For one thing, so far we have established only that pure presidentialism is bad; we have by no means established that its "mixed" progeny—semipresidentialism—is equally bad. Secondly, so far we know what we are dismissing but not what we are adopting. What is "parliamentarism"? The label by no means denotes a simple, uniform entity.

The only common denominator of systems that we call parliamentary is that they require governments to be appointed, supported, and, as the case may be, discharged by parliamentary vote. But to say that governments are supported by a parliament is not saying much. It does not even begin to explain why the polities in question display strong or feeble government, stability or instability, effectiveness or immobilism, and in sum good, or mediocre, or even detestable performance. As we look further into the matter we find that there are at least three major varieties of parliamentary system: at one extreme the English type of premiership or cabinet system, in which the executive forcefully prevails over parliament; at the other extreme the French (Third and Fourth Republic) type of assembly government, which makes governing a near impossibility; and a middle-of-the-way formula of party-controlled parliamentarism. So what are we getting into? Parliamentarism may fail us just as much and as easily as presidentialism. If we wish the alternative to presidentialism to be a parliamentary system, we still have to decide *which parliamentarism* and to make sure that the exit from pure presidentialism does not simply lead, along a path of least resistance, to pure parliamentarism, that is, to assembly government and misgovernment.

If we are concerned, as I assume we are, with substance, then the straightforward question is: what is a good, and what is a bad, polity performance? Juan Linz and Arturo Valenzuela endorse parliamentarism over presidentialism on the major ground that presidential systems are "rigid" while parliamentary systems are "flexible" and that flexibility is to be preferred to rigidity. Their underlying assumption is risk minimization; and the full argument thus is that a flexible system is far less exposed to risk, on account of its self-correcting mechanisms, than a rigid one. Valenzuela puts it in a nutshell: "The crises of parliamentary systems are crises of government, not regime."[6] The point is well taken, and I certainly agree. However, the argument of the people who endorse presidentialism (an argument that is much repeated today in Italy) is that effectiveness is to be preferred to paralysis, and that parliamentary systems (as Italians know them) are immobilist and inefficient. Note that this, too, can be turned into a risk-minimizing argument, namely, that ineffective and squabbling government is self-delegitimizing and conducive, in the long run, to regime crisis.

Does the above break the issue at an even fifty-fifty? Not quite, because the argument cannot be left at that. To begin with, it cannot be assumed that flexibility is unqualifiedly a good thing or even the major factor at play. On the other hand, is it truly the case that presidentialism provides for strong and efficient government?

Pure presidentialism, or the American-type presidential system, hinges on the division and separation of power between president and congress.[7] And the fact that the American system has long coped with its problems does not detract from the fact that a divided power structure engineers paralysis and stalemates better than any other.[8] And, indeed, does the American system still work? Looking back, we see that the division of power has been tempered, in reality, by undivided (consonant) majorities—the coinciding of the president's majority with the parliamentary one—and, in custom, by consociational practices, especially bipartisan concurrence in foreign politics. But undivided majorities and bipartisan consociationalism no longer are the prevailing pattern.[9] The Clinton administration beginning in 1993 represents, in this respect, an exception. Most previous administrations since 1957 attest to an antagonistically divided polity whose two component elements perceive their electoral interest to be, across the board, the failure of the other institution. For a Democrat-controlled Congress to go along with a Republican president is to help another Republican presidency. Conversely, a minority president (in Congress) seeking to restore undivided government is prompted to run against Congress, playing, as it were, the blame game.

Thus the answer to the question whether presidentialism provides for effective government is, with reference to its most acclaimed incarnation, no. Ironically, the belief that presidential systems are "strong" systems draws on the worst possible structural arrangement (divided power defenseless against "divided government") and fails to realize that the American system works *in spite of* its constitution— hardly *thanks to* its constitution. To the extent that it is still able to perform, it requires, in order to unblock itself, three factors: ideological or, better, pragmatic flexibility, weak and undisciplined parties, and locality-centered politics. On these three counts a president can win over the congressional votes that he may need in exchange for constituency favors. We thus end up with the institutionalization of pork barrel politics—nothing much to be admired.[10] And what we have, structurally, is in fact a weak state.

The conclusion that might suggest itself on the basis of the foregoing is that if presidentialism has virtues, they are to be sought in the semi- or quasi-presidential systems based on power sharing (as in the French Fifth Republic), not on power separation.[11] The problem with power sharing is, to begin with, that the formula lacks the simple neatness of power separation. Even so, "power sharing" does not defy pinpointing. The authority structure in which a chief executive is called to perform may place the premier as:

1. a first *above unequals*
2. a first *among unequals*
3. a first *among equals*

All are power-sharing formulas in that they all exclude a power concentration in just one person, in a *primus solus,* as in the case of the American president (whose government is only his private cabinet). But they are indeed very different formulas. A British prime minister stands as a *primus* above unequals; that is, he has a free hand in picking and firing truly subordinate ministers. Mitterand has been a *primus* both above and among unequals (when sharing power with Chirac, an "imposed" premier). The German chancellor is a *primus* more among unequals than among equals. A prime minister in an ordinary parliamentary system is a *primus inter pares,* a first among equals, and thus not much of a *primus.* We can, of course, bicker about the examples. Nonetheless, the criterion that underpins the three formulas is neat enough.

A first *above unequals* is a chief executive who is the party leader, who cannot easily be unseated by a parliamentary vote, and who appoints and changes cabinet ministers at his or her pleasure. This "first" rules over the ministers and indeed overrules them. A first *among unequals* may not be the party leader and yet cannot be unseated by a mere no-confidence parliamentary vote and is expected to remain in office even when his cabinet members change. This "first" can unseat ministers but cannot be unseated by them. Finally, a first *among equals* is a prime minister who falls with his cabinet, who generally must take on the governmental team "imposed" ministers, and who has little control over the team (better described as a nonteam whose untouchables play their own game).

The significant point is that the formulas in question outline a scale of power-sharing arrangements that cuts across, and *undercuts*, the presidential-parliamentary dichotomy. For one, the scale indicates that an English prime minister can govern far more effectively than an American president. This entails that the presidential *primus solus* formula cannot be credited with any exclusive "governing merit." Furthermore, the scale suggests that there is no net advantage in replacing a *primus solus* with a *primus inter pares*. Indeed, a prime minister who cannot control his ministers (because he cannot fire them), and who does not even have a free hand in choosing them, cannot be expected to be really in charge. So the power-sharing formulas that hold "governing promise" are (1) first above unequals, and (2) first among unequals. This is the same as suggesting that the interesting cases are, on the one hand, the semipresidential systems (whose range extends from France to Finland) and, on the other hand, the premiership systems (ranging from England to Germany).

My stance is, then, that semipresidentialism can improve presidentialism and, similarly, that semiparliamentary systems (if I may so call the *Kanzler* or premiership formulas) are better than plain parliamentary ones. Within the aforesaid range of "mixed" polities, do I have a specific favorite? Not really. That political form is best that best applies. That is tantamount to saying that at this stage of the argument context becomes essential. By context I mean, at the very least, (1) the electoral system, (2) the party system, and (3) the political culture or degree of polarization.

Proceeding swiftly and scantily by illustration,[12] the English premiership system assumes single-party government (it would founder with coalition government), which in turn assumes a single-member district system that engenders a two-party system. Let it be noted that single-party government also calls for the strict party discipline that obtains in Westminster (a discipline that is just as necessary to Westminster as it is necessarily absent from "divided" presidentialism).[13] However, the winner-take-all system is inadvisable when a polity is polarized or characterized by a heterogeneous political culture. Indeed, without proportional representation (and coalition governments) the integration of the externally created parties of a century ago—mainly Socialist and Catholic parties—into the liberal democratic state would have been extremely hazardous. Proportional representation and coalitions are thus essential safety devices for "difficult" societies.

But we should not corner ourselves into a plurality–proportional representation dichotomy any more than into a presidential-parliamentary one. Proportional representation can be corrected by thresholds (the German *Sperrklausel*) or by majority premiums. The German chancellorship system is sustained not only by the constitutional requirement of the constructive vote of no confidence (a barrier against negative majorities) but also by the 5 percent barrier to representation. Another corrective is the double-ballot runoff system, which is indeed a "soft" majoritarian electoral formula. These devices must be kept in mind because efficient government is almost impossible with coalitions that reflect a highly polarized party system and that are therefore characterized by high coalitional heterogeneity. The gist is that any electoral system that penalizes the most distant, that is, extreme (most leftist and most rightist) parties benefits the governability requirement.

As context is brought into the picture one also comes to understand better that a pure assembly-centered parliamentary system can be just as risky and dysfunctional as a pure presidential system. The parliamentary systems that are most frequently cited as stable and working democracies are the Scandinavian ones (Sweden and Norway), Japan, and, since 1982, Spain. It so happens that these countries all owe, or owed, their working credentials to a predominant party pattern (one party obtains an absolute majority of seats) that brings about long periods (in Japan, 39 years) of single-party government. The consociational theory (and practice) of democracy may allow us to add a couple of countries to the list of working democracies, plus Switzerland (which is, however, a highly anomalous case). Even so, the list of performing parliamentary systems is a relatively short one. Can it be extended on the basis of the argument that a number of so-called unstable democracies (parliamentary ones, to be sure) are unstable only "in appearance"? I think not.

To begin with, stability of what? Of the regime, or of governments? I value immensely the first one, that is, "stable democracy." But the shine of stable democracy should not be unduly extended to cover "stable government." Despite much loose talk to the contrary, stable democracy is not undermined by unstable governments but rather by impotent or bad government—which is another matter. Government stability represents mere *duration,* and governments can be both long lived and impotent: their duration is by no means an indicator of efficiency or efficacy. Indeed, in most parliamentary systems that require government by coalition, governments prolong their survival by doing next to nothing. In this setting the little that coalition governments can do is usually done in the first six months—the initial period in which they cannot decently be overthrown. After that, they are left to gain time by staying still. Thus the problem is not longevity, how long governments last, but whether governments *govern*, whether they perform as decision makers or as decision shunners. And, let it be reiterated, *stable* government is not a sufficient condition for *effective* government: the former need not engender the latter.

What, then, is the worth of the argument that unstable (short-lived) governments do not matter as long as the political personnel that rotates in office is stable (i.e., the same)? The notion here is that apparent instability is remedied, in substance, by an underlying continuity. However, if governmental stability is, as I have just held, a misdirected concern, then the notion of "personnel stability" is, by the same token, a nonremedy. I would add, pressing the point further, that the argument is flawed and that by endorsing it we just make matters worse. The honorable Yellow, we discover, has occupied cabinet positions for some thirty years, as minister of tourism, then treasury, then foreign affairs, then environment, then education, and finally state holdings. Wonderful for him—his personal stability in office is indisputable. But in what way is his personal stability a system-serving one, a stability that benefits the polity? I search in vain for an answer—unless it lies in the Peter Principle: people rise to their level of incompetence. Indeed, by endlessly dropping whatever expertise he may have acquired along the way, the honorable Yellow disseminates all around the discontinuity (not the continuity) of his unending incompetence. And the reason why the honorable Yellow is an everlasting minister of everything is precisely that he well knows that his staying power has nothing to do with his performance in office (nor, incidentally, with his natural intelligence) and everything to do with his intraparty factional maneuverings. And if this is what "substantial stability" truly stands for, then we are better off without it.

Wrapping my case together, parliamentary systems owe their name to the premise that the parliament is sovereign. This founding assumption sustains assembly government in principle, is in fact easily conducive to it, and thereby is also conducive to feeble, inconstant, and all in all poor governing. If this development is called "pure parliamentarism," then it has proven itself to be a nonworking solution. In its stead so-called parliamentary government works (works better) when its name is somewhat of a misnomer, that is, when it is an "impure" solution that keeps a lid on the sovereignty of parliament. English- or German-type *Kanzlerdemokratie* on the one hand, predominant party systems on the other, and party discipline (over MPs) across the board, all see to it that the sovereign (parliament) does not govern. Even so, a prior condition has yet to be entered in the argument—namely, that parliamentary democracy cannot perform (in any of its varieties) unless it is served by *parliamentarily fit* parties, that is to say, parties that have been socialized (by failure, duration, and appropriate incentives) into being relatively cohesive or disciplined, into behaving, in opposition, as responsible opposition, and into playing, to some extent, a rule-guided fair game.

These are underlying and diffuse conventions of the constitution that do not lend themselves to precise underpinning. But assume, for the sake of the argument, that Latin American countries decided to switch from presidentialism to parliamentarism. Would their parliamentary performance be any better than the assembly-rule performance of much of continental Europe all the way up to the twenties and thirties? I very much doubt it. The bulk of Latin America does not have, and is still far from acquiring, parliamentarily fit parties. Brazil eminently speaks to the point; and since Brazil appears to buy the idea that it could remedy its ills by transforming itself into a parliamentary system, let me pause on the Brazilian case.

Probably no country in the world currently is as antiparty, both in theory and in practice, as Brazil. Politicians relate to their party as a *partido de aluguel,* as a rental. They freely and frequently change party, vote against the party line, and refuse any kind of party discipline on the ground that their freedom to represent their constituency cannot be interfered with.[14] Thus parties are powerless and volatile entities, and the Brazilian president is left to float over a vacuum, an unruly and eminently atomized parliament. For these dire conditions a cure is being sought in the adoption of a parliamentary system that would require parties to solidify because they would be required to sustain a parliament-derived government. But I very much fear that this will not and cannot happen.

There is no comparative or historical evidence to support the Brazilian expectation. Compared to the Brazilian parties, the German ones during the Weimar period were "model parties"; yet their fragmentation was never overcome and their parliamentary performance between 1919 and 1933 neither improved nor provided governability. Nothing changed in the behavior or the nature of parties during the Third and Fourth French Republics. The average duration of governments over the forty-year period of the Third Republic (1875–1914) was nine months. And the same would apply to prefascist Italy. The point is that party solidification and discipline (in parliamentary voting) has never been a feedback of parliamentary government. If a system is assembly based, atomized, unruly, magmatic, on its own inertia it will remain as it is. I cannot think of any party system that has evolved into a veritable "system" made of strong, organization-based mass parties on the basis of *internal* parliamentary learning. The metamorphosis from an unstructured to a "structured" party system has always been triggered by *exogenous* assault and contagion. The earlier parties of notables and of opinion either perished or changed their ways in response to the challenge of "externally created" (and largely antisystem) religious and socialist mass parties characterized by strong ideological ties and fervor.

All the foregoing elements are notably absent in Brazil. Furthermore, Brazil displays an antiparty creed and rhetoric (let alone typically antiparty electoral legislation) that makes any kind of parliamentarily fit parties not only unlikely but altogether inconceivable. Putting it the other way around, the entire Brazilian political culture and tradition nurtures *parliamentarily unfit* parties. That under such circumstances a parliamentary experience would lead Brazil out of chaos into some kind of efficient parliamentary government is, in my opinion, against all odds.

On the other hand there are, in Latin America, three countries that might conceivably afford—in terms of their party system—a switch to parliamentarism, namely, Chile and two-party Argentina and Venezuela (since 1973). Chile has the most Europeanlike multiparty arrangement of the continent. However, Chile also has a past of "polarized pluralism," of strong polarization coupled with high party fragmentation. With this background, would Chile be wise to adopt a parliamentary system? I doubt it. If Chileans were to abandon their presidential system, they would be well advised, in my opinion, to seek a semipresidential, not a parliamentary, solution.

Argentina currently is, instead, a two-party presidential system that comes close to enjoying undivided majorities.[15] As a purely conjectural question, would Argentina benefit from a parliamentary transformation? Again, I doubt it. Argentina's parties are not "solid" parties. What keeps them together and brings about their coalescence is the presidential system, that is, the overriding importance of winning a nondivisible prize: the presidency.[16] I would thus expect a different arrangement to bring about a party fragmentation that Argentina does not need. All told, then, Venezuela appears to be the one South American country that can afford, on the basis of its two strong and disciplined parties, to run the risk of a parliamentary experiment. I am thus prompted to conclude that should Latin America enter the path of parliamentarism, the variety that would most probably emerge across most of it would be the assembly variety at its worst.[17]

Do not get me wrong: my case against "pure parliamentarism" does not lessen in the least my opposition to "pure presidentialism." The first problem with American-type presidentialism is, as we have seen, that the division of power requires undivided majorities. This we have discovered to be a rare and difficult condition to meet. But I am wary of presidentialism also on a second, somewhat future-oriented count, namely, the new politics, which I call videopolitics.[18] With videopolitics the all-decider can easily be an outsider (like Fujimori in Peru and Collor in Brazil) and will turn out to be, more and more, the winner of a video match eminently decided by looks and "sound bites" lasting ten seconds (their average duration in the 1988 American presidential election). If so, presidentialism becomes a gambling event. Video elections are supposed to bring about transparence, truly "visible politics." Alas, no. What we are actually given, under the guise of visibility, is largely a display of petty appearances that cover up the substance and leave the issues in greater darkness than ever. So, the long and the short of my brief is that the popular, direct election of presidents provides no safeguards and no buffers against a disastrous election (mis-election) of the *primus solus*—and that this will be ever more the case. More than ever before, videopolitics promises to put in office dilettantes or poll-monitored robots (whose true faces are never unveiled) stuck with populist campaign promises. To be sure populist and demagogic appeals are nothing new. But videopolitics magnifies their impact and easily becomes an ideal vehicle of bad politics. By the same token, then, videopolitics is a risk multiplier.

The risk still exists, but its virulence is considerably lessened, in semipresidential systems in which the president is popularly elected into a dual authority structure and the prime minister must obtain a vote of confidence in the parliament. Here a presidential candidate runs on a programmatic platform but is not entitled (even if he or she may, in fact, trespass) to make specific policy promises because actual policies fall under the jurisdiction of the prime minister and his parliamentary majority.

Scholars are wary of French-type presidentialism on account of the possibility of a split majority, one of which elects the president while the other supports the premier and his government. Would this eventually repeat the American "divided government" paralysis discussed earlier? Maybe. But maybe not, for French-type presidentialism, unlike the American model, is not based on the division of power, and this enfeebles the analogy. Indeed, a virtue of the semipresidential formula is precisely that it can cope with split majorities. They enfeeble the president and force him into cohabitation with a prime minister of a different party; but this engenders a strengthened premier, who can and will find a coalitional majority for his government.[19] Thus semipresidentialism can solve the problem that pure presidentialism cannot solve.[20]

It should furthermore be acknowledged that in the French formula the direct election of the president has played an important and positive role in that it has "presidentialized" the party system, forcing it into a bipolar mold.[21] This is not a fortuitous outcome. Since the presidential office is a nondivisible win, presidentialism counters "proportional politics."

The English sing the praises of proportional representation; the Italians, of the single-member district system. Latin Americans are advised to adopt parliamentarism, which the French have dropped with relish. We are generally correct in our criticism of the polity under which we live but often wrong in assessing the alternatives and their hoped for benefits. I believe that the case *against* the two extremes, pure presidentialism and pure parliamentarism, is a strong one. But I am prepared to admit that the case *for* semipresidentialism is not strong. My positive evaluation of French-type semipresidentialism is clearly tentative, in the "maybe" mold.[22] Turning to the other mixed alternative—the semiparliamentary one—the problem is that the English- and German-type premiership systems perform as they are intended to perform only under a set of favorable conditions. If the English system ceased to be a two-party system (third parties have not managed, thus far, to break single-party governance), or if the German polity became (as it appears in the process of becoming) more fragmented and more polarized than it has been thus far, one might well fear a relapse into "bad parliamentarism."[23]

While the thrust of my argument admittedly is that our best hope lies in mixed solutions, what is of essence, hopes aside, is that we must make as sure as our fallibility permits that we are not moving out of the frying pan into the fire.

Notes

I have greatly benefited from the responses to a first draft of this essay of Michael Coppedge, Arend Lijphart, Juan Linz, Scott Mainwaring, and Arturo Valenzuela. My debt to their comments and suggestions is gratefully acknowledged.

1. On the European cases see the overview of Stefano Bartolini, "Sistema partitico e elezione diretta del capo dello stato in Europa," *Rivista italiana di scienza politica* 2 (1984): 223–42. Portugal adopted a French-type system in 1976, but the 1982 revision of the constitution has drastically clipped the power of the presidency.

2. Uruguay has displayed uncharacteristic constitutional oscillations between "quasi-presidentialism" (1830, 1934, 1942, 1966) and not (1918, 1952), but I definitely consider its present system (following the 1973 coup and the 1973–84 interruption) a presidential one. That the legislature may censure ministers and, conversely, that the president is empowered to dissolve the legislature represent a deviation from the U.S. model but not one that contradicts my defining criteria of presidentialism or affects the substance.

3. L. Diamond, J. Linz, and S. M. Lipset, eds., *Democracy in Developing Countries*, 4 vols. (Boulder: Lynne Rienner, 1989), preface, p. xviii.

4. Ecuador is in near permanent crisis; Bolivia between 1952 and 1982 underwent some seventeen military interventions; Honduras and Guatemala perform messily and largely under de facto military control; and the Dominican Republic is currently back from *dictablanda* to military dictatorship.

5. It will be noted that my list does not include South Korea; this is because its presidentialism has been only a 1988–90 interregnum. I also exclude Mexico, whose undeniable success record since the 1930s belongs to a pattern of "authoritarian presidentialism" (albeit limited by a firmly adhered to nonreelection principle) sustained by a hegemonic party arrangement, as I have called it. However, Mexico's electoral reform of 1989 allows (in principle) for alternation in power, which proposes as a democratic possibility a presidential formula (that reverses the American one) based on undivided concentration of power. Finally, I leave aside Sri Lanka not only on account of its dubious constitutional performance but also because I am inclined to consider its 1978 constitution semipresidential.

6. Arturo Valenzuela, chap. 6. Another drawback of presidential systems is, in the analysis of Linz (see chap. 1), its zero-sum implication. Here the counterargument might be that (1) when American presidentialism has performed, it has done so (as we are about to see) in "consociational" far more than in zero-sum manner and that (2) zero-sum outcomes characterize all the plurality, winner-take-all electoral systems. In the latter respect, a zero-sum game of politics is conceived (positively) as one of the factors that sustain "governability." The zero-sum point thus appears to cut in many ways.

7. There has been much quibbling about this "division-separation." R. E. Neustadt asserted that the founding fathers did not create a government of "separated powers" but, instead, "a government of separated institutions *sharing* power" (*Presidential Power* [New York: Wiley, 1960], p. 33). Charles O. Jones corrects: we now "have a government of separated institutions *competing for* shared power" ("The Separated Presidency," in *The New American Political System*, 2d ed., edited by A. King [Washington, D.C.: AEI, 1990], p. 3), then speaks of a "truncated system" (p. 5); and note his title. So, we come back to separation. To make the point simple: separation consists of "separating" the executive from parliamentary support, whereas power sharing means that the executive stands on, and falls without, the support of the parliament.

8. Let it be underscored that we can have checks and balances without power separation.

Indeed, all constitutional systems are systems of checks and balances. The American formula is, in fact, unique in checking and balancing power by dividing it.

9. As pointed out by J. L. Sundquist, the 1988 election of George Bush "was the sixth time [1956, 1968, 1972, 1980, 1984] in the last nine presidential elections that the electorate chose to split the government between the parties. . . . This is something new in American politics. When Dwight D. Eisenhower took his second oath of office in 1957, he was the first chief executive in seventy-two years . . . to confront . . . a Congress of which even one house was controlled by the opposition party. . . . In the fifty-eight years from 1897 through 1954, the country experienced divided government during only eight years—all in the last half of a presidential term—or 14 percent of the time. Yet in the thirty-six years from 1955 through 1990, the government will have been divided . . . for two-thirds of that period." ("Needed: A Political Theory for the New Era of Coalition Government in the United States," *Political Science Quarterly* 4 [1988]:613–14).

10. To be sure, the belief that presidential systems are "strong" systems is also contradicted by the Latin American experience. As Scott Mainwaring sums up, "Most Latin American presidents have had trouble accomplishing their agendas. They have held most of the power for initiating policy but have found it hard to get support for implementing policy. . . . The common tendency to characterize Latin American presidents as all-powerful is misleading" ("Presidentialism in Latin America," in *Latin American Research Review* 25, no. 1 [1990]:162, 171).

11. It should be well understood that "semi-" does not imply in the least "a regime type that is located midway along some continuum," as suspected by Matthew Soberg Shugart and John M. Carey, *Presidents and Assemblies: Constitutional Design and Electoral Dynamics* (New York: Cambridge UP, 1992), p. 23. *Semi-* is a latin prefix, more than two thousand years older than our notion of continuum! It is unfortunate, in my mind, that on this unwarranted understanding Shugart and Carey propose the confusing label of "premier presidentialism."

12. I largely draw, in what follows, from my *Parties and Party Systems* (New York: Cambridge UP, 1976), passim. For the impact of electoral systems in particular, see my chapter, "Faulty Laws or Faulty Method?" in *Electoral Laws and Their Political Consequences*, edited by B. Grofman and A. Lijphart (New York: Agathon, 1986).

13. This applies only to the English kind of premiership system. It does not apply to Germany—the feeble case of the category—which has neither the single-member district system, nor bipartism, nor single-party government.

14. An excellent account of this state of affairs is Scott Mainwaring, "Politicians, Parties and Electoral Systems: Brazil in Comparative Prospective," *Comparative Politics*, Oct. 1991, pp. 21–43.

15. President Alfonsín had a slight majority, in 1983–87, in the chamber of deputies, but not in the senate; and President Menen has, since 1989, a majority in the senate but not in the low chamber. This is not, then, a clear-cut status of undivided majority. Historically, and aside from the Perón periods, only President Frondizi (1958–62) had a majority in both houses of the congress.

16. Guillermo Molinelli in a private conversation calls to my attention that "the Radical and Perónist parties have traditionally been internally centralized parties . . . and prone to 'centralist' public policies and attitudes, on ideological grounds." He is obviously right in pointing out that the presidential prize is not, by itself, a sufficient condition of bipartism (as attested by most Latin American presidentialisms). However, my sense is that the presidential factor becomes weightier as ideological differences decline. Spelled out, a presidentialism based on two parties is favored by: (1) the centrality of the presidency; (2) having

parties that perform as principal competitors for the presidency; (3) requiring an absolute majority winner (with a double-ballot system); (4) the coinciding of parliamentary and presidential elections (in order to obtain a coattail effect).

17. For an assessment of the various levels of "institutionalization" (and its absence) of parties across Latin America, see Scott Mainwaring and Timothy Scully, eds., *Building Democratic Institutions: Parties and Party Systems in Latin America* (Stanford: Stanford UP [forthcoming]), esp. chap. 1.

18. For the overall argument see my "Video-Power," *Government and Opposition*, Winter 1989, pp. 39–53.

19. These power shifts do not amount, however, to an alternation between presidentialism (when the presidential and parliamentary majorities coincide) and parliamentarism (when they do not), as M. Duverger suggests—a suggestion that blows up the "mixed" nature of the system. See "A New Political System Model: Semi-Presidential Government," *European Journal of Political Research* 8, no. 2 (1980):186. No. A French president never is like an American president; nor does he ever become, even at the nadir of his power, as powerless as a parliamentary president. In both respects Duverger's understanding is misleading.

20. The point is illustrated by the cohabitation between President Mitterand and the Gaullist premier Chirac in the 1980s, and it is seemingly confirmed, thus far, by the cohabitation between Mitterand and Premier Balladur imposed by the 1993 election.

21. Bipolar is more correct than "bipolarized," for the latter term is easily misread to mean "increased polarization," whereas the absolute majority required for winning the presidency has in fact brought about centrist candidates, centripetal competition, and therefore a much reduced polarization.

22. Thus in other writings I outline a different kind of semipresidentialism. See G. Sartori, "Le riforme istituzionali—Tra buone e cattive," *Rivista italiana di scienza politica* 3 (1991); and, further, *Seconda Repubblica? Sì, ma bene* (Milan: Rizzoli, 1992). But see especially my forthcoming work, *Comparative Constitutional Engineering* (New York: New York UP, 1994).

23. The gist is that semiparliamentarism requires low levels of polarization, which is, in turn, the single most important variable (see G. Sani and G. Sartori, "Polarization, Fragmentation and Competition," in *Western European Party Systems*, edited by Hans Daalder and Peter Mair [Beverly Hills: Sage, 1983], pp. 307–40).

4

ALFRED STEPAN AND CINDY SKACH

Presidentialism and Parliamentarism in Comparative Perspective

THE STRUGGLE to consolidate the new democracies—especially those in Eastern Europe, Latin America, and Asia—has given rise to a wide-ranging debate about hard choices concerning economic restructuring, economic institutions, and economic markets.[1] A similar debate has focused on democratic *political* institutions and *political* markets. This literature has produced provocative hypotheses about the effects of institutions on democracy. It forms part of the "new institutionalism" literature in comparative politics, which holds as a premise that "political democracy depends not only on economic and social conditions but also on the design of political institutions."[2]

One fundamental political-institutional question that has only recently received serious scholarly attention concerns the impact of different constitutional frameworks on democratic consolidation.[3] Although the topic has been increasingly debated and discussed, little systematic cross-regional evidence has been brought to bear on it. This is unfortunate, because constitutions are essentially "institutional frameworks" that in functioning democracies provide the basic decision rules and incentive systems concerning government formation, the conditions under which governments can continue to rule, and the conditions by which they can be terminated democratically. More than simply one of many dimensions of a democratic system,[4] constitutions create much of the overall system of incentives and organizations within which the other institutions and dimensions found in the many types of democracy are structured and processed.

Study shows that the range of existing constitutional frameworks in the world's long-standing democracies is narrower than one would think.[5] With one exception (Switzerland), every existing democracy today is either presidential (as in the United States), parliamentary (as in most of Western Europe), or a semipresidential hybrid of the two (as in France and Portugal, where there is a directly elected president and a prime minister who must have a majority in the legislature).[6] In this chapter we pay particular attention to contrasting what we call "pure parliamentarism" with "pure presidentialism."[7] Each type has only two fundamental characteristics, and for the purposes of our classification these characteristics are necessary and sufficient.

A pure parliamentary regime in a democracy is a system of mutual dependence:

1. The chief executive power must be supported by a majority in the legislature and can fall if it receives a vote of no confidence.

2. The executive power (normally in conjunction with the head of state) has the capacity to dissolve the legislature and call for elections.

A pure presidential regime in a democracy is a system of mutual independence:

1. The legislative power has a fixed electoral mandate that is its own source of legitimacy.

2. The chief executive power has a fixed electoral mandate that is its own source of legitimacy.

These necessary and sufficient characteristics are more than classificatory. They are also the constraining conditions within which the vast majority of aspiring democracies must somehow attempt simultaneously to produce major socioeconomic changes and to strengthen democratic institutions.[8]

Pure parliamentarism, as defined here, was the norm in the democratic world following World War II.[9] However, so far in the 1980s and 1990s, all the new aspirant democracies in Latin America and Asia (Korea and the Philippines) have chosen pure presidentialism. And to date, of the approximately twenty-five countries that now constitute Eastern Europe and the former Soviet Union, only three—Hungary, the new Czech Republic, and Slovakia—have chosen pure parliamentarism.[10]

We question the wisdom of this virtual dismissal of the pure parliamentary model by most new democracies and believe that the hasty embrace of presidential models should be reconsidered. In this chapter we bring evidence in support of the theoretical argument that parliamentary democracies tend to increase the degree of freedom that facilitates the momentous tasks of economic and social restructuring facing new democracies as they simultaneously attempt to consolidate their democratic institutions.

It is not our purpose in this article to weigh the benefits and the drawbacks of parliamentarism and presidentialism. Our intention is to report and analyze numerous different sources of data, all of which point in the direction of a much stronger correlation between democratic consolidation and pure parliamentarism than between democratic consolidation and pure presidentialism. We believe our findings are sufficiently strong to warrant long-range studies that test the probabilistic propositions we indicate.[11]

Constitutional Frameworks: Constructing Relevant Data

We were able to construct a data set about party systems and consolidated democracies. Since we are interested in the lessons about party systems in long-standing consolidated democracies, we include the countries of the Organization of Economic Cooperation and Development (OECD). There were forty-three consolidated democracies in the world between 1979 and 1989.[12] Excluding the "mixed cases" of Switzerland and Finland, there were thirty-four parliamentary democracies, two semipresidential democracies, and only five pure presidential democracies.[13] We used the powerful, yet relatively simple, formula devised by Markku Laakso and Rein Taagepera to measure the "effective" number of political parties in the legislatures of these forty-one political systems.[14] Of the thirty-four parliamentary democracies, eleven had between three and seven effective political parties.[15] Both of the semipresidential democracies in this universe had between three and four effective political parties. However, no pure presidential democracy had more than 2.6 effective political parties. These data indicate that consolidated parliamentary and semipresidential democracies can be associated with a large number of parties in their legislatures, whereas consolidated presidential democracies are not associated with the type of multiparty coalitional behavior that facilitates democratic rule in contexts of numerous socioeconomic, ideological, and ethnic cleavages and of numerous parties in the legislature. The currently empty column in table 4.1 of long-standing presidential democracies with "3.0 or more" effective legislative parties is probably one of the reasons why there are so few continuous presidential democracies.

The Finnish political scientist Tatu Vanhanen published an important study of democratic durability that incorporates the nuances in individual countries' socioeconomic structures. Hence, it provides another data set for testing our hypothesis regarding constitutional frameworks.[16]

Vanhanen constructed a political Index of Democratization (ID) based on (1) the total percentage of the vote received by all parties except the largest vote getter and (2) the total percentage of the population that voted. He has also constructed a socioeconomic Index of Power Resources (IPR) based on six variables: (1) degree of decentralization of nonagricultural economic resources, (2) percentage of total agricultural land owned as family farms, and percentage of population (3) in universities, (4) in cities, (5) that is literate, and (6) that is not employed in agriculture. His major hypothesis is that all countries above his threshold level of 6.5 on his Index of Power Resources "should be democracies," and all countries below his minimum level, 3.5 index points, "should be non-democracies or semi-democracies." He has constructed his indexes for 147 countries for 1980 and 1988.

Vanhanen's hypothesis was broadly confirmed in that 73.6 percent of the countries that were above 6.5 in his IPR qualified as democracies as measured by his Index of Democratization. In his regression analysis with these indexes, Vanhanen

Table 4.1. A Laakso-Taagepera Index of Effective Political Parties in the Legislatures of Continuous Democracies, 1979–1989

Parliamentary		Semipresidential		Presidential	
≥ 3.0 parties	< 3.0 parties	≥ 3.0 parties	< 3.0 parties	≥ 3.0 parties	< 3.0 parties
	Kiribati[b]				
	Nauru[b]				
	Tuvalu[b]				
	Botswana 1.3				
	St. Vincent 1.4				
	Dominica 1.5				
	Jamaica 1.5				
	Bahamas 1.6				
	Trinidad and				
	Tobago 1.6				
	Barbados 1.7				
	St. Lucia 1.7				USA 1.9
	New Zealand 2.0				Colombia 2.1
	Canada 2.0				Dominican
	United Kingdom 2.1				Republic 2.3
	India 2.1				Costa Rica 2.3
	Greece 2.2				
	Austria 2.4[a]				Venezuela 2.6
	Australia 2.5				
	Solomon Islands 2.5				
	Mauritius 2.5				
	Spain 2.7				
	Ireland 2.7[a]				
	Japan 2.9				
West Germany 3.2					
Norway 3.2		France 3.2			
Sweden 3.4					
Luxembourg 3.4		Portugal 3.6			
Israel 3.6					
Netherlands 3.8					
Italy 3.9					
Papua New					
Guinea 4.0					
Iceland 4.3[a]					
Denmark 5.2					
Belgium 7.0					

Source: See nn. 12, 14 for explanation of the Laakso-Taagepera index formula, criteria for inclusion into this universe of continuous democracies, and data used to construct this table.

Note: Switzerland and Finland are "mixed" systems with 5.4 and 5.1 "effective" political parties, respectively. See n. 13 for why we classify Finland, until 1988, as a mixed rather than a semipresidential regime.

   a. See n. 15 for why Duverger (and we) classify Austria, Ireland, and Iceland as parliamentary rather than presidential regimes.

   b. Traditionally in Kiribati, all candidates for the unicameral legislature—the Maneaba—have fought as independents. In 1985 various Maneaba members who were dissatisfied with government policies formed a Christian Democrat opposition grouping. The government grouping then "is generally known as the National Party, although it does not constitute a formal political party." It is more accurate to refer to Kiribati's "parties" as "pro" and "anti" assembly groupings, of which there are a total of two. See J. Denis and Ian Derbyshire, *Political Systems of the World* (Edinburgh: W. and R. Chambers, 1989), p. 724. This is also true in Tuvalu, where there are no formal political parties, and in Nauru, where there are loosely structured pro- and antigovernment groupings. See Arthur Banks, *Political Handbook of the World* (Binghamton: CSA Publishers, State University of New York, 1989), pp. 422, 627.

Table 4.2. Significant Democratic Over- and Underachievers: Comparison of Pure Parliamentary and Pure Presidential Systems

	Total Countries	Democratic Underachievers	Democratic Overachievers
Pure parliamentary systems	37	6 (16.2%)	31 (83.8%)
Pure presidential systems	22	12 (54.6%)	10 (45.5%)

Source: Vanhanen, *The Process of Democratization* (see n. 16), pp. 75–79, 94–97, presents data for his Index of Democratization and his Index of Power Resources. We determined whether the systems were parliamentary, presidential, or "other" using the references contained in the source note to table 4.5. "Other" includes semipresidential, one-party, and ruling monarchy.
Note: Overachiever and underachiever ratings are based on residuals in Vanhanen's regression analysis with his Index of Power Resources and his Index of Democratization for 1980 and 1988.

found the correlation (r^2) between the ID and the IPR equal to .707 in 1980 and .709 in 1988. Approximately 76 percent of the 147 countries tested by Vanhanen had small residuals and deviated from the regression line by less than one standard error of estimate.

However, thirty-six countries in 1980 and thirty-four in 1988 had negative or positive residuals larger than one standard error of estimate. These seventy large-residual cases indicate that about 24 percent of the variance in Vanhanen's regression analysis is unexplained. Vanhanen noted that "large positive residuals indicate that the level of democratization is considerably higher than expected on the basis of the average relationship between ID and IPR [we will call these cases "democratic overachievers"], and large negative residuals indicate that it is lower than expected [we will call these "democratic underachievers"]." He then asks "how to explain these deviations that contradict my hypothesis? I have not found any general explanation for them."[17]

Vanhanen's unexplained variance—his democratic over- and underachievers—constitutes a data set with which to test our hypothesis regarding constitutional frameworks. Of the total seventy deviating cases in his 1980 and 1988 studies, fifty-nine occurred in constitutional frameworks we have called "pure parliamentary" or "pure presidential" (thirty-seven and twenty-two cases, respectively). When we analyze democratic underachievers in Vanhanen's set, we find that presidential systems had a democratic underachiever rate 3.4 times greater than did the parliamentary systems. Further, parliamentary systems in Vanhanen's set were 1.8 times more likely than presidential systems to be democratic overachievers. (See table 4.2.)

Another set of data concerns both comparative capacity to be democratic survivors and vulnerability to military coups. Since we are concerned primarily with countries that are making some effort to construct democracies, we restrict our analysis to those countries in the world that qualified on the Gastil Political Rights Scale as democracies for at least one year between 1973 and 1989. Only 77 of the 168 countries in the world met this test. In an attempt to control for economic development as an intervening variable that might independently influence political sta-

Table 4.3. Regime Type of Fifty-three Non-OECD Countries That Experimented with Democracy between 1973 and 1989

	Regime Type during Democracy		
	Pure Parliamentary	Pure Presidential	Semipresidential or Mixed
Countries that were democratic for at least one year during 1973–89	28	25	0
Countries that were continuously democratic for 10 consecutive years during 1973–89	17	5	0
Democratic survival rate	61%	20%	NA

Source: Criteria for inclusion in this universe of countries are based on the Gastil Democracy Scale and the Coppedge-Reinicke Polyarchy Scale (see n. 5).

bility, we eliminate from this section of our analysis the twenty-four OECD countries. This leaves a data set of fifty-three non-OECD countries that experimented with democracy for at least one year between 1973 and 1989. Of these, twenty-eight countries were pure parliamentary, twenty-five were pure presidential, and surprisingly none were either semipresidential or mixed. Only five of the twenty-five presidential democracies (20 percent) were democratic for any ten consecutive years in the 1973–89 period; but seventeen of the twenty-eight pure parliamentary regimes (61 percent) were democratic for a consecutive ten-year span in the same period. Parliamentary democracies had a rate of survival more than three times higher than that of presidential democracies. Pure presidential democracies were also more than twice as likely as pure parliamentary democracies to experience a military coup. (See tables 4.3 and 4.4.)

Another source of relevant data concerns the set of countries, ninety-three in all, that became independent between 1945 and 1979.[18] During the ten-year period between 1980 and 1989 only fifteen of the ninety-three merit possible classification as continuous democracies. Since we are interested in evolution toward and consolidation of democracy, we examine the regime form that these countries chose at independence. Forty-one countries functioned as parliamentary systems in their first year of independence, thirty-six functioned as presidential systems, three functioned as semipresidential systems, and thirteen functioned as ruling monarchies. At this stage of our research, we are impressed by the fact that no matter what their initial constitutional form, not one of the fifty-two countries in the nonparliamentary categories evolved into a continuous democracy for the 1980–89 sample period, whereas fifteen of the forty-one systems (36 percent) that actually functioned as parliamentary systems in their first year of independence not only evolved into continuous democracies but were the only countries in the entire set to do so. (See table 4.5.)

Table 4.4. Regime Type of Non-OECD Countries That Experienced Military Coups while Democracies during 1973–1989

	Regime Type at Time of Coup		
	Pure Parliamentary	Pure Presidential	Semipresidential or Mixed
Countries that were democratic for at least one year during 1973–89	28	25	0
Countries that experienced military coups while democracies	5	10	0
Military coup susceptibility rate	18%	40%	NA

Source: Data for incidence of military coups are found in Arthur Banks, *Political Handbook of the World* (Binghamton: CSA Publishers, State University of New York, 1989) and Peter J. Taylor, *World Government* (Oxford: Oxford UP, 1990). For regime type at time of coup, see sources cited in table 4.5.
Note: We define a military coup as an unconstitutional removal of the executive by or with the aid of active-duty members of the domestic armed forces.

If the data in table 4.5 were strictly numerical observations, the chances that this distribution would occur randomly would be less than one in one thousand. But we realize that the quantification of this qualitative data masks important realities, such as the fact that the classes catch some countries that were always ademocratic or even antidemocratic. We do not rule out the hypothesis that the more democratic countries chose parliamentary systems at independence. Also, the fact that many of the "democratic survivors" are island states and that all but two (Papua New Guinea and Nauru) are former British colonies should be taken into account.[19] We can control for the British colonial legacy, however, by isolating the fifty former British colonies from our original set of ninety-three. Of the thirty-four from this subset that began independence as parliamentary systems, thirteen (38 percent) evolved into continuous democracies for the 1980–89 period. Of the five former British colonies that began as presidential systems, not one evolved into a democracy for the 1980–89 period.[20] Similarly, not one of the eleven former British colonies that began independence as ruling monarchies evolved into a continuous democracy for 1980–89. This suggests that factors other than British colonial heritage are related to democratic evolution and durability in these countries. Moreover, the fifteen democratic survivors in our set survived despite challenges such as tribal riots, linguistic conflicts, economic depressions, and mutinies. They therefore constitute a set of countries for which the constitutional form may be crucial in explaining democratic durability.

The comparative tendency for different constitutional frameworks to produce legislative majorities can also be ascertained. This is relevant to our central question because majorities help to implement policy programs democratically. Examining evidence from our set of non-OECD countries that were democratic for at least one year from 1973 to 1987, we note that in presidential democracies the exec-

Table 4.5. Regime Type of the Ninety-three Countries That Became Independent between 1945 and 1979 and the Countries from this Set That were Continuous Democracies between 1980 and 1989

Parliamentary (N = 41)		Presidential (N = 36)		Semipresidential (N = 3)	Ruling Monarchy (N = 13)
Bahamas	Malta	Algeria	Madagascar	Lebanon	Bahrain
Bangladesh	Mauritius	Angola	Malawi	Senegal	Burundi
Barbados	Nauru	Benin	Mali	Zaire	Cambodia
Botswana	Nigeria	B. Faso	Mauritania		Jordan
Burma	Pakistan	Cameroon	Mozambique		Kuwait
Chad	Papua New Guinea	Cape Verde	Niger		Lesotho
Dominica	St. Lucia	CAR	Philippines		Libya
Fiji	St. Vincent	Comoros	Rwanda		Maldives
Gambia	Sierra Leone	Congo	São Tomé		Morocco
Ghana[b]	Singapore	Cyprus	Seychelles		Oman
Grenada	Solomon Islands	Djibouti	Syria		Qatar
Guyana[b]	Somalia	Eq. Guinea	Taiwan		Tonga
India	Sri Lanka[b]	Gabon	Togo		United Arab
Indonesia	Sudan	Guinea	Tunisia		Emirates
Israel	Suriname	Guinea Bissau	Vietnam (N)		
Jamaica	Swaziland	Ivory Coast	Vietnam (S)		
Kenya	Tanzania	Korea (N)	Yemen (S)		
Kiribati	Trinidad and Tobago	Korea (S)	Zambia		
Laos	Tuvalu				
Malaysia	Uganda				
	W. Samoa				

Continuous Democracies 1980–89					
(N = 15/41)		(N = 0/36)		(N = 0/3)	(N = 0/13)
Bahamas	Nauru				
Barbados	Papua New Guinea				
Botswana	St. Lucia				
Dominica	St. Vincent				
India	Solomon Islands				
Israel	Trinidad and Tobago				
Jamaica	Tuvalu				
Kiribati					

Sources: See n. 5 for definitions of the Coppedge-Reinicke Polyarchy Scale and the Gastil Democracy Scale, upon which the table is based. Data for determining regime type at independence are found in Arthur Banks, *Political Handbook of the World* (Binghamton: CSA Publishers, State University of New York, 1989); Albert P. Blaustein and Gisbert H. Flanz, eds., *Constitutions of the Countries of the World*, vols. 1–19 (Dobbs Ferry, N.Y.: Oceana Publications, 1990); *Keesing's Contemporary Archives; Europa World Yearbook;* Peter J. Taylor, ed., *World Government* (Oxford: Oxford UP, 1990); Ian Gorvin, ed., *Elections since 1945* (Chicago: St. James Press, 1989), and the country studies of the *Area Handbook Series* (Washington, D.C.: Federal Research Division, U.S. Library of Congress, various years). Note: Results of a Pearson's chi-squared test with this data allow us to reject the null hypothesis that the above distribution is random. The chances of observing this distribution randomly are less than one in one thousand.

a. Although Cape Verde became independent in 1975, its first constitution was not promulgated until 1980. For the first five years of independence, Cape Verde appears to have functioned as a presidential system.

b. Sri Lanka was certainly and Ghana and Guyana appear to have been parliamentary democracies upon independence in 1948, 1957, and 1966, respectively. In 1960 Ghana changed to a presidential system, and in 1966 it experienced a military coup. The changes to a strong semipresidential system in Sri Lanka (1978) and a presidential system in Guyana (1980) were followed by increased restrictions of political rights and civil liberties. The last years that Sri Lanka and Guyana were classified as democracies on the Gastil Democracy Scale were 1982 and 1973, respectively. Ghana was classified as a democracy on this scale only in 1981–82.

Table 4.6. Regime Type in Non-OECD Countries, 1973–1987, and Years in Which Executive's Party Had a Legislative Majority

		Years in Which Executive Had a Legislative Majority	
	Years of Democracy[a]	Total	Percentage[b]
Parliamentary years	208	173	83%
Presidential years	122	58	48%

Source: Data concerning legislative seats and the executives' party affiliations were found in *Keesing's Contemporary Archives;* Ian Govin, *Elections since 1945: A Worldwide Reference Compendium* (Chicago: St James Press, 1989); Thomas T. Mackie and Richard Rose, *The International Almanac of Electoral History* (London: Macmillan, 1991); *Chronicle of Parliamentary Elections and Developments* (Geneva: International Centre for Parliamentary Documentation, 1973–89).

a. Includes all non-OECD countries that qualified as democracies for at least one year during the 1973–87 period, according to the Gastil Polyarchy Scale ten-year evaluation (see n. 5). Countries that became independent after 1979 are excluded.

b. We consider an executive to have had a legislative majority each year in which his or her party held at least 50 percent of the legislative seats in the country's lower house for parliamentary frameworks and in both houses for presidential frameworks. Coalitional majorities formed after the elections for legislative seats in the parliamentary frameworks are not included here. Therefore, the parliamentary years in which prime ministers actually governed with legislative majorities is likely to be higher than 83 percent. The norm in Western Europe, for example, is the coalitional, not single-party, legislative majority. See Kaare Strom, *Minority Government and Majority Rule* (Cambridge: Cambridge UP, 1990.)

utive's party enjoyed a legislative majority less than half of the time (48 percent of the democratic years). Parliamentary democracies, in sharp contrast, had majorities at least 83 percent of the time. (See table 4.6.)

A final set of data concerns the duration and reappointment of cabinet ministers in presidential versus parliamentary frameworks. These data relate to the issue of continuity in governance. Some minimal degree of ministerial continuity or prior ministerial experience would seem to be helpful in enhancing the political capacity of the government of the day to negotiate with state bureaucracies and with national and transnational corporations. Using a number of recent studies, we have examined all ministerial appointments during the years of democratic rule in Western Europe, the United States, and Latin America between 1950 and 1980. Two major findings emerge. First, the "return ratio" of ministers (that is, the percentage who serve more than once in their careers) is almost three times higher in parliamentary democracies than in presidential democracies. Second, the average duration of a minister in any one appointment is almost twice as long in parliamentary democracies as it is in presidential democracies. Even when only those countries with more than twenty-five years of uninterrupted democracy are included in the sample, the findings still hold.[21] The conclusion is inescapable: ministers in presidential democracies have far less experience than their counterparts in parliamentary democracies.

The Contrasting Logics of Pure Parliamentarism and Pure Presidentialism

Let us step back from the data for a brief note about the type of statements that can be made about political institutions and democratic consolidation. The status of statements about the impact of institutions is not causally determinative (*A* causes *B*) but probabilistic (*A* tends to be associated with *B*). For example, Maurice Duverger's well-known observation about electoral systems is a probabilistic proposition: it holds that systems with single-member districts where a simple plurality wins the seat tend to produce two-party systems, whereas electoral systems with multimember districts and proportional representation tend to produce multiparty systems.[22] The fact that Austria and Canada are exceptions to his proposition is less important than the fact that nineteen of the twenty-one cases of uninterrupted democracy in postwar industrialized countries conform to his proposition.[23]

A probabilistic proposition in politics is more than a statistical assertion. It entails the identification and explanation of the specific political processes that tend to produce the probabilistic results. And to establish even greater confidence in the proposition, one should examine case studies to explain whether and how the important hypothesized institutional characteristics actually came into play in individual cases.[24]

Whatever the constitutional framework, consolidating democracy outside of the industrialized core of the world is difficult and perilous. The quantitative evidence we have brought to bear on presidentialism and parliamentarism would assume greater theoretical and political significance if a strong case could be made that the empirically evident propensities we have documented are the logical, indeed the predictable, result of the constitutional frameworks themselves. We believe that such a case can be made.

The essence of pure parliamentarism is mutual dependence. From this defining condition a series of incentives and decision rules for creating and maintaining single-party or coalitional majorities, minimizing legislative impasses, inhibiting the executive from flouting the constitution, and discouraging political society's support for military coups predictably flows. The essence of pure presidentialism is mutual independence. From this defining (and confining) condition a series of incentives and decision rules for encouraging the emergence of minority governments, discouraging the formation of durable coalitions, maximizing legislative impasses, motivating executives to flout the constitution, and stimulating political society to call periodically for military coups predictably flows. Presidents and legislatures are directly elected and have their own fixed mandates. This mutual independence creates the possibility of a political impasse between the chief executive and the legislative body for which there is no constitutionally available impasse-breaking device.

Here, then, is a paradox. Many new democracies select presidentialism because they believe it to be a strong form of executive government. Yet our data show that between 1973 and 1987 presidential democracies enjoyed legislative majorities less than half of the time. With this relatively low percentage of "supported time" and the fixed mandates of the presidential framework, executives and legislatures in these countries were "stuck" with one another, and executives were condemned to serve out their terms. How often did these executives find it necessary to govern by decree-law—at the edge of constitutionalism—in order to implement the economic restructuring and austerity plans they considered necessary for their development projects?

Our evidence shows that, in contrast to presidentialism, the executive's party in parliamentary democracies enjoyed a majority of seats in the legislature more than 83 percent of the time period under study. For the remaining 17 percent of the years, parliamentary executives, motivated by the necessity to survive votes of confidence, formed coalition governments and party alliances in order to attract necessary support. When they were unable to do this, the absence of fixed mandates and the safety devices of the parliamentary institutional framework allowed for calling rapid new elections, the constitutional removal of unpopular, unsupported governments through the vote of no confidence, or simply the withdrawal from the government of a vital coalition partner.

Parliamentarism entails mutual dependence. The prime minister and his or her government cannot survive without at least the passive support of a legislative majority. The inherent mechanisms of parliamentarism involved in the mutual dependency relationship—the executive's right to dissolve parliament and the legislature's right to pass a vote of no confidence—are deadlock-breaking devices. These decision rules do not assure that any particular government will be efficient in formulating policies; nor do they assure government stability. But the decision mechanisms available in the parliamentary framework do provide constitutional means for removing deadlocked or inefficient governments (executives and parliaments). The danger that a government without a majority will rule by decree is sharply curtailed by the decision rule that allows the parliamentary majority (or the prime minister's coalition allies or even his or her own party) to call for government reformation.

Why is it logical and predictable that military coups are much more likely in pure presidential constitutional frameworks than in pure parliamentary ones? Because, as we discussed above, parliamentary democracies have two decision rules that help resolve crises of the government before they become crises of the regime. First, a government cannot form unless it has acquired at least a "supported minority" in the legislature; second, a government that is perceived to have lost the confidence of the legislature can be voted out of office by the simple political vote of no confidence (or in Germany and Spain by a positive legislative vote for an alternative government). Presidentialism, in sharp contrast, systematically contributes to impasses and democratic breakdown. Because the president and the legislature have separate and fixed mandates, and because presidents more than half of the time find themselves frustrated in the exercise of their power due to their lack of a legislative majority, presidents may often be tempted to bypass the legislature and rule by decree-law. It is extremely difficult to remove even a president who has virtually no consensual support in the country or who is acting unconstitutionally; it usually requires a political-legal-criminal trial (impeachment), whose successful execution requires exceptional majorities.[25] Thus, even when the socioeconomic crises are identical in two countries, the country with the presidential system is more likely to find itself in a crisis of governance and will find it more difficult to solve the crisis before it becomes a regime crisis.[26] Such situations often cause both the president and the opposition to seek military involvement to resolve the crisis in their favor.

Guillermo O'Donnell documented a phenomenon observed in the new Latin American democracies in his extremely interesting (and alarming) article on "delegative democracy," a conceptual opposite of representative democracy.[27] Key characteristics of delegative democracy include (1) presidents who present themselves as being "above" parties, (2) institutions such as a congress and a judiciary that are viewed as "a nuisance," with accountability to them considered an unnecessary impediment, (3) a president and his staff who are the alpha and omega of politics, and (4) a president who insulates himself from most existing political institutions and interactions and becomes the sole person responsible for "his" policies. We suggest that these characteristics of O'Donnell's delegative democracy are some of the predictable pathologies produced by the multiple logics of the presidential framework. Consider the following: Presidential democracy, due to the logic of its framework, always produces (1) presidents who are directly elected and (2) presidents with fixed terms. Presidential democracy often produces (1) presidents who feel they have a personal mandate and (2) presidents who do not have legislative majorities. Thus, the logic of presidentialism has a strong tendency to produce (1) presidents who adopt a discourse that attacks key political institutions (the legislature and parties) and (2) presidents who increasingly attempt to rely upon a direct appeal to the people and a discourse that marginalizes organized political and civil groups. Delegative democracy can no doubt exist in the other metainstitutional frameworks; however, the multiple logics of pure parliamentarism seem to work against delegative democracy.

Why are there many enduring multiparty parliamentary democracies but no long-standing presidential ones? In a parliamentary system, the junior political parties that participate in the ruling coalition are institutional members of the government and are often able to negotiate not only which ministries they will receive but who will be appointed to them. All members of the coalition have an incentive to cooperate if they do not want the government of the day to fall. In these circumstances, democracies with four, five, or six political parties in the legislature can function quite well.

There are far fewer incentives for coalitional cooperation in presidentialism. The office of the presidency is nondivisible. The president may select members of political parties other than his own to serve in the cabinet, but they are selected as individuals, not as members of an enduring and disciplined coalition. Thus, if the president's party (as in President Collor's party in Brazil) has less than 10 percent of the seats in the legislature, the president rules with a permanent minority and with weak coalitional incentives. On a vote-by-vote basis, the president may cajole or buy a majority, but repeated purchases of majorities are absolutely inconsistent with the principled austerity plans of restructuring that face most East European and Latin American democracies.

Evidence demonstrates that East European or Latin American political leaders who believe their countries, for historical reasons, are inevitably multiparty in political representation are playing against great odds if they select a presidential system. Brazil's high party fragmentation, for example, has contributed to a presidential-legislative deadlock that has frozen the law-making process in an already fragile democracy. Party fragmentation, the lack of party discipline, and general party underdevelopment in Brazil have been exacerbated by an electoral system that combines proportional representation with an open list. The 1990 elections yielded 8.5 effective parties in the Brazilian chamber of deputies and 6.0 in the senate.[28] These numbers seem alarmingly high considering that all the long-standing, pure presidential democracies reported in table 4.6 had fewer than 2.6 effective political parties.

Moreover, the closer a country approaches the ideal types of "sultanship," "totalitarianism," or early "posttotalitarianism," the "flatter" are its civil and political societies.[29] In these circumstances, adopting the constitutional framework of presidentialism in the period of transition from sultanship, totalitarianism, or early posttotalitarianism reduces the degree of freedom for an emerging civil and political society to make a midcourse correction because heads of government have been elected for fixed terms (as in Georgia). In contrast, the Bulgarian transition had significant parliamentary features that allowed an emerging political society to change the prime minister (and the indirectly elected president) so as to accommodate new demands.

In Poland, where constitutional reformers are flirting with the idea of strengthening the role of the president, party fragmentation is even greater than in Brazil; the effective number of parties in the Polish Sejm after the 1991 legislative elections was 10.8.[30] Most of these parties in the Polish legislature, like those in Brazil, lack clear programs and exist as mere labels for politicians to use for election into office.[31] Our data suggest that Poland would be playing against the odds were it to move toward a purely presidential system.

Also flowing from the logic of the constitutional framework are the questions of why ministers serve short terms in presidential democracies and why they are rarely reappointed. Because presidents do not normally enjoy majorities in the legislature, they resort to rapid ministerial rotation as a device in their perpetual search for support on key issues. In parliamentary systems, by contrast, coalitional majorities make rapid turnover unnecessary. Furthermore, key ministers usually have long and strong associations with their political parties and are often reappointed as government coalitions form and reform during the life of their careers. In presidential democracies, ministers are strongly associated with a particular president, leave office when the president does, and normally never serve as a minister again.

Conclusion

Let us consider the question that follows from the data. Why does pure parliamentarianism seem to present a more supportive evolutionary framework for consolidating democracy than pure presidentialism? We believe we are now in a position to say that the explanation of why parliamentarism is a more supportive constitutional framework lies in the following theoretically predictable and empirically observable tendencies: its greater propensity for governments to have majorities to implement their programs; its greater ability to rule in a multiparty setting; its lower propensity for executives to rule at the edge of the constitution and its greater facility at removing a chief executive who does so; its lower susceptibility to military coup; and its greater tendency to provide long party or government careers, which add loyalty and experience to political society.

The analytically separable propensities of parliamentarism interact to form a mutually supporting system. This system, qua system, increases the degree of freedom politicians have as they attempt to consolidate democracy. The analytically separable propensities of presidentialism also form a highly interactive system, but they work to impede democratic consolidation.

Notes

This chapter appeared in *World Politics* 46 (Oct. 1993), 1-22, under the title, "Constitutional Frameworks and Democratic Consolidation: Parliamentarism and Presidentialism." It is reprinted with permission. The study grew out of an exchange at a December 1990 meeting in Budapest of the East-South System Transformations Project, which brought together specialists on Eastern Europe, Southern Europe, and South America. When we were discussing topics for future research and dividing up our collective work, Adam Przeworski lamented that although there were assertions in the literature about the probable impact of different types of institutional arrangements on democratic consolidation, no systematic data were available. In his notes about the Budapest meeting, Przeworski reiterated that "we seem to know surprisingly little about the effects of the particular institutional arrangements for their effectiveness and their durability. Indeed, the very question whether institutions matter is wide open." See Przeworski, "Notes after the Budapest Meeting" (University of Chicago, 11 Jan. 1991), p. 10. We acknowledge the careful reading and/or comments of Adam Przeworski, Jack Snyder, Douglas Rae, Juan Linz, Mike Alvarez, Martin Gargiulo, Lisa Anderson, Anthony Marx, Gregory Gause, and Joel Hellman. The usual caveats apply.

1. See, e.g., Stephan Haggard and Robert R. Kaufman, eds., *The Politics of Economic Adjustment* (Princeton: Princeton UP, 1992); Adam Przeworski, *Democracy and the Market: Political and Economic Reforms in Eastern Europe and Latin America* (Cambridge: Cambridge UP, 1991); and Christopher Clague and Gordon C. Rausser, eds., *The Emergence of Market Economies in Eastern Europe* (Cambridge: Blackwell, 1992).

2. James G. March and Johan P. Olsen, "The New Institutionalism: Organizational Factors in Political Life," *American Political Science Review* 78 (Sept. 1984): 738. For a pioneering early work exemplifying this approach, see Maurice Duverger, *Political Parties* (New York: Wiley, 1954). Other important works that explore the causal relationship between institutions such as electoral systems and political parties, and democratic stability include Gio-

vanni Sartori, *Parties and Party Systems: A Framework for Analysis* (Cambridge: Cambridge UP, 1976); Douglas Rae, *The Political Consequences of Electoral Laws* (New Haven: Yale UP, 1967); William H. Riker, *The Theory of Political Coalitions* (New Haven: Yale UP, 1962); B. Grofman and A. Lijphart, eds., *Electoral Laws and Their Political Consequences* (New York: Agathon, 1986); Rein Taagepera and Matthew Soberg Shugart, *Seats and Votes* (New Haven: Yale UP, 1989); and Matthew Soberg Shugart and John M. Carey, *Presidents and Assemblies: Constitutional Design and Electoral Dynamics* (New York: Cambridge UP, 1992). An important work in the neo-institutionalist literature that focuses on legislatures and structure-induced equilibrium is Kenneth Shepsle, "Institutional Equilibrium and Equilibrium Institutions," in *Political Science: The Science of Politics,* edited by Herbert F. Weisberg (New York: Agathon, 1986). See also Mathew D. McCubbins and Terry Sullivan, eds., *Congress: Structure and Policy* (Cambridge: Cambridge UP, 1987).

3. There is a growing literature on this question. Much of it is brought together in the present volume. However, no article in this valuable collection attempts to gather systematic global quantitative data to address directly the question raised in the title of the book and by Przeworski. Linz first appeared in print on this subject in a brief "Excursus on Presidential and Parliamentary Democracy," in Linz and Alfred Stepan, eds., *The Breakdown of Democratic Regimes* (Baltimore: Johns Hopkins UP, 1978). His much cited seminal "underground" paper with the same title as this book was first presented at a workshop on "Political Parties in the Southern Cone," Woodrow Wilson International Center, Washington, D.C., 1984; see also Linz, "The Perils of Presidentialism," *Journal of Democracy* 1 (Winter 1990). See also Scott Mainwaring, "Presidentialism, Multiparty Systems, and Democracy: The Difficult Equation" (Kellogg Institute Working Paper 144, University of Notre Dame, Sept. 1990).

4. We agree with Philippe C. Schmitter's argument that there are many types of democracies and that "consolidation includes a mix of institutions." See Schmitter, "The Consolidation of Democracy and the Choice of Institutions," East-South System Transformations Working Paper 7 (University of Chicago, Department of Political Science, Sept. 1991), p. 7. See also Schmitter and Terry Karl, "What Democracy Is . . . And Is Not," *Journal of Democracy* (Summer 1991); the authors list eleven important dimensions that provide a matrix of potential combinations by which political systems can be differently democratic.

5. We realize that any effort to operationalize the concept of "democracy" so that it can be used to classify all the countries of the world is inherently difficult. Fortunately, two independently designed efforts attempt this task. One, by Michael Coppedge and Wolfgang Reinicke, attempted to operationalize the eight "institutional guarantees" that Robert Dahl argued were required for a polyarchy. Based on their assessment of political conditions as of mid-1985, the authors assigned values to 137 countries on a polyarchy scale. The results are available in Coppedge and Reinicke, "A Measure of Polyarchy" (paper presented at the Conference on Measuring Democracy, Hoover Institution, Stanford University, 27–28 May 1988; and in Coppedge and Reinicke, "A Scale of Polyarchy," in *Freedom in the World: Political Rights and Civil Liberties, 1987–1988,* edited by Raymond D. Gastil (New York: Freedom House, 1990), pp. 101–28. Robert A. Dahl's seminal discussion of the institutional guarantees needed for polyarchy is found in his *Polyarchy: Participation and Opposition* (New Haven: Yale UP, 1971), pp. 1–16.

The other effort to operationalize a scale of democracy is the annual Freedom House evaluation of virtually all the countries of the world. The advisory panel in recent years has included such scholars as Seymour Martin Lipset, Giovanni Sartori, and Lucian W. Pye. The value assigned for each year from 1973 to 1987 can be found in Gastil, *Freedom in the World,* pp. 54–65. In this chapter, we call a country a "continuous democracy" if it has received no higher a scale score than 3 on the Coppedge-Reinicke Polyarchy Scale for 1985 and no higher than a 2.5 averaged score of the ratings for "political rights" and "civil liberties" on the Gastil Democracy Scale for the 1980–89 period.

6. On the defining characteristics of semipresidentialism, see the seminal article by Maurice Duverger, "A New Political System Model: Semi-Presidential Government," *European Journal of Political Research* 8, no. 2 (1980). See also Duverger, *Echec au roi* (Paris: Albin Michel, 1978), and *La monarchie républicaine* (Paris: R. Laffont, 1974).

7. For a discussion of the semipresidential constitutional framework, its inherent problem of "executive dualism," and the exceptional circumstances that allowed France to manage these problems, see Alfred Stepan and Ezra N. Suleiman, "The French Fifth Republic: A Model for Import? Reflections on Poland and Brazil," in *Politics, Society and Democracy: Comparative Studies*, edited by H. E. Chehabi and Alfred Stepan (Boulder: Westview, forthcoming).

8. Alfred Stepan will develop this argument in greater detail in a book he is writing entitled "Democratic Capacities/Democratic Institutions."

9. For example, in Arend Lijphart's list of twenty-one continuous democracies since World War II, seventeen were pure parliamentary democracies, two were mixed, one was semipresidential, and only one, the United States, was pure presidential. See Lijphart, *Democracies: Patterns of Majoritarian and Consensus Government in Twenty-one Countries* (New Haven: Yale UP, 1984), p. 38.

10. The norm is a directly elected president with very strong de jure and de facto prerogatives coexisting with a prime minister who needs the support of the parliament. As of April 1993, only Hungary and the newly created Czech Republic and Slovakia had opted for a pure parliamentary constitutional framework. Despite having directly elected presidents, Slovenia, Estonia, and Bulgaria have strong parliamentary features. In Slovakia and Estonia presidents are now selected by the parliament. Bulgaria, however, has moved from an indirectly to a directly elected president. For political, legal, and sociological analyses of constitution making in East European transitions, see the quarterly publication *East European Constitutional Review*, which is part of the Center for the Study of Constitutionalism in Eastern Europe at the University of Chicago. The center was established in 1990 in partnership with the Central European University.

11. Duration analysis would be particularly appropriate because it estimates the *conditional* probability that an event will take place (for example, that a democracy will "die" by undergoing military coup), given that a regime has survived for a given period of time as a democracy. This conditional probability is in turn parameterized as a function of exogenous explanatory variables (such as constitutional frameworks). The sign of an estimated coefficient then indicates the direction of the effect of the explanatory variable on the conditional probability that a democracy will die at a given time. Such models allow us to estimate whether democracies exhibit positive or negative "duration dependence": specifically, whether the probability that a democracy will die increases or decreases with increases in the duration of the spell. Mike Alarez, a Ph.D. candidate in political science at the University of Chicago, is creating the data and the appropriate statistical techniques and implementing the duration analysis as part of his dissertation. Adam Przeworski, too, has embarked on such research. See also Nicholas M. Kiefer, "Economic Duration Data and Hazard Functions," *Journal of Economic Literature* 26 (June 1988).

12. We consider a country to be a "consolidated democracy" if it has received no higher a scale score than 3 on the Coppedge-Reinicke Polyarchy Scale for 1985 *and* no higher than a 2.5 average of the ratings for "political rights" and "civil liberties" on the Gastil Democracy Scale. Countries that met these joint criteria for every year of the 1979–89 decade are considered "continuous consolidated democracies." See n. 18 herein.

13. Duverger calls Finland semipresidential because the president has significant de jure and de facto powers; it should be pointed out, however, that from 1925 to 1988 the Finnish president was not so much directly elected as indirectly chosen by party blocs. The candidates normally did not campaign in the country, and though parties put the names of their candidates on the ballot, the electoral college votes were not pledges and often entailed deliberations and multiple balloting, leading Shugart and Carey to conclude that the presidential election system in Finland from 1925 to 1988, "given its party-centered character . . . was not much different from election in parliament." See Shugart and Carey, *Presidents and Assemblies*, pp. 212–21, 226–28, quote at p. 221. We consider Finland to have been a "mixed" constitutional system until 1988.

14. Laakso and Taagepera, "'Effective' Number of Parties: A Measure with Application to West Europe," *Comparative Political Studies* 12 (Apr. 1979). The formula takes into account each party's relative size in the legislature, as measured by the percentage of seats it holds. The "effective" number of parties is "the number of hypothetical equal-size parties that would have the same total effect on fractionalization of the system as have the actual parties of unequal size." The formula for calculating the effective number of parties (N) is

$$N = \frac{1}{\sum\limits_{i=1}^{n} pi2}$$

where pi = the percentage of total seats held in the legislature by the ith party. For each country listed in table 4.1, we determined the number of seats held in the lower or only house of the legislature at the time of each legislative election between 1979 and 1989. Then, we calculated the effective number of political parties (N) for each of these election years and multiplied by the number of years until the next legislative election.

15. Austria, Ireland, and Iceland have directly elected presidents, but we do not classify them as semipresidential; we concur with Duverger that they are not de facto semipresidential, since "political practice is parliamentary." See Duverger, "A New Political System Model," p. 167.

16. See Tatu Vanhanen, *The Process of Democratization: A Comparative Study of 147 States, 1980–1988* (New York: Crane Russak, 1990).

17. Ibid., p. 84.

18. We use the date of independence since it was usually within one year of independence that new constitutions were drafted and approved in these countries. We exclude from our analysis those countries that became independent after 1979 because we want to see which of these countries were then continuously democratic for the ten-year period 1980–89. This gives us a sample of time between World War II and 1979.

19. Myron Weiner observes that "most of the smaller, newly independent democracies . . . are also former British colonies" and puts forth the hypothesis that "tutelary democracy under British colonialism appears to be a significant determinant of democracy in the Third World." See Weiner, "Empirical Democratic Theory," in *Competitive Elections in Developing Countries*, edited by Myron Weiner and Ergun Özbudun (Durham: Duke UP, 1987), esp. pp. 18–23, quote at p. 19. This question is also addressed by Jorge Dominguez, "The Caribbean Question: Why Has Liberal Democracy (Surprisingly) Flourished?" in *Democracy in the Caribbean: Political, Economic, and Social Perspectives* (Baltimore: Johns

Hopkins UP, 1993). Dominguez discusses how these Caribbean democracies have faced (and survived) severe economic crises. He attributes their democratic stability to the legacy of British institutions (including, but not limited to, the Westminster parliamentary model) and the prodemocratic disposition of the countries' leadership.

20. The five former British colonies that chose presidential systems within one year of independence were Zambia, Cyprus, Malawi, Seychelles, and South Yemen.

21. See Jean Blondel, *Government Ministers in the Contemporary World* (Beverly Hills, Calif.: Sage, 1985), esp. app. 2, pp. 277–81; Mattei Dogan, *Pathways to Power: Selecting Rulers in Pluralist Democracies* (Boulder: Westview, 1989); Waldino C. Suárez: "Argentina: Political Transition and Institutional Weakness in Comparative Perspective," in *Comparing New Democracies: Transition and Consolidation in Mediterranean Europe and the Southern Cone,* edited by Enrique A. Baloyra, (Boulder: Westview, 1987); Suárez, "El gabinete en América Latina: Organización y cambio," *Contribuciones,* no. 1 (Jan.–Mar. 1985); and Suárez, "El poder ejecutivo en América Latina: Su capacidad operativa bajo regímenes presidencialistas de gobierno," *Revista de estudios politicos,* no. 29 (Sept.–Oct. 1982).

22. See Duverger, *Political Parties.*

23. For a discussion of Duverger's proposition in the context of modern industrialized democracies, see Lijphart, *Democracies,* pp. 156–59.

24. A growing literature of case studies examines the influence of constitutional frameworks on stability or breakdown in developing countries. See, e.g., David M. Lipset, "Papua New Guinea: "The Melanesian Ethic and the Spirit of Capitalism, 1975–1986," in *Democracy in Developing Countries: Asia,* edited by Larry Diamond, Juan J. Linz, and Seymour Martin Lipset, (Boulder: Lynne Rienner, 1989), esp. pp. 3–413. Lipset discusses how the constitutional framework came into play to prevent regime breakdown in Papua New Guinea. See also Dominguez, "The Caribbean Question."

25. Schmitter and Karl, "What Democracy Is," quite correctly build into their definition of democracy the concept of accountability. But except in the United States, where a president can be directly reelected only once, no president in a long-standing democracy, once in office, can be held politically accountable by a vote of the citizens' representatives. The accountability mechanism is so extreme and difficult—with the political-legal-criminal trial that needs exceptional majorities (impeachment)—that the accountability principle in presidentialism is weaker than in parliamentarism.

26. For theoretical differentiation between crises of government and crises of regime, see Juan J. Linz and Alfred Stepan, eds., *The Breakdown of Democratic Regimes* (Baltimore: Johns Hopkins UP, 1978), esp. p. 74.

27. See O'Donnell, "¿Democracia delegativa?" *Novos estudios* CEBRAP, no. 31 (Oct. 1991).

28. These numbers were calculated using the Laakso/Taagepera formula and the data reported in *Keesing's Record of World Events* (1990) and Arthur S. Banks, ed., *Political Handbook of the World* (Binghamton: CSA Publishers, State University of New York, 1991).

29. This argument is developed in Juan J. Linz and Alfred Stepan, "Problems of Democratic Transition and Consolidation: Eastern Europe, Southern Europe and South America" (book manuscript), pt. 1.

30. This is developed in Stepan and Suleiman, "The French Fifth Republic."

31. For a discussion of how both the political culture and the institutional structure in Brazil contributed to the country's weak party system, see Scott Mainwaring, "Dilemmas of Multiparty Presidential Democracy: The Case of Brazil" (Kellogg Institute Working Paper 174, University of Notre Dame, 1992). See also Mainwaring, "Politicians, Parties, and Electoral Systems: Brazil in Comparative Perspective," *Comparative Politics* 24 (Oct. 1991).

EZRA N. SULEIMAN

Presidentialism and Political Stability in France

In HIS FAMOUS SPEECH at Bayeux (Normandy) on June 16, 1946—the speech that contained the outlines and principles of what was to become twelve years later the constitution of the Fifth Republic—General de Gaulle observed that "the Greeks in earlier times used to ask the sage Solon, 'What is the best Constitution?' He used to reply: 'Tell me first for what people and at what epoch.'"[1]

While no one particular constitutional arrangement ensures democratic stability and effective government, an institutional form of governance may exercise a strong influence on the whole political process. Institutional arrangements derive their importance from the influence they exercise on the context within which conflicts are resolved. They do not guarantee the resolution of conflicts. If ethnic or religious conflicts are especially acute, no institutional form of democratic governance may be capable of resolving them peacefully. Lebanon, which for many years was presented to the world as the model of a pluralistic, consociational society, ultimately found its form of government to be extremely fragile. It may have been Lebanon's geopolitical context (a negligible factor in the case of consociational societies like Holland) that showed how fragile the Lebanese state was in the face of a crisis. Nonetheless, the crisis was probably too acute to be resolved by any form of democratic institutional arrangement.

Constitutional arrangements can allow for the resolution of what might be called moderate or routine conflicts, which are inherent in democracies. The collective interests of diverse communities, or political parties, tend toward ensuring that the system does not break down. But once a major crisis occurs (the entry of the Palestine Liberation Organization into Lebanon, the Algerian war and its consequences for France), the capacity to resolve conflicts collapses. Constitutional arrangements are therefore generally judged by their capacity to contribute to conflict resolution that avoids institutional breakdown, as well as to handle threats to the political order.

The case of France is especially germane to a project that seeks to understand the impact of presidentialism on political stability or instability. Since the introduction of the presidential regime in 1958, and its reinforcement in 1962,[2] the French political system has undergone vast changes. The most important of these changes have been reinforced executive authority, government stability, and a more coherent party system. The central question that needs to be dealt with, then, is: Are the post-1958 changes in the political system attributable to the constitutional change from a parliamentary to a presidential system?

All the more significant is this question in view of the fact that the French constitution of 1958 has had an enormous appeal to many countries who have looked at this document as a model for import or imitation. In France itself a general consensus has developed that the 1958 constitution is responsible for the political changes that have taken place. This is understandable perhaps in light of the fact that from 1870 to 1958 (excluding, of course, the Pétainist interlude of 1940–44), France had a democratic form of government, on the whole unstable but viable, in which multiple parties were able to form governments that simply changed when they could not deal with crises. The system collapsed when it was confronted by a major crisis. The years 1940–44 and 1954–58 (the years of the Algerian war) convinced many that a strong executive authority was needed precisely to ensure the continuity of the state in times of crises. Managing political crises without creating a governmental vacuum was the obsession of the drafters of the Gaullist constitution.

And yet there is strong evidence—some of which is presented in this chapter—to suggest that the drafters of the 1958 constitution were taken by surprise by subsequent developments in the political system. They did not anticipate many of the most important changes that have characterized the political system since 1962, and indeed it seems fairly clear that they did not even grasp all the implications of a presidential system. Few people reading the constitution in 1958, or even several years later, could have predicted the developments that have taken place in the political system. Mendès-France, perhaps as harsh a critic of the new régime as was to be found, was nevertheless not alone in thinking that authoritarianism was bound to be the hallmark of the new presidential system. As late as 1964 he was able to declare that "there is not a single example in history, neither in France nor in any other country in the world, and not in any epoch, where a monopolization of power in the hands of a single man (even if he does not make a despotic and bloody use of this power)—no, there are no examples where such a concentration of power did not lead to disaster."[3]

That Mendès-France may have erred in seeing the seeds of despotism in the 1958 constitution did not prevent the drafters and supporters of that constitution from failing to anticipate the subsequent development of political institutions. The French political system, in addition to providing political stability, has developed in ways that would not have met the approval of the drafters of the 1958 constitution. France, then, has succeeded in developing a strong executive authority and remaining a democratic society. My task in this chapter, therefore, is, first, to ask why and in what ways the presidential system has contributed to political stability in France. Secondly, I will examine the ways in which the presidential system has shaped the political system and has in turn been affected by it.

The main reason why the French constitution of 1958 has a great appeal to a number of countries grappling with a variety of constitutional arrangements is that France appears to have avoided the clash of two competing legitimacies that has been the bane of many presidential systems. In fact, Juan Linz's central argument regarding the inherently unstable nature of presidential systems is based on the clash likely to ensue between executive and legislative powers when both are endowed with electoral legitimacy. This, then, is the third question that I will try to answer: Why has France avoided the clash between presidential and legislative institutions?

One other aspect of French constitutional engineering that has caught the attention of Latin American and Asian countries is the dual executive system, which consists of both a president and a prime minister. But the dual executive system does not function in a predetermined way. It can allow for considerable executive coherence and cooperation when the hierarchy between the two offices is clearly established. The system may also entail a minimum of conflict when a prime minister seeks to attain a degree of autonomy. Finally, it may lead to two competing legitimacies. Such a conflictual relationship can occur when a president is elected by universal suffrage and a prime minister chosen by the president represents a majority party in the assembly that is in opposition to the presidential majority.

It should be clear from the outset that the Fifth Republic has not provided political stability for France because it introduced the presidential or the dual executive system. No institutional arrangement can be seen independently of the unforeseen changes that it engenders. Nor can it be seen independently of other simultaneous and autonomous changes that influence it. In the French case, as will be seen, the presidential system has provided political stability because it has been accompanied by simultaneous transformations of other political institutions, many of which were neither foreseen nor desired. Lest it be forgotten, a caveat is in order: the system I am describing is some thirty years old, which is very young for a constitution. The flexibility of the system is its major strength, but it also comes with considerable costs.

Consolidation of the Regime

For the first time since the Revolution of 1789, there is no longer conflict in France about what kinds of political institutions are best suited to the society. Changes in government and elections are no longer occasions for changing or promising to change the politicoinstitutional structure of the society. It is generally accepted, by the Left and the Right, that the constitution of 1958 has given France the political stability it lacked under the Third and Fourth Republics. Indeed, it has even been argued that the French Revolution that began in 1789 is finally over because the two-hundred-year struggle and search for a viable institutional setup has reached its culmination.[4]

In some sense, "everyone is a Gaullist today" because it is no longer acceptable to criticize the institutions that came into being with the constitution of 1958. At most, if there is debate, it revolves around the kind of electoral system that ought to be instituted. This is about the only disagreement that can be observed amid the general consensus on existing political institutions.

Acceptance of the institutions created by the 1958 constitution was gradual. In the earlier years, the hostility of the Left to the presidential system, to the personalization of power, to the decapitation of the parliament—to what François Mitterrand attacked as "le coup d'état permanent"[5]—was uncompromising. In 1964, Mitterrand, addressing the prime minister, vigorously attacked the constitution. "The provisions of the Constitution which stipulate that 'the executive branch determines and implements national policy' and 'is accountable to Parliament' have now become empty phrases. . . . The present regime, in which you appear at times to be the unobtrusive head of State and, at other times, to be the Prime Minister, resembles more the relationship between an absolute ruler and his favorite than a valid Constitution for all citizens." Pompidou's response was equally stinging, qualifying Mitterrand as a man of the past and assuring him that the future did not belong to him because he did not understand its direction. "Whatever may be the future conditions of political conflict, the nation will only give its full confidence to those who, unhesitatingly, vow to preserve the basis for a stable regime: a head of State who is really that."[6]

Stability was what the country lacked, and stability was what the new Gaullist constitution provided. Whatever the costs of this executive stability, it was, according to its founders and defenders, what the country needed. And no party that assumes power under this constitution is likely to want to alter it in any way. Barely two months after he acceded to the presidency in May 1981, Mitterrand declared in an interview, "I shall exercise, to their fullest extent, the powers conferred upon me by the Constitution. Neither more nor less. . . . The political institutions were not conceived for my benefit. But those institutions suit me well."[7] As Debré noted, "He who declares today that 'France now is what she is because of General de Gaulle' would hardly be contradicted."[8]

The Search for Stability

The constitution of 1958 was a reaction to the instability of the Third and Fourth Republics, as well as to the incapacity of a weak executive to respond to national crises.

A strong executive and political stability were seen to go hand in hand. The Fourth Republic, it was believed, could provide neither because it was a "régime des partis," a regime that the Gaullists never ceased to vilify and to undermine. In his press conference of May 19, 1958, de Gaulle explained the cause for his having left power abruptly in 1946: "And then when I saw that political parties had resurfaced, like the émigrés [under the Restoration] who had forgotten nothing and learned nothing, and, as a consequence, that it had become impossible for me to govern in a proper way, well, I withdrew from public office."[9]

What was the "régime des partis"? It consisted of (1) multipartism, (2) parliamentary supremacy, and (3) governmental instability. For opponents, the three characteristics were linked.

That the Fourth Republic was characterized by a multiparty system is evident. But the point is that it was a polarized party system and the parties themselves were without strong discipline and organization. Consequently, no party could achieve a parliamentary majority. The parties were constituted more as associations of elected officials bearing the same political labels than as organizations with a deep anchoring in the society. As Borella observes:

> Under the Third Republic, as under the Fourth, what was called party government was, above all, a supple parliamentary system, without a predetermined majority, in which the center of political decision-making was located within the elected chambers. Therefore, well before 1958, a party system existed based on groupings within Parliament, or, as the British would say, on parliamentary parties. But these elected committees, unlike those in Great Britain, lacked a base or support in French society as a whole.[10]

Historians and analysts of the Fourth Republic's political system have disagreed about the causes of its instability and eventual collapse. The ills have been attributed to the constitution, to ideological divisions, to multipartism, to the electoral laws, and to the personal ambitions of politicians.[11] The party system did not permit the governments of the Fourth Republic to possess genuine authority, and it granted the parliament the powers of making and unmaking governments. Every government of the Fourth Republic was a coalition of diverse political families (socialists, radicals, and liberal Catholics) that sometimes (until May 1947) even included communists. Because the parties were internally divided and because governments were often subjected to assaults by the forces of the extreme left and extreme right, no government could survive a struggle with the parliament.

The lack of authority of the Fourth Republic was manifested above all by governmental instability. Between 1946 and 1958, twenty-five governments were formed, and of the fifteen prime ministers who led them only two (Henri Queuille and Guy Mollet) lasted more than a year. The parliament's power to consume governments explains in part the absence of stable executives. But the power of parliament was also derivative of the party system. As Vincent Wright notes, "The problem of the Fourth Republic was not that it was dominated by the parties but rather that those parties which formed successive coalition governments were so internally divided and so undisciplined in their parliamentary behavior."[12]

But an unstable governmental system can still enjoy a long life, as the Italian political system testifies. For a governmental system based on coalitions and frequent changes in governments to endure, one condition seems necessary: the absence of a costly crisis. The Third Republic survived the Dreyfus affair, financial scandals, and the ideological divisions of the 1930s. It did not survive the German invasion. Similarly, the Fourth Republic survived the Indochina conflict, the departure of the communists from the government, the granting of independence to Tunisia and Morocco. It could not, however, survive the Algerian war. It must be said, therefore, that the Fourth Republic would have probably endured had the Algerian war not divided the society to the point of making possible the return to power of General de Gaulle.[13]

The fact, then, that political parties were undisciplined, poorly structured, rudimentary in organization, and incapable of obtaining majorities did not amount to a death warrant for the regime. Yet, in what sense did the Fourth Republic merit the epithet, a "régime des partis"? In attacking the Fourth Republic as the "régime des partis" critics were in fact attacking a parliamentary system of government, that is, a parliamentary system that escaped the control of party organizations. As the principal author of the 1958 constitution, Michel Debré, noted:

> The serious error of previous Republics is to have replaced national sovereignty with parliamentary sovereignty by a simple play on words. During each of its elected terms, the National Assembly had the right to do anything it pleased while the other branches of government were simply subordinate. The abuse of power was all the more evident as it became clear that parliamentary sovereignty was a phrase to mask the unlimited power of political parties, that is to say, of party leaders.[14]

Like many opponents of the Fourth Republic, Debré confused a parliamentary regime with a "régime des partis." In fact, what characterized the Fourth Republic was precisely the weakness of parties and of their leadership. The party leadership ("états-majors") often did not control its own deputies. The founders of the Fifth Republic came to abhor the role that parties played. They sought a presidential regime in which the chief executive was "above parties" and could govern without them.

Yet, as will be seen, the Fifth Republic has turned out to be more a "regime of parties" than was the Fourth Republic, and a regime in which the party leadership exercises veritable control over the elected deputies. Philip Williams observed that the Fourth Republic "failed because it was incapable of providing a government with authority."[15] Yet this was surely a consequence rather than a cause of political instability. For what has occurred under the Fifth Republic is that political parties have come into their own and now dominate the parliament. Hence, the maturation of the political system—or political stability—has come about as a result of the creation of a genuine "régime des partis."

The Executive in the New Constitution

The constitution of the Fifth Republic reacted to the previous republic's inability to act authoritatively. The three principles that were not accepted in 1944—and whose rejection led to de Gaulle's twelve-year-long, self-imposed exile at Colombey-les-Deux-Eglises—found approval in 1958 with the drafting of the new constitutional text. Michel Debré, the main author of the 1958 constitutional document, has described these guiding principles thus:

> For the stability and authority of the executive I used an idea that found favor later, the idea of a republican monarch. In the second place, what was needed was a genuine parliamentary system, that is, a cabinet that directs the actions of the government and the work of parliament whose activity is organized and whose will is not all-powerful. And finally, a method of election which, while ensuring as cohesive a majority as possible, permits solid cooperation between the cabinet and parliament, and thus greater government stability.[16]

The principles on which the Fifth Republic constitution is built are complex and can lend themselves to different interpretations. For the text itself allows for both the separation of executive and legislative powers, with the former no longer dependent on the latter, and the preservation of a parliamentary system. The regime can therefore function as a presidential one, as it has for most of the years of the Fifth Republic, or it can function much like a parliamentary regime, as it did between 1986 and 1988, when the president's leadership was considerably compromised.

Nonetheless, "what is striking to observers today and what seems to be the critical point, is the new importance accorded to the president of the Republic by the political institutions."[17] The president, according to the constitutional text, is "the protector of National independence, of territorial integrity," and has the responsibility for ensuring that "the Constitution is respected" and for ensuring "the continuity of the State" (article 5). The constitution also enables the president to take important actions at certain times: article 16 grants him emergency powers; article 12 gives him power to dissolve the National Assembly; and article 11 allows him to bypass the parliament and submit certain issues to a referendum.

Now, these prerogative powers, which can be used in national crises, allow the president to take decisive steps when an emergency arises. De Gaulle was haunted by the ineffectiveness of Albert Lebrun, the last president of the Third Republic, in 1940. But the use of these constitutional provisions is likely to reflect a breakdown in the political process. The decision to bypass the parliament and to submit an issue to the people would entail a rift in executive-legislative relations, just as dissolution of the National Assembly would generally involve a political crisis.[18] Constitutional provisions that grant the president extraordinary powers are used only when other efforts have failed to control or change events. But their presence in the constitutional text was designed to overcome the chief handicap of the Fourth Republic: the paralysis of executive authority in the face of a major national crisis. The extraordinary powers of the president could not—and have not—determined the political process and the manner in which it has evolved during the years of the Fifth Republic.

The error of both the founders of the Fifth Republic and their strongest critics was that they believed that the extraordinary powers granted the president would determine the political system. For the former, the extraordinary powers in the constitutional text guaranteed the president preeminence in the political process. For the latter, this preeminence guaranteed that a genuinely democratic form of government could not flourish. Both defenders and critics of the constitutional text failed to understand that extraordinary powers were intended to be used only in extraordinary circumstances and that democratic political institutions would continue to have their role.

The unique feature of the French constitutional system, and the one that has aroused the greatest interest in countries seeking answers to their constitutional problems, is the dual executive system. The president sits at the top of the political structure. He is not *primus inter pares.* He is elected by popular vote and has the constitutional authority to name the prime minister and, on the recommendations of the latter, the ministers in the cabinet. "The branches of government should be separate instead of merged into one," said de Gaulle. "That is to say, they should not emanate from the same source." Because the president is responsible for the continuity of the executive and of the state, the logic was that he had to possess the authority to dissolve the assembly and the right to go over the head of the assembly by calling for referendums. "In order to fulfill his role as arbiter, thereby removing him from the details of everyday politics, he will not possess sufficient authority if he continues to be elected only by Parliament."[19]

The separation of powers between executive and legislative functions—the executive no longer being at the mercy of the assembly—is a key innovation of the 1958 constitution. It was the referendum of October 28, 1962, which called for the election of the president of the republic by universal suffrage, that represented a turning point in the history of the Fifth Republic. "It replaces the moribund parliamentary 'republican tradition' with a new political system that permits the coexistence of the republican system with a strong executive."[20]

The election of the president by popular vote did create a strong and durable (the president's term is seven years) executive. But it did not do away with the complexity of the constitutional system, which while curtailing the role of parliament, nonetheless requires constituted governments to have its approval. Hence, governments can only be emanations of parliamentary majorities. Moreover, the constitution accords the prime minister considerable powers. Article 20 states that "the

Government shall determine and direct the policy of the nation," and article 21 adds that "the Prime Minister shall direct the operation of the Government."

The constitutional text of 1958 therefore allows for the existence of two competing legitimacies—presidential and parliamentary—simply because both are elected by popular vote. That de Gaulle had in fact created two distinct legitimacies was something that he refused to recognize, at least at the outset of the Fifth Republic. In his press conference of January 31, 1964, he showed his characteristic interpretation of the new presidential office. He refused to accept the fact that the presidential office did not have a monopoly on political authority. "The indivisible authority of the state," he noted, "is entirely given to the president by the people who elected him. There exists no other authority, neither ministerial, nor civil, nor military, nor judicial that is not conferred or maintained by him." And yet, the constitutional text makes it abundantly clear that the National Assembly is elected, as Duverger noted, "by the people, as is the president, and that it is, like him, endowed with a part of national sovereignty."[21]

Because of the two "national sovereignties," or two legitimacies expressly recognized by the constitution, much ink was spilled between 1958 and 1986 by constitutional experts on the possibility of a grave constitutional crisis in the event of the election of a legislative majority that was different from the majority that had elected the president. The president can dissolve the National Assembly if the majority it contains is not to his liking. He cannot be made to resign if, subsequent to his dissolving the National Assembly, the opposition again obtains a majority. In such an instance, the president can only appoint a government that has the confidence of the National Assembly, that is, a government composed of members of the opposition party. This is what occurred between 1986 and 1988 and again in 1993.

That the introduction of the presidential system in France has contributed to political stability is scarcely deniable. It has not destabilized the political process in the same way that it has in a number of other countries. This outcome was certainly not evident at the outset, in part because the new regime did not gain immediate acceptance and in part because the constitution allows for the existence of two competing legitimacies. To understand the basis of political stability in France it is not sufficient to dwell on the constitutional provisions that underlie the executive system. The executive system fits into and is supported by other institutions that have themselves undergone transformations. As I pointed out at the outset, the presidential system interacts with other institutions. It is shaped by and shapes those other less formal institutions. If presidentialism has contributed to political stability, it has done so because other institutions have made this possible.

Political stability in France as well as the functioning of the presidential system since 1958 have been conditioned as much by the transformation of the party system as by the constitutional changes, that is to say, as much by the *unforeseen* consequences of the constitution as by the constitution itself.

Presidentialism and the Party System

It is difficult to understand why the founders of the Fifth Republic believed that presidentialism would limit the importance of political parties. We know that the constitutional document was hastily drafted.[22] But believing that a presidential regime circumscribes the role of political parties suggests that the drafters of the constitution had little understanding of the workings of presidential regimes. Perhaps this has turned out to be a blessing in disguise, for the transformation of the party system under the Fifth Republic has been the central underpinning of the presidential system and probably the key element in the accompanying political stability.

Despite the scorn heaped on political parties by the founders of the 1958 constitution, the fact is that this constitution gave parties immediate recognition. With respect to article 4 of the new text,[23] which defines and recognizes the democratic role of political parties, Debré writes, "I am just as determined as Guy Mollet to preserve it. . . . But recognizing the [legitimate] role of political parties does not mean opening the door to party government. It is not a paradox to affirm that the Republican Constitution, by ending the parliamentary system of government, intended to halt domination by parties and yet [this Constitution] was the first to recognize their existence and their importance."[24]

Regardless of how de Gaulle and his supporters perceived the role of parties, whose banishment was one of their central objectives, it is undeniable that what Debré called the "omnipotence of the parties" has not occurred. Indeed, the contrary has taken place. The presidential system led in an unexpected way to the transformation of the party system and to a new mode of party organization. Consequently, the Fifth Republic's political system has been characterized not just by a presidential (or semipresidential) system but also by organized and disciplined national parties. These two changes, one made in the constitutional text, the other an unanticipated consequence, must be seen in tandem in order to comprehend the new political system. In effect, the presidential system derives its strength from the support it receives from a majority party. Without that support in the National Assembly, presidential power is considerably diminished, as is revealed when we discuss the 1986–88 period, under the Fifth Republic, when the president was obliged to govern without a majority party.

Political parties have, in effect, become machines for nominating, supporting, and helping elect presidential candidates. It may be a paradox, as François Borella has observed, that "the Fifth Republic, founded in opposition to party government, is the first truly partisan regime that France has ever known."[25] Indeed, the transformation of the party system has introduced for the first time a governing majority and an opposition in France. As Georges Lavau noted, "The very idea of a permanent majority did not exist in the political tradition of previous Republics. The tradition inherited from the revolution of the left and of the right, which under the Third and Fourth [Republics] was expressed in an electoral bipolarization, has only very rarely been the basis for the separation between the executive and the opposition."[26] As Pierre Avril notes, "We have moved from a system composed of six autonomous poles to a dualist system subdivided into bilateral two-headed poles ('the Gang of Four'). This double two-headed polarity was brought to a quasi-equilibrium in 1978, but the rise of the Socialist Party to the rank of dominant party in 1981 restored the symmetry, on the left, of the Gaullist movement's domination over the other camp during the previous period."[27]

The composition of the National Assembly reflected these changes in the party system. Between 1958 and 1973, French political parties represented in the assembly, though they remained numerous, began to define themselves according to a bipolar, Left-Right scale. After 1973, a process of consolidation effectively reduced the number of parties to a handful.

What has engendered this restructuring of parties, which has made it possible to have a majority and an opposition even with what is essentially a multiparty system? Two factors are responsible: the presidential system and the change in the electoral law.

The institution of the presidency and the election of the president by popular vote have formed alliances within the Left and within the Right. Conquering the highest office has stimulated a restructuring of the parties—at least of the parties who wished to share power—because without alliances obtaining a majority is extremely difficult. The presidential system has bipolarized elections, so that the system is one that has "two principal poles, each composed of several separate parties forced to cooperate with each other in order to win the presidential election and to govern with a parliamentary majority which reflects that cooperation."[28]

The bipolar tendency of the party system since 1962 has considerably reduced the weight of the center and of the extremist parties.[29] It has also engendered a similar restructuring on the Left and the Right.[30] The desire to be part of the majority ("vocation majoritaire"), both presidential and legislative, has forced this regrouping. Even the center parties have tried to integrate themselves into one camp or the other. As Lancelot notes, "Between the Gaullists and the Left, the centrist parties have also tried to join together in a potential governing majority. Even if, on the whole, this effort has not been successful, it is part of the same dynamic process." The result is that while "six major forces opposed each other in the electoral arena of 1958, only four contenders [joined battle] in the early 1970s" (106). A fleeting familiarity with American presidentialism would have indicated to the drafters of the 1958 constitutional text that the American two-party system is a derivative of the presidential form of government.

Because parties nominate candidates and because the electoral system contains two rounds, there is a tendency toward "nationalization" of parties. The major political parties on the Left and the Right regroup to support a single candidate. The electoral system practiced for the years of the Fifth Republic, except for the 1986 legislative elections, has been the *scrutin majoritaire* (single-member districts) with two rounds. Again, alliances and regroupings occur between the two rounds among the parties that have a "vocation majoritaire." The sort of electoral system of proportional representation—used throughout the years of the Fourth Republic—excluded the election of a majority party. An electoral system based on winner-take-all, single-member districts encourages the "majority vocation" of parties. This is further encouraged by the two-round electoral system.[31]

It remains important, however, to emphasize that the presidential system led to a bipolarization of elections. François Mitterrand was one of the first opposition leaders to recognize that the presidential system obliged the socialists to ally with the communists because that was the only means of achieving a presidential majority. And just as General de Gaulle, "who detested parties, created the first great majority party in the country,"[32] so Mitterrand created the first majority party on the Left. The development of governing parties in the Fifth Republic is a singular achievement for a regime created to undermine the influence of political parties. And yet, it is largely to this unforeseen development that the Fifth Republic owes its stability.

The Presidency and Legislative Legitimacy

The presidential regime in France has not merely transformed the party system; it has become dependent on the new party system. The political system of the Fifth Republic is characterized by an interplay of three distinct majorities: presidential, parliamentary, and governmental.[33] Presidential power is exercised effectively and unambiguously when all three majorities coincide.

When the presidential majority coincides with the parliamentary majority, the legislature can become a "transformative" arena.[34] But, as has occurred in the Fifth Republic, legislatures have generally been controlled by governments. The control of the legislature by a government is possible under one condition only: when a majority party exists. This is what accounts for the profound transformation of the French political system in the Fifth Republic. This is a critical change, and it is what might be called a nonconstitutional, or extraconstitutional, change because there was no way to predict this development from a reading of the constitutional text.

The rise of a majority party should be viewed in conjunction with other constitutional changes, for these were important and they significantly altered the power relationship between the executive and the legislature. The constitutional document limits the sphere of the law. Article 34 defines the areas over which the parliament has jurisdiction. Article 39 states that "the initiative for laws belongs concurrently to the Prime Minister and to the Members of Parliament." In practice, the government has come to have complete control over the legislative process. The government also controls parliament's agenda. Deputies no longer have power over financial matters. The government even has the power to impose the budget by ordinance after seventy days of debate have elapsed. Alteration of the committee structure of the parliament has made these groups far less effective and powerful than they used to be. The government can even prevent the introduction of amendments by insisting on a "package vote" *(vote bloqué)*.

The constitution of 1958 had as one of its main goals an alteration of (or a diminution in) the powers of the legislature. Michel Debré described what he meant by the idea that "the Republic had to acquire the attributes of government":

> Three truly basic attributes were required: an executive with its own authority stemming from both its mode of selection and its powers; a parliamentary system, meaning on one hand a cabinet backed by a majority within an assembly and thus able to guide this majority as well as head the administration but also on the other hand, a parliament that should carry out its legislative duties and act as a control without infringing on the executive; and third, an election method as close as possible to the British-American system, the one used by the first French Republicans, election by majority vote.[35]

Presidents have come to recognize (and François Mitterrand is the first president to have had the experience) that presidential power can only be exercised to the full when it is buttressed by a parliamentary majority. Giscard d'Estaing warned the French people on the eve of the 1978 legislative elections: "You may choose to put into effect the Common Program. That is your right. But if you do choose it, it will be put into effect. Do not believe that the Constitution grants the President the means to oppose it. And I would have shirked my duty had I not warned you."[36] The power of dissolution therefore introduced a certain degree of flexibility into the political system. A newly elected president can seek to change the composition of the National Assembly if a different parliamentary majority exists from the one that supported his election. Mitterrand never had any doubt that the dissolution of the National Assembly would be his first act if he were elected president of the republic in 1981.[37]

In dissolving the National Assembly immediately upon his election, both in 1981 and in 1988, Mitterrand was able to avoid a deadlock in the political system caused by differing presidential and parliamentary majorities. The power of dissolution, which had been used on only two previous occasions in the Fifth Republic (October 9, 1962, and May 30, 1968), enables a president to exercise considerable pressure on the parliament. It is a power that Giscard preferred not to use, thus effectively making himself a prisoner of his own uneasy coalition with the Gaullists for his entire term. Mitterrand, on the other hand, showed that using the power to dissolve the National Assembly can give the president the parliamentary majority he needs to carry out his programs and can allow him to exercise authority over a government of his choosing and over the parliament. Mitterrand again dissolved the assembly in 1988, a move that allowed him to pick a Socialist prime minister.

One of the central arguments relating to the conflict that is likely to ensue between a president and a legislature in any presidential system has to do with the supposed need to render the government and the bureaucracy more efficacious. In the attempt to carry out this task, presidents have often found themselves in conflict with the legislature. The French political system instituted in 1958 appears to have avoided this potential conflict because generally one of two situations is likely to prevail: either the presidential and legislative majorities coincide, in which case presidential dominance of the legislative process is pretty much assured, or the legislative majority turns out to be different from the presidential majority, in which case the government emanates from the legislature and so is in a position to dominate it. In both cases, party government exists.

The Cohabitation Experience, 1986–1988

The years 1986–88 are instructive for any analysis of presidential power in France. Between 1981 and 1986 the president enjoyed a comfortable majority in the National Assembly. He dominated the government, and through the government and the party he dominated the parliament. The parliamentary bipolarization of the parties has led to a majority-opposition split in voting on issues, which ties the individual deputy to his party in a way that was not called for when party organizations could not impose sanctions on recalcitrant representatives. The deputy's career now depends on the good will of his party, for there is a price to be paid for disloyalty to the party. In a system of organized, hierarchically structured parties, the deputy cannot be a free agent.[38]

The parties organize to get their presidential candidate elected. They also recognize that their own fate depends to some extent on the fate of their candidates. The Socialist party supported President Mitterrand between 1981 and 1986 because it had become a majority party, and it became a majority party because it had become a "presidentializing" party. The pressure that the party brought to bear on the president between 1986 and 1988 to run for a second term derived from the belief that only if the socialist president were reelected could the party hope to become a majority party again.

The support of a majority party in the assembly is critical for presidential power. Between 1986 and 1988, the socialist president lost much of his power. With a Right-dominated assembly he was obliged to call a prime minister from the rightist wing to form a government. The policy process came to be dominated by the government. Hence, two legitimacies emanating from a popular vote—legislative and presidential—coexisted.

While this period came to be known as a time of "cohabitation," the fact remains that the president did not govern.[39] He exercised "power" in a way appropriate to the new situation. He presided over the meetings of the council of ministers, he represented the nation in international settings, and he used his powers of signature to influence policies. But he was no longer in a position to determine policies, to have his own legislative agenda, or to allocate funds.

The founders of the Fifth Republic, even if they made government responsible to the parliament, nonetheless believed they were giving birth to a presidential system. They believed that the president should not be responsible to the parliament in any way. Yet making the president's term independent of the legislature's did not make him independent of the legislature for matters of policy. Again, a better acquaintance with the American presidential system might have alerted the drafters of the constitution to some of the pitfalls they were creating for themselves. Ministers in the Fifth Republic may have to appear in the parliament (even though they are constitutionally compelled to resign their seats once they are appointed as ministers), but a president never sets foot there. This "irresponsibility" of the president before the parliament was thought to assure the primacy of the executive over the parties and the legislature. The years 1986–88 showed that without the backing of a majority party the president's role is reduced; it exceeds the role played by presidents in earlier republics but certainly bears no relationship to the Gaullian view of the office.

It is possible that what happened once will not recur and that a president may seek to act more aggressively with a government of the opposition than was the case between 1986 and 1988. But an aggressive president who lacks a parliamentary majority is not likely to accomplish very much because the parliament majority determines the government that the president can appoint. The president cannot appoint a prime minister who does not enjoy the confidence of the assembly.

Finally, presidential power depends on the support of a majority party, which itself depends to a considerable extent on an electoral system that encourages consolidation and regrouping of parties rather than one that allocates seats in parliament on the basis of proportional representation.

The election of two majorities—presidential and parliamentary—has led to conflicts but not to crises because when a presidential majority is recreated in the parliament conflict is unlikely to arise; and when two majorities conflict, it is the president who assumes a secondary role. The lesson of the Fifth Republic is that no president can exercise power without the support of a majority party in the National Assembly.[40] An even more important lesson, based on the 1986–88 experience, is that the constitutional text of 1958 is far more flexible than was initially recognized. It contains a safety valve that avoids the clash and crises of two popularly elected legitimacies by permitting the political system to function now as a presidential system, now as a parliamentary system.

Consequences and Problems of Presidential Regimes

The presidential regime in France is only thirty-odd years old. It has not given rise to a major constitutional crisis, and it has weathered potential crises (such as the coexistence of a right-wing legislative majority and a left-wing president between 1986 and 1988 and since 1993). Beyond the political stability it has provided, however, it has had a profound impact on other political institutions.

The presidential system raises the political stakes for political parties and for politicians to far greater heights than does a parliamentary system. There is a winner-take-all aspect to a presidential system, particularly when the president is elected for a seven-year term. Such a system shapes and brings into the political orbit institutions (such as the civil service) that might have remained relatively unpoliticized. It also shapes politicians' perceptions of politics and of the policies that ought to be followed. Finally, the presidential system tends to dichotomize, even if it gives the impression of polarizing, the party and political system.[41]

Presidentialism and Administrative Politicization

The French have always prided themselves on having, if not stable governments, at least a stable group of highly competent, dedicated civil servants. These civil servants represented the mythical neutrality of the state. They kept the machinery of the state turning. This explanation had the force of logic on its side: civil servants obtained power by default, not through winning a conflict. Under the Fifth Republic, civil servants have come to power openly, fulfilling their appetites for a diversity of posts and activities that transcend the administration proper. They have not needed to replace elected politicians or to oppose themselves to elected politicians. They came to assume political roles and, as a consequence, destroyed even the myth of a civil service group that oversees the neutral conduct of the state apparatus. The presidential system has openly polarized and politicized the state administration.

Much has been written in recent years about the politicization of the French bureaucracy.[42] And yet the belief remains that this is a fairly contained phenomenon, unlike the "spoils system" that obtains in the United States. For the most part, many scholars believe France has not become like the United States, which supposedly experiences an institutional "witch-hunt" with the arrival of a new president.

Despite important changes in the political and administrative spheres over the past thirty years, this myth has retained much of its force. But the reality is altogether different because it is France today rather than the United States that more closely approaches, if not a spoils system, a genuine politicization of administrative personnel. This development has come about as a result of two simultaneous factors: on the one hand, the institutions under the state's control remained in the hands of a single political force (the Center Right) for almost twenty-five years; on the other hand, the political system became a presidential one, a factor that assumed considerable importance in light of the fact that presidentialism was superimposed on a centralized administrative structure.

A newly elected American president has far more restricted powers of nomination than his French counterpart. There are about three million federal civil servants. A president names between twenty-five hundred and three thousand of them, and the most important (cabinet secretaries, Supreme Court justices, even ambassadors) have to be confirmed by the senate. Implicit in this power to effect changes at the top of the administrative hierarchy is the recognition that a president needs to have officials loyal to him and his policies, even at the cost of a certain degree of instability. But beyond the power to name a relatively small number of federal officials, an American president has little time to devote to placing officials at state and local levels. Nor does he possess the power to place officials in other sectors of the economy and society.

Let us look closely at what now takes place in France. First, with respect to the central administration, the highest officials get changed sooner or later after the arrival of a newly appointed government. Then there are changes that take place in other sectors where the state is present: the nationalized industries and banks, education, culture, and the audiovisual media. In short, there is practically no sector where the government does not have a say in nominating directors.

The acceleration of this development during the past thirty years is the result of the bipolarization of the political (and party) system and of the presidentialization of this system. One immediate consequence of this development is that anyone in or aspiring to an important position must choose a side. And this includes higher civil servants, academic chancellors, radio and television journalists, artists, musicians. The candidate who triumphs in a presidential election has at his disposition an enormous trough to feed those who supported him. This power is all the greater because the political system is *centralized, dichotomized,* and *presidential.* The candidate who wins can bestow the fruits of power during his term. If the opposition party wins the next elections, all is lost and the cycle starts over.[43]

The appropriation of this power of nomination by a president may not have been inevitable. It became so as a result of the political moves instituted by the Center Right between 1958 and 1981. This political majority gradually began distributing posts to its own loyalists. It began by colonizing the upper reaches of the civil service, then extended this practice to the nationalized sector and, finally, to sectors that had traditionally escaped the clutches of political nominations. Having been excluded from the administrative, industrial, financial, and cultural sectors for twenty-five years, the Left in 1981 proceeded to name its own loyalists to posts in all these sectors.

In addition to the practice instituted by the Center Right, the new constitution encouraged the politicization of all institutions linked to the state. The result was to give the power of nomination to a president who knows few controls, and that power is unlike the power possessed by any democratically elected head of state. In Germany, the federal system limits the chancellor's power of nominations. In Italy, the sharing of power by several political parties ensures that no one wins or loses all. In the United States, decentralization and congressional power severely limit the president's power in this domain. In France, on the other hand, centralization and presidentialism give the president remarkable powers to name personnel in a variety of areas, including the higher civil service (which itself includes sectors as varied as transportation, justice, the police, the postal service, and education), the museums, the theater, the opera, the audiovisual media, banks, industries, insurance companies. In other words, the power of nomination touches a variety of areas that are not normally considered political.

The presidential system, in short, today obliges those aspiring to top positions in a variety of public and semipublic sectors to take sides in a political context. For the most part, only political loyalists will be rewarded. Rewarding political loyalists is not, strictly speaking, a "spoils system," which implies a total disregard for professional competence. Nominations in France can always be justified by a minimal level of competence because France produces an elite whose members may not always be technically qualified for specific posts but are rarely wholly incompetent.[44] But there is little doubt that managing a career through political considerations is becoming more important than possessing professional qualifications, which alone are no longer of major importance.[45]

Presidentialism and Political Strategy

The activity, strategy, and ambitions of parties and politicians are all directed toward presidential elections. The concentration on presidential elections is an aspect of French presidentialism that has received little attention. The regrouping of political parties that took place on both sides of the political spectrum during the 1970s was uniquely influenced by the presidential system. Mitterrand's strategy of making himself president and bringing the Left to power was based on the need to capture the highest office.

Today, the internal conflicts of the Right seem much akin to the conflicts that the Left experienced in the 1960s and 1970s. After repeated losses at presidential, legislative, and municipal elections, as well as being saddled with leaders who have demonstrated their penchant for losing elections, the Right finds itself challenged by its own groups, who are anxious to prepare for the 1995 presidential elections. The conflict within the Right today has, to be sure, ideological, generational, and personal aspects. But at bottom it is about who will represent the Right in the 1995 presidential elections. Speaking about Giscard d'Estaing's heading the list of rightist candidates for the European elections in 1989, Dominique Baudis, the mayor of Toulouse and one of the leaders of the Young Turks who once challenged the elders, revealed what the conflict was really about:

> What I fear is that on June 19 [after the European elections], M. Giscard d'Estaing will interpret the results as the consecration of his leadership over the opposition, while M. Jacques Chirac will see things totally differently and therefore the fight will start over again on June 19. The nightmare might be another primary fight, in 1995 when the next presidential election takes place, pitting M. Chirac against M. Giscard d'Estaing just as in 1981, fourteen years earlier.[46]

The Left experienced the same internal conflicts in the 1960s and 1970s. When Mitterrand had lost two presidential elections and led the Socialist party to municipal and legislative defeats, he too was challenged by a "younger" generation, led by Michel Rocard, the former prime minister, who had branded the Socialist party's leadership "archaic."

But presidential politics not only determines the strategies of parties; it also determines their policies when they are in power. The policies of the right-wing government between 1986 and 1988 were geared toward preparing for the presidential elections of 1988. The policies of the leading politicians in the Socialist party today are undertaken with an eye toward the 1995 presidential elections.

Under the prime ministership of Michel Rocard, the government's policies became moderate, even modest. The government had no intention of reforming or redoing society. It wanted to be seen as a government that *manages* the nation's economy responsibly. Rocard did not launch any major reforms, and his moderate policies were intended to attract the centrist voters to him in 1995, or earlier should the president's office become vacant.

Other leading contenders for the presidency continue to devise strategies to gain support through their policies. The extent to which the election of the president every seven years shapes the political (and policy) process requires much greater attention than it has hitherto received.

Tendencies toward Dichotomization

The regrouping of political forces and the Left-Right choices in elections have been heavily influenced by the presidential system. "The Constitution of the Fifth Republic has polarizing consequences,"[47] concludes a major study of voting in France. This perceived "polarizing" effect has had the consequence of causing spectacular changes in public policies.

After the Left won the presidency and obtained a majority in the National Assembly in 1981, it believed that it enjoyed a mandate to "change the society." It disregarded the international economic order and followed economic policies that ran counter to the exigencies of the world economy. The Socialists undertook a massive industrial and financial nationalization program. This was followed by numerous costly social programs and some important social legislation. After 1983, it was clear that France could not afford to follow the economic policies of 1981.[48] Consequently, the Left took note that the vote that brought it to power in 1981 was more a reflection of a desire for change in government (after twenty-three years of a center-right government) than for a change in society.

Oddly enough, this message was lost on the Right also. When the center-right coalition gained a majority in the 1986 legislative elections, they believed that this vote constituted a rejection of socialism and immediately undertook a massive denationalization program. They privatized a public television station, major industrial groups, and banks. The new ideology of the Right was contained in the new words, "liberalism" and the "market," and came to be seen as equally extremist as

the position the Left had adopted in 1981. As a consequence, two years of governing by the Right led to the reelection of Mitterrand as president and to the election
of a new assembly with a leftist majority. The Right did not commit the same error
when it won the legislative elections in 1993.

The "extremist" policies adopted by the parties of the Left and the Right between 1981 and 1988 derived to a considerable extent from a misunderstanding of
the presidential system. The need to develop an identity has led political parties to
believe that elections should be fought on ideological grounds. Since the president
can dissolve the National Assembly in an attempt to obtain his own majority, the
legislative elections have also tended to be fought on heavily ideological grounds.

After the elections of 1988, both presidential and legislative, the Left appears to
have understood (aided, in part, by a narrow legislative victory) that the French
electorate was not seeking a series of so-called leftist policies; hence, the policy of
opening toward the center (modest as it is for the time being) that has resulted in
the entry of a few centrist politicians into the government and the absence of major
structural reforms by the Rocard government.

The existence of two blocks—Left and Right—has resulted from the presidential system and from the electoral system. Until recently, the "two-block" system
has implied ideological polarization. But there is evidence to suggest that what
Lancelot calls the increasing "nationalization" of French politics (resulting from a
multiplication of national elections—referendums and presidential elections) has
had the effect of detaching the voter from his traditional orientation.[49] In other
words, there may well be coming onto the horizon a "new French voter" less at-
tached to a party or a movement and more easily able to shift his vote from one side
to the other. How else can one explain the reelection of Mitterrand in May 1988 and
of a leftist legislative majority in June 1988?

Beyond the development of the more mobile, less entrenched "new French
voter," the critical development in the dichotomization of political party conflicts
is the deideologization of this conflict. Presidential systems may in an earlier phase
give rise to ideological conflicts between the two main parties on either end of the
ideological spectrum, but in due course these parties tend to vie for the center and
so approximate what Kirchheimer referred to as "catch-all" parties.

Tendencies toward Cooperation

The presidential system in France has brought a definite measure of stability to
a political system that was not as unstable as it appeared to be and not as ineffectual
as it has been portrayed. The much maligned Fourth Republic was responsible for
a spectacular transformation of the postwar French economy, even if it had not
been able to generate sufficient authority to fight a bitter colonial war.

The presidential system has reduced the number of polarized political blocs,
even if it has not in reality reduced the number of parties. What is often forgotten

is that the bipolarization of the Fifth Republic's political system has consisted of coalitions that form two blocs. This means therefore that no political party can count on a totally loyal base for support.

The political system, like the party system, has appeared more coherent because the electoral system obliges cooperation within each bloc. But the power of the presidency is itself dependent on the party system and on the electoral system because, as noted earlier, a presidency without a majority in the National Assembly is more than a figurehead but far less than what de Gaulle intended the office to be.

Presidential elections also encourage cooperation among rival political parties because the stakes are high. A presidential term lasts seven years, and losing a presidential election means a long wait in the opposition. Hence, apparent polarization is inevitable because such an election has to be fought, contrary to what de Gaulle had intended, on a partisan basis. As de Gaulle came to recognize, though a president may wish to see himself as above parties, he cannot forgo party support when he is a candidate or when he is elected.

Hence, the presidential regime in France, relying as it has on the single-member constituency ("winner-take-all") electoral system, has given rise to a duality of political forces that has weakened the forces of the center but that obliges the two major blocs to push toward the center. The elections, then, have the appearance of polarization, but politics is based on cooperation among different political forces within each side. The new French voter, free to vote differently in presidential, legislative, municipal, and European elections, tends to reduce the polarization of politics and policies.

The Dual Executive System

The most unusual feature of the constitution of the Fifth Republic is the existence of two executives, a president and a prime minister. The constitution grants both considerable authority. In most instances, the relationship between a president and a prime minister coming from the same party has, sooner or later, turned sour.[50]

It is true that the dual executive system introduces a certain flexibility into the political system. The president can change prime ministers and the government without calling for new elections. He can: constitute a coalition that can obtain the confidence of the National Assembly; influence the conflict among the various factions within his own party by the way he chooses to constitute a government; and preserve the integrity of his office by sanctioning his own government for unfortunate results of particular policies.

Until 1974, the president of the republic was unquestionably the dominant figure. After the election of Giscard d'Estaing to the presidency, prime ministers came to carve out a degree of autonomy for themselves.[51] Giscard's two prime ministers, Jacques Chirac and Raymond Barre, attempted to gain a degree of autonomy, as have Mitterrand's prime ministers. Laurent Fabius even once went so far as to express being "troubled" when the president received General Jaruselski. Fabius came to be known for his expression, "Lui c'est lui, moi c'est moi."

One much overlooked feature of the dual executive system, insofar as the policy-making process is concerned, is that it dilutes central control and authority without granting the advantages of decentralization.[52] The reason for this lies in the competitive element that the system introduces. As a result of the competition between president and prime minister, other ministers and their bureaucracies circumvent decisions made by the head of the government (the prime minister) and appeal to the Elysée. Interministerial committees play a whole set of games trying to guess where Matignon and the Elysée stand on a particular issue.[53] Whatever is decided and subsequently arbitrated by Matignon is not always considered a closed matter. A displeased minister often solicits the Elysée's intervention, or the Elysée on its own develops a viewpoint on an issue that is different from that of the prime minister and his staff.

The dual executive system, in effect, gives rise to three distinct legitimacies, one of which (governmental) depends on the legislature's composition. Hence, the constitution allows for a presidential majority that is distinct from a legislative majority, but it also allows for the formation of a government that neither coincides with the presidential majority nor emanates from a clear legislative majority. In this instance, the government is at the mercy of what may turn out to be a shifting (and hence fragile) legislative majority.

It is perhaps paradoxical that the control by a single political party of all the key political institutions does not obviate intergovernmental conflicts, whereas the sharing of power by two political parties does so to a much larger extent. In the period of "cohabitation," or coexistence, between a socialist president and a conservative government—the period that began after the March 16, 1986, legislative elections—the conflicts between the two executives' teams had little effect on the policy process. The reason is that, contrary to what had been the general prediction, there was less room for conflict because it was indisputable that the government determined policies and not the president. Under cohabitation, no minister could do what had become a regular practice under the previous socialist governments; the prime minister was the chief executive, and his arbitration was final. The president may have the power to refuse to sign an ordinance, but he cannot refuse to sign a law, cannot instruct ministers to adopt policies, and above all, cannot arbitrate conflicts among ministers. Only the prime minister controls the ministers of the government. Aware of the ways in which a prime minister's authority is compromised, Prime Minister Jacques Chirac warned the ministers in his government at the first cabinet meeting that under no circumstances were they to have recourse to the president. Only the minister of defense and the minister of foreign affairs were permitted to move freely between the Elysée and Matignon. Chirac was not about to see his authority as prime minister undermined as it had been in 1974–76, when Giscard d'Estaing was president and Chirac was prime minister. Yet, had Chirac not had the support of a clear majority in the National Assembly he would have had far less authority over his ministers, and the presidential system would have functioned as simply a parliamentary system characterized by a lack of a distinct majority.

Conclusion

The presidential system in France has functioned in a stabilizing manner. It has provided the society with a stable executive (whether presidential or, as between 1986 and 1988 and since 1993, governmental), and it has provided the context within which politics takes place. The length of the presidential term tends to block options for many politicians and institutions. If the president has a comfortable majority in the National Assembly, that assembly is ruled by the president's party and scarcely plays an independent legislative role; such is the case with most legislatures. As for civil servants, their careers are more and more affected by the party in power and by the president himself. Hence, they find themselves obliged to make choices among the various presidential candidates. They are rewarded for their support if their candidate wins and relegated to insignificance if he loses. The power of nomination at the president's disposal is subject to no control when he is powerful in office—that is, when he is able to control the government and the parliament.

When a president loses his majority in parliament he comes face to face with a rival legitimacy. He can claim that he will retire for the remainder of his term to one of his châteaus and leave the running of the government to the newly elected majority, which is what Giscard intended to do had the Left won the legislative elections in 1978. Alternatively, he can remain in office, lean on the legitimacy of his own election, and exercise whatever power (both positive and negative) the constitution grants him. In this instance, the president's power is mostly negative, consisting in the ability to refuse to countersign decrees and sanction nominations. This power, already reduced, has to be used sparingly.

Presidential power turns out to be a flexible power that depends on the support of other institutions. It can go from being, as one of Mitterrand's ministers described it, "nearly dictatorial" to an inability to govern or to initiate policies. France has accepted this kind of presidency because, in the end, the country did not want to give unrestricted power at all times to one office. The one thing that was not foreseen was the development of political parties. Once majority parties came into existence, they dominated the legislative process and became the underpinning of presidential power.

The presidential system in France has been able to provide political stability over the past thirty years mostly because rival parliamentary and presidential legitimacies have existed for only two years. But the system has built-in potential complications that have so far not had to be dealt with because they have not occurred. While it may be able to handle two rival legitimacies (which the president's power of dissolution can put an end to), it may have a more difficult time dealing with rivalry among presidential, governmental, and parliamentary legitimacies. In other words, when no party wins a majority in parliament, a majority on the Left or the Right does in fact exist. But it must be put together in much the same way a government of the Fourth Republic was put together. Consequently, the government will not really control the parliament, and the president will not control either institution. But this is not likely to be the norm. Since a president is elected for a seven-year term, he is likely to be able to obtain a parliamentary majority for at least one legislative term, that is, for five years. The same is likely to recur whether he is reelected for a second term or whether the opposition candidate is elected. Hence, the system may alternate between being presidential and being parliamentary, but the probabilities are high that it will be fully presidential for more than two-thirds of the time.

It seems clear, however, that the 1958 French constitution is a delicate instrument that should be emulated only with extreme caution by more divided societies. One would not want to see a president who is head of the armed forces and a prime minister who can pass legislation without a parliamentary vote (as article 49.3 of the French constitution permits the prime minister to do) take their roles with equal seriousness. Moreover, stability of the stand-off kind is not without costs. The government in 1986–88 and after the 1993 elections had its eye fixed on the presidential elections. Most governmental actions became part of a strategy for winning the presidential election. As the Greek sage might have said, in another era the French constitution of 1958 might have been very unsuitable for France.

Notes

I wish to thank Arend Lijphart, Juan Linz, Seymour Martin Lipset, Giovanni Sartori, William Schonfeld, and Arturo Valenzuela for their very helpful comments on an earlier version of this paper. Walter Murphy broadened my horizons on the subject of constitutionalism and corrected my misconceptions, and for this I owe him special thanks.

This chapter was written under the auspices of the Center of International Studies, Princeton University, and was also supported by the German Marshall Fund of the United States.

1. Cited in Michel Debré, *Trois républiques pour une France: memoires 1946–1958* (Paris: Albin Michel, 1988), p. 347. See also General de Gaulle, *Discours et messages* (Paris: Plon, 1970).

2. A referendum in 1962 approved the election of the president by universal suffrage. The first presidential election took place in 1965.

3. Cited in Jacques Fauvet, "Mendès-France ou l'exercice solitaire de l'opposition," *Le monde*, 18 Oct. 1989. See also vol. 5 of Pierre Mendès-France, *Préparer l'avenir 1963–1973* (Paris: Gallimard, 1989).

4. F. Furet, J. Julliard, and P. Rosanvallon, *La république du centre* (Paris: Editions du Seuil, 1988). .

5. François Mitterrand, *Le coup d'état permanent* (Paris: Plon, 1964).

6. Cited in S. Coignard and J. F. Lacan, *La république bananiére* (Paris: Belfond, 1989), p. 29.

7. *Le monde*, 2 July 1981. Cited also ibid.

8. Debré, *Trois républiques pour une France*, p. 319.

9. De Gaulle, *Discours et Messages.*

10. François Borella, *Les partis politiques dans la France d'aujourd'hui,* 4th ed. (Paris: Editions du Seuil, 1981), p. 8.

11. For varying interpretations of the Fourth Republic, see Philip M. Williams, *Crisis and Compromise: Politics in the Fourth Republic* (New York: Doubleday Anchor, 1966); Jacques Fauvet, *La France dechirée* (Paris: Fayard, 1957); Nathan Leites, *On the Game of Politics in France* (Stanford: Stanford UP, 1959); Herbert Luethy, *France against Herself* (New York: Meridian Books, 1954); Duncan MacRae, *Parliament, Parties and Society in France, 1949–1959* (New York: St. Martin's Press, 1967); Georgette Elgey, *La république des illusions, 1945–1951* (Paris: Fayard, 1965); and *La république des contradictions, 1951–1954* (Paris: Fayard, 1968); Paul-Marie de la Gorce, *Apogée et mort de la IV République* (Paris: Grasset, 1979); and Jacques Julliard, *La IV République* (Paris: Calmann-Levy, 1968).

12. Vincent Wright, *The Government and Politics of France* (London: Hutchinson & Co., 1979), p. 14.

13. See Stanley Hoffmann's essay, "The Rulers: Heroic Leadership in Modern France," in his *Decline or Renewal? France since the 1930s* (New York: Viking, 1972), pp. 63–110.

14. Debré, *Trois républiques pour une France,* p. 370.

15. Philip M. Williams, *The French Parliament: Politics in the Fifth Republic* (New York: Praeger, 1968), p. 15.

16. Michel Debré, "The Constitution of 1958: Its *Raison d'Etre* and How it Evolved," in *The Fifth Republic at Twenty,* edited by William G. Andrews and Stanley Hoffmann (New York: State U New York P, 1980), p. 17.

17. Serge Berstein, *La France de l'expansion. I. La République gaulliénne 1958–1969* (Paris: Editions du Seuil, 1989), p. 18.

18. De Gaulle dissolved the National Assembly in 1962 after the Pompidou government was censured. He dissolved the National Assembly in May 1968 after the crisis of that month. Mitterrand dissolved the assembly in 1981 and in 1988.

19. Cited in Debré, *Trois républiques pour une France,* pp. 355–56.

20. Berstein, *La France de l'expansion,* pp. 113–14.

21. Maurice Duverger, *Echec au roi* (Paris: Albin Michel, 1978), p. 143.

22. See Nicholas Wahl, *The Fifth Republic: France's New Political System* (New York: Random House, 1959).

23. This article states: "Political parties and groups shall play a part in the exercise of the right to vote. They shall be formed freely and shall carry on their activities freely. They must respect the principles of national sovereignty and of democracy."

24. Debré, *Trois républiques pour une France,* p. 370.

25. François Borella, *Les partis politiques dans l'Europe des neuf,* (Paris: Editions du Seuil, 1979), p. 407.

26. Georges Lavau, "Reflexions sur le régime politique en France," *Revue française de science politique,* Dec. 1962.

27. Pierre Avril, *Essai sur les partis* (Paris: LGDG, 1986), p. 191. This work contains an excellent summary of the historical development of the French party system.

28. Borella, *Les Partis politiques dans la France d'aujourd'hui,* p. 33.

29. See Frederic Bon and Jean-Paul Cheylan, *La France qui vote* (Paris: Hachette, 1988).

30. See Alain Lancelot's excellent summary of this phenomenon, *Les élections sous la Ve République* (Paris: Presses Universitaires de France, 1988), pp. 103–6.

31. Pierre Avril also accords a considerable importance in the restructuring of French political parties to referenda and to the presidential power of dissolution. Avril believes that

both these factors contributed heavily to the formation of majorities. See his *Essai sur les partis*, pp. 193–98. See also Colette Ysmal, *Les partis politiques sous la Ve République* (Paris: Montchrestien, 1989).

32. Duverger, *Echec au roi*, p. 99.

33. See Jean-Louis Quermonne, *Le gouvernement de la France sous la Ve République* (Paris: Dalloz, 1983).

34. Nelson W. Polsby, "Legislatures," in *Handbook of Political Science*, edited by Fred I. Greenstein and Polsby (Reading, Mass.: Addison-Wesley, 1975), 5:277.

35. Debré, "The Constitution of 1958," p. 17.

36. *Le monde*, 29–30 Jan. 1978.

37. François Mitterrand, *Ici et maintenant* (Paris: Fayard, 1980), p. 41.

38. For an elaboration on the role of the deputy in the Fifth Republic, see Ezra N. Suleiman, "Toward the Disciplining of Parties and Legislatures," in *Parliaments and Parliamentarians in Democratic Politics* (New York: Holmes & Meier, 1986), pp. 85–103.

39. See Harvey Feigenbaum, "Recent Evolution of the French Executive," *Governance* 3, no. 3 (1990): 264–78.

40. On the effects of conflicting majorities, see Jean-Louis Quermonne, *L'alternance au pouvoir* (Paris: Presses Universitaires de France, 1988), pp. 88–122.

41. I am grateful to Giovanni Sartori for suggesting to me that the data showing the trend toward polarization do not mean greater ideological divisions. Hence the term "dichotomization" might be preferred to "polarization."

42. On the politicization of the civil service, see Francis de Baecque and J.-L. Quermonne, *Administration et politiques sous la V République* (Paris: Presse de la Fondation Nationale de Sciences Politiques, 1981). See also Jacques Chevallier, "La gauche et la haute administration sous la cinquième République," in *La haute administration et la politique* (Paris: Presses Universitaires de France, 1988), pp. 9–48.

43. The presidential system forces civil servants to place their bets on a presidential candidate. The party system requires the parties to reward party activists. See Ezra Suleiman. "Hauts fonctionnaires: le mythe de la neutralité," *Le monde*, 27 Feb. 1986, and "Toward the Disciplining of Parties and Legislators," pp. 79–105.

44. See Ezra N. Suleiman, "From Right to Left: Bureaucracy and Politics in France," in *Bureaucrats and Policy-Making* (New York: Holmes & Meier, 1984), pp. 107–36.

45. See Monique Dagnaud and Dominique Mehl, *L'élite rose* (Paris: Editions Ramsay, 1988).

46. *Le monde*, 21 Apr. 1978.

47. Bon and Cheylan, *La France qui vote*, p. 428.

48. See David Cameron, "The Colors of a Rose: On the Ambiguous Record of French Socialism" (Center for European Studies Working Paper, Harvard University, 1988).

49. Lancelot, *Les elections sous la Ve Republique*, pp. 107–8.

50. I treat this relationship in some detail in my "Presidential Government in France," in *Presidents and Prime Ministers*, edited by Richard Rose and Ezra N. Suleiman (Washington, D.C.: American Enterprise Institute, 1980), pp. 106–21.

51. See Duverger, *Echec au roi*, pp. 144–46.

52. This is treated in some detail in Ezra Suleiman, *Private Power and Centralization in France* (Princeton: Princeton UP, 1987), where these issues are elaborated through an analysis of a specific public policy issue.

53. Thierry Pfister, *A Matignon au temps de l'union de la gauche* (Paris: Hachette, 1985), pp. 122–32.

Notes on Contributors

Arend Lijphart is professor of political science, University of California, San Diego. His specialization is comparative politics, with special interests in democratic states, ethnically divided societies, and constitutional design. He is the author of *The Politics of Accommodation: Pluralism and Democracy in the Netherlands; Democracy in Plural Societies: A Comparative Exploration; Democracies: Patterns of Majoritarian and Consensus Government in Twenty-one Countries; Electoral Systems and Party Systems: A Study of Twenty-seven Democracies, 1945–90*, and other books. His edited books include *Parliamentary versus Presidential Government*, and he has written numerous articles in leading international journals on comparative politics and democratic theory.

Juan J. Linz is Sterling Professor of Political and Social Science at Yale University. He holds degrees in law, political science, and sociology and has contributed to books on authoritarianism, fascism, political parties, nationalism, religion, and politics. He is the author of *Crisis, Breakdown, and Reequilibration*, volume 1 of a four-volume work, *The Breakdown of Democratic Regimes*, which he co-edited with Alfred Stepan, and of "Totalitarian and Authoritarian Regimes" in *Macropolitical Theory*, volume 3 of the *Handbook of Political Science*, edited by Fred L. Greenstein and Nelson W. Polsby. He is co-author and editor, with Larry Diamond and S. M. Lipset, of *Democracy in Developing Countries*. He has written extensively on the transition to democracy in Spain and is co-authoring with Alfred Stepan a book titled *Problems of Democratic Transition and Consolidation: Southern Europe, South America, and Eastern Europe*. In 1987 he was awarded the Premio Príncipe de Asturias de Ciencias Sociales, and he holds honorary degrees from the Universidad Autónoma de Madrid, Georgetown, Granada, and Marburg.

Giovanni Sartori is Albert Schweitzer Professor in the Humanities, Columbia University, New York City. His fields of interest are political theory, comparative politics, and social science methodology. His major works are *Parties and Party Systems: A Framework for Analysis; La Politica: Logica e Metodo in Scienze Sociali; The Theory of Democracy Revisited;* and *Elementi di Teoria Politica*. Among the volumes he has edited, two recent ones are *Social Science Concepts: A Systematic Analysis*, and *La Comparazione in Scienze Sociali*.

Cindy Skach is a Ph.D. candidate in Political Science at Columbia University. She is currently conducting research on electoral systems, political party polarization, and democratic consolidation at Heidleberg University on a fellowship from the German Academic Exchange.

Alfred Stepan has written books on the military, the state, and democratization. His most recent book, co-authored with Juan J. Linz, is *Problems of Democratic Transition and Consolidation: Eastern Europe, Southern Europe, and South America* (forthcoming). He is also the editor, with Linz, of *The Breakdown of Democratic Regimes* (1978). He has taught at Yale University and Columbia University and is now rector and president of the Central European University in Budapest and Prague.

Ezra N. Suleiman is IBM Professor in International Studies and chairman of the Committee for European Studies at Princeton University. He is the recipient of a Guggenheim Fellowship, a German Marshall Fund of the U.S. Fellowship, a Fulbright Senior Research Fellowship, and a Fellowship of the American Council of Learned Societies. He is the author or co-author of *Politics, Power and Bureaucracy in France; Elites in French Society; Industrial Policies in Western Europe; Parliament and Parliamentarianism in Democratic Societies; Presidents and Prime Ministers; Bureaucrats and Policymaking;* and *The Politics of Public Sector Reform and Privatization.*

Arturo Valenzuela is professor of government and director, Center for Latin American Studies, Georgetown University. His research interests include the origins, consolidation, and breakdown of democratic regimes, authoritarianism, political parties, and the nature and functioning of democratic regimes. He is the author of *Political Brokers in Chile: Local Government in a Centralized Polity, The Breakdown of Democratic Regimes: Chile,* and with Pamela Constable, *A Nation of Enemies: Chile under Pinochet.* He is co-author or co-editor of *Chile: Politics and Society* and *Military Rule in Chile* (with J. Samuel Valenzuela), *La Opción Parlamentaria para América Latina* (with Juan J. Linz and Arend Lijphart), and *The Failure of Presidential Democracy* (with Juan J. Linz). He has been a visiting scholar at Oxford University, the University of Chile, the Catholic University of Chile, the University of Florence, and the University of Sussex. Prior to joining the Georgetown faculty, he was a professor of political science and director of the Council on Latin American Studies at Duke University.

Index

Library of Congress Cataloging-in-Publication Data

The Failure of presidential democracy / edited by Juan J. Linz and Arturo Valenzuela.

    p.   cm.

    Issued also in a 1 v. hardbound ed.

    Includes bibliographical references and index.

    Contents: v. 1. Comparative perspectives — v. 2. The Case of Latin America.

    ISBN 0-8018-4640-4 (pbk. : v. 1 : acid-free paper). — ISBN 0-8018-4784-2
(pbk. : v. 2 : acid-free paper)

    1. Presidents.   2. Cabinet system.   3. Democracy.   4. Representative government and repre-
sentation.   5. Latin America—Politics and government—Case studies.   6. Presidents—Latin
America—Case studies.   I. Linz, Juan J. (Juan José), 1926– .   II. Valenzuela, Arturo, 1944–
JF255.F35   1994
321.8'042—dc20   93-27222